James William Buel, Giuseppe Verdi

The Great Operas

The Romantic Legends upon which the Masters of Song have Founded their

Famous Lyrical Compositions

James William Buel, Giuseppe Verdi

The Great Operas
The Romantic Legends upon which the Masters of Song have Founded their Famous Lyrical Compositions

ISBN/EAN: 9783744793063

Printed in Europe, USA, Canada, Australia, Japan

Cover: Foto ©Thomas Meinert / pixelio.de

More available books at **www.hansebooks.com**

The Great Operas

The Romantic Legends upon which
the Masters of Song have Founded
Their Famous Lyrical Compositions

INTRODUCED BY

GIUSEPPE VERDI

LAST OF THE GREAT COMPOSERS

Edited by

JAMES W BUEL, Ph.D

The Société Universelle Lyrique

London Paris Berlin Philadelphia

Contents of Section Five

The Prophet

AFTER THE ORIGINAL PAINTING BY [illegible]

[illegible] *Who am I*

[illegible]

[illegible]

[illegible]

And you knew me not [illegible] *ungrateful man.*

Act IV. Scene [illegible]

THE PROPHET.

Music by Meyerbeer.—Words by Scribe.

PROBABLY the least satisfactory of Meyerbeer's several imposing, picturesque, and tunefully descriptive music dramas is "The Prophet," notwithstanding it was the most carefully elaborated of his several works, and a period of thirteen years elapsed between it and "The Huguenots." It excels the latter in spectacular effects, but a sacrifice of the melodious is made to the declamatory, for which reason the opera is much less pleasing, from a strictly musical view-point, though its pageantry is impressively great. The fault, however, lies chiefly with the librettist, for notwithstanding Scribe's cleverness in dealing with other subjects, clearly he lacked ability to represent, with sustained interest, the psychological character which constitutes the theme of "The Prophet." So ill-defined is his attempt that the Anabaptist leader, instead of standing as a type of the miraculously endowed, is brought to a level scarcely above that of an impostor. It is proper to explain that early in the sixteenth century a considerable part of Germany became profoundly agitated by religious fanaticism that had its rise with a sect known as the "Anabaptists," which we must believe was inspired by a spirit of hatred of the rich rather than a purpose to propagate Christian faith or to combat the heretical tendencies that conflicting creeds engendered. The leader of this new sect was Bockelson, a tailor of Leyden, who came to be known as John of Leyden. He was a man of great valor and a born leader, who rallied about him so large an armed following that he soon made himself master of a considerable territory, and established his capital at Munster, where he was coronated, and maintained himself with royal pomp for several years, until defeated by the army of Germany. During his rulership John taught his followers that he was divinely born and commissioned, a belief which they the more readily accepted because his ranks were composed of the ignorant classes, and chiefly because all property was held by them in common, thus furnishing the earliest example in Germany of pure socialism. Upon this historic incident Scribe constructed his lyric drama, the plot of which may be thus summarized:

John, an innkeeper of Leyden, falls in love with Bertha, a maid of Dordrecht, and would prosecute his suit favorably but for the unfortunate fact that Count Oberthal, lord of the domain, refuses his consent to the marriage, having a design to espouse the girl himself. Bertha is seized and detained by the count, but after a time she contrives to escape and flees to her lover, who gives her protection. Oberthal at length secures the person of Fides, John's aged mother, and by threatening her with death, as the alternative, induces John to surrender Bertha. This outrage, characteristic of the common vice of the nobles of the time, so enrages John that, burning for revenge, he joins the Anabaptists, a revolutionary sect pledged to the destruction of the power of the aristocratic classes. By the operation of some strange influence John is hailed as the promised Messiah, and is immediately elevated to leadership of the sect. The Anabaptists are now marshaled in a great army, and lay siege to Munster, which quickly falls into their hands, and in the Cathedral John is not only crowned but is also solemnly proclaimed the Son of God. During the ceremony of investiture Fides recognizes in John her son, whom she had believed was slain by a false prophet, and she follows the army to Munster, hoping to obtain a revenge. She rushes forward to embrace him, but John pretends that he does not know her, realizing that to admit a mortal relationship would destroy the holy regard in which he is held by the populace, and compels her to confess her mistake. The unhappy mother is seized and carried away to prison for her audacity, but as soon as he has the opportunity of doing so, John visits her in her cell to seek pardon for his action, explaining his situation in a manner that serves to excuse him. He desires to liberate his mother and to fly the country ere his true character be ascertained by the people, but this he is prevented from doing by discovery of a plot against him by jealous Anabaptist leaders. Finding that there are no other means for frustrating their designs upon his life, John contrives to have a powder-mine laid beneath the palace, and calling the leaders together, upon a pretence, when they are feasting he blows up the building, and perishes, together with all the conspirators and his mother, in the holocaust.

Act I.—The opening scene represents a country view near Dordrecht, at the back of which is a glimpse of the River Meuse, on the right a fortified château, on the left farms, and a mill before which are sacks of corn and rustic tables. After a spirited chorus by peasants and mill-boys, Bertha appears upon the scene and renders a cavatina, expressive of blissful emotions at the prospect of her early marriage. As the song concludes, Fides arrives, travel-stained and excited, and is joyfully greeted by Bertha, who has been expecting her to bring news of John. This expectation is not disappointed, for with manifestation of intense satisfaction, Fides delivers the message that John, her son, has sent her to bring his affianced to Leyden at once that the bans may be celebrated. Bertha betrays a diffidence because of her situation as a poor orphan, but Fides reassures her by declaring that no other maid in Dordrecht is so fair and amiable, nor one so worthy of her son, who, she takes pains to represent, is the owner of a favored inn that does a thriving business, the finest indeed in Leyden. Bertha is quite persuaded and would gladly go to consummate her happy anticipations, but she reminds Fides that she is a vassal and cannot marry or quit the country without permission of her sovereign, Count Oberthal, whose battlemented castle stands upon the hill. Fides, most anxious to conduct the girl to her son, proposes to go at once and solicit Oberthal's consent, but at this moment three Anabaptists, Zacharias, Jonas and Matthias, show themselves, at sight of whom Fides shrinks back, alarmed by their sombre and sinister appearance. Bertha promptly explains that they are holy ministers, preaching sacred doctrines among the people. The three, in fact, are leaders of the revolt in Westphalia, whose mission it is to spread the insurrection, but their design is secretly conducted under the guise of pious men, until finding their purpose opportune they inveigh against the oppressions of the nobles. Speciously they represent that all the lands rightfully belong to the masses, whose toil has made them valuable, and anathematizing the lords who hold the people in vassalage, exhort their hearers to rise and throw off the yoke of bondage, promising when this is done the rich shall be humbled, all property, castles and lands shall be held in common, all taxes shall disappear, and freedom will rule, without distinction of classes. As if inspired, the three Anabaptists lift their voices in a stirring trio of supplication to God for aid in establishing liberty through a rising of the people against their masters, which so enthuses the peasants that they arm themselves with pitchforks, axes, and clubs, and advance to attack the castle.

"Fides, good mother, you [illegible]"

In the succeeding scene the peasants have marched to the doors of the castle, making an outcry that brings Count Oberthal to the door with a company of his guests. At sight of him, instead of attacking, the peasants are dismayed and attempt to hide their weapons, but the Count divines their intent and addresses them in an amiable tone, requesting to know if their threatening words and angered feelings are not incited by the gloomy Puritans who go about the country preaching impious doctrines and striving to create popular unrest. The three Anabaptists dolefully lament the blindness of the people, and the hardships laid upon them by unfeeling lords, but Oberthal turns to Jonas and exposes him as a knavish butler driven from the castle because of his drunkenness, and to more thoroughly humiliate the agitators, Oberthal orders his soldiers to beat them off by laying on their backs with sheathed swords. The peasants and Anabaptists disappearing, Bertha and Fides timidly draw near and make obeisance to the Count, who receives the girl with such flattering words that she is much frightened. Fides bids her take courage, and the two join in a pretty romanza, beseeching the Count to give consent to the marriage of Bertha and John. But Oberthal is so deeply fascinated by Bertha's beauty that he refuses to grant the necessary permission, designing to possess her himself. The two protest that such decision reflects the will of a cruel tyrant, for which boldness, in disputing his right, Oberthal orders his retainers to seize the offending women and confine them as prisoners in the castle where they shall be retained to wait his royal pleasure. As the Count passes through the gates which close behind him, peasants and the three Anabaptists return to the stage. Having been witnesses to the outrage, they threaten the castle again, by violent outcry and demonstration, which scene terminates the first act.

Act II.—When the curtain rises again it is upon a scene in the hostelry of John in Leyden, and the action is introduced by a waltz and drinking-chorus, in which many people participate. John waits upon his numerous customers with unusual cheerfulness, thinking the while of his mother's mission to bring Bertha, who he believes will soon become his wife. In a few minutes the three Anabaptists, Zacharias, Jonas and Matthias, enter the tavern, and take seats at a table, but Jonas suddenly fixes his eyes upon John and calls the attention of his companions to the striking likeness the inn-keeper bears to a portrait of David that hangs in the Munster Cathedral. Inquiry of the peasants elicits from them the information that he is famous for valor and strength and knows his Bible by heart. This convinces the Anabaptists that John is the immortal one for whom they have been seeking, the chosen Son of Heaven to preach the truth on earth. In a few moments John dismisses the peasants and takes a seat at a table to wait the coming of his mother and Bertha.

The three fanatics, finding their opportunity at hand, approach John, who appears to be gloomily engaged with his thoughts, and Zacharias, striking him familiarly upon the shoulder, sympathetically inquires what cloud is passing over his mind? To this question, addressed by a stranger, John affects some surprise, but desiring counsel, he replies with confidence that he is awaiting his mother and intended bride, but their delay in coming causes him great uneasiness, especially since last night an evil presage has troubled his mind. Urged to explain, John prays that the knowledge of the three may be able to interpret a strange dream that has twice been repeated, which he proceeds to describe in a recitative: That he seemed to be standing under the vast dome of a splendid temple where he had been crowned, and the people prostrating themselves proclaimed him David, Son of the Most High. Upon a shrine, where offerings were being made, there was written in fire the words, "Woe! woe to thee!" and that when he attempted to seize his sword a vast surge of blood swept it away. To escape the gory flood he mounted the throne, but this too was carried by the flood, and as he was borne upon the tide, the lightning grew fierce, and great flames arose around him; while Satan clutched his soul, a mighty clamor was set up from the earth, amid which hellish cries were heard, "May he be forever cursed!" From out this din infernal, one single voice was distinguishable, which, though feeble, addressed a prayer for mercy that Heaven listened to, and hope was thereby inspired.

Such beauty for me would be best! And for you! No, I'll not permit it.

The Anabaptists regard the dream as a prefigurement of John's destiny, and interpret it as a means employed by God for calling him to rule over the nation, thus declaring: "In so mysterious a dream Heaven itself speaks to us, the future discovers toils to thee; thou, John, shalt reign." There is created by this incentive and invitation two emotions, one restraining, the other propelling, which engage in violent conflict. John, the peasant, shrinks from assuming the mighty responsibilities that must be borne by a ruler, yet having faith in the interpretation of his dream, he is almost persuaded to accept the alluring prospect that worldly ambition holds forth. While halting between two inducements, his thoughts, grasping at every motive, revert to Bertha, who, like himself, is only a peasant, ignorant of the ways and burdens of sovereignty, and he reflects that to gain a crown it must be at the sacrifice of the one who possesses his heart. This reminder, for the moment, determines him as to his action, and he makes choice of his preference to be husband of Bertha, under a thatched roof, where love abides without care, rather than to be king of the mightiest nation of the world, and expresses his ambition in a noble romanza:

> "Oh, there's a sweeter empire far,
> Which long has been my guiding star;
> Oh, thou my joy, my greatest gain,
> If in thy faithful heart I reign," etc.

The three Anabaptists insist that John shall set off with them—that duty demands his services, promising that on the morrow he shall be crowned king of Germany, but he resists their entreaties, protesting that he has no desire for royal pomp, since nuptial couch is far more pleasing, bringing a felicity such as no crown can ever feel. The Anabaptists go out, declaring that he shall be king. Relieved of their sinister presence, John falls again into pleasant anticipations of his approaching bliss, but is aroused soon by the sounds of horses' hoofs and clash of arms. On the next instant Bertha runs in and cries for protection against a cruel tyrant who is pursuing her. She runs and hides herself in a recess under the stairway as Oberthal and soldiers appear at the door. The odious Count hurriedly explains that while conducting two female prisoners through a thick wood one of them suddenly broke away and fled with such speed that she could not be overtaken, but she has been tracked to this house and he demands that she be immediately brought forth, threatening to execute the other prisoner, who is John's mother, in his presence, if the girl is not produced. John pleads for the life of his mother, freely offering his own to satisfy the Count's vengeance, but Oberthal refuses, and directs his soldiers to bring in Fides, who appearing, she falls on her knees before her son, extending her arms in supplication for his help. A soldier lifts a battle-axe above the trembling woman's head, at which terrible sight John runs up to Bertha and drags her forth, directing her to follow the soldiers. She is received half-fainting by the monster, and as the soldiers bear her away John falls in a chair heart-broken.

Fides presently recovers sufficiently to minister to her son, and in probably the most dramatic of Meyerbeer's arias she blesses him for his noble sacrifice to save her life, begging him now to be courageous, not doubting that the Lord will strengthen his arm to redeem Bertha from the cruel despot. She passes out, with revenge in her heart, as the hymn of the Anabaptists is heard, which serves to rouse John from his despair and to inspire him with a fury against Oberthal and all that belong to the class of nobles. When the Anabaptists enter they find the wretched man eager to embrace their proposal. His mightiest ambition is to destroy Oberthal, and being told that this revenge may be quickly satisfied by following their counsel, John begs to be at once instructed as to his duty. Jonas replying for the three, tells him they are appointed to be the interpreters of Heaven's will, able to read the future, and to discover the divine one who has been sent to deliver the people from their oppressors. The three

"Ah! Why! Heaven's thunder
Is not hurled against the wicked!"

thereupon declare that the signs of Messiahship are on his brows, and that he is that same one who, more divinely inspired than was the maid, Joan of Arc, is to save the nation. John is persuaded to believe all that is thus told him, finding confirmation in the visions that have appeared to him in many dreams, and he therefore asks the three to show him the path to glory.

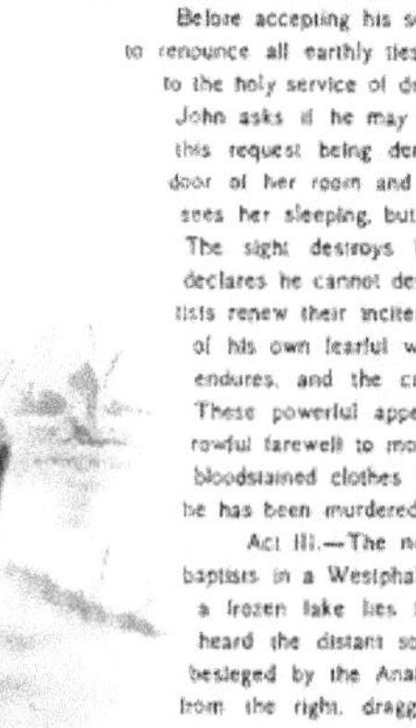

Before accepting his services the Anabaptists require John to renounce all earthly ties, that he may better devote his life to the holy service of destroying the impious race of tyrants. John asks if he may not say farewell to his mother, but this request being denied, he sorrowfully approaches the door of her room and opening it a little way looks in and sees her sleeping, but murmuring a prayer for his safety. The sight destroys his resolution, and in anguish he declares he cannot desert his mother. The three Anabaptists renew their incitements, reminding him of God's call, of his own fearful wrongs, of the sufferings that Bertha endures, and the crown that awaits his holy service. These powerful appeals decide him, and bidding a sorrowful farewell to mother, home, he departs, leaving some bloodstained clothes behind that his mother may believe he has been murdered, thus concluding Act II.

Act III.—The next act opens in the camp of Anabaptists in a Westphalian forest. The time is winter, and a frozen lake lies in the background, beyond which is heard the distant sound of battle, for Munster is being besieged by the Anabaptists. A party of soldiers enter from the right, dragging in men, women and children prisoners, all richly dressed to indicate their relations to the noble class. Matthias and chorus point to the captives, and dancing about them, rejoice at the Anabaptists' victory, and gloat over the prospect of destroying, root and branch, all the hated heads and offspring of the privileged nobles. Zacharias returns from the battle with a troop of followers, and flourishing his battle-axe as a sign of victory, he renders a spirited pæan, in which he recounts the valor of the Anabaptists in their conflict with the vassals of oppressors, whose vast numbers have been vanquished and trodden under foot. Having finished his song of exultation, Zacharias reports that the Anabaptists have fought since early dawn, and the fruits of victory are not confined to glory achieved, for the peasants are hastening hither with great stores of provisions to feed the hungry warriors, for whom they entertain patriotic sympathy and hold in high appreciation. Matthias piously observes that it is manna from heaven to recompense the holy battalions of God's army!

A merry scene follows the entrance of sutlers and purveyors from across the frozen lake, who bring many kinds of tempting food, which is exchanged with the soldiers for trophies of the battlefield. The girls remove their skates and commence a lively dance, accompanied by ballet music, while the hungry men satisfy their appetites, after which, as night is advancing, they put on their skates again and depart across the lake. Darkness rapidly falls on the scene, and the sentinels being placed, the tired soldiers seek repose, leaving Zacharias and Matthias alone. The latter asks his lieutenant what news from Munster? to which reply is made that Oberthal stoutly refuses to surrender the castle, and that action to reduce the place must be quickly taken, or the cause of the Anabaptists will be ruined, for the Emperor is hurrying with a large army to the assistance of the Count. Zacharias thereupon advises that three hundred men be sent to storm the castle, under the cover of darkness. At this juncture Jonas and a party of soldiers appear at the door of Matthias' tent, leading Oberthal, whom they captured while he was wandering in a neighboring wood. His identity, however, is not detected in the darkness, and to the better prevent discovery he offers to join the sect, and takes the oath required, to respect the cotters' rights, to take from the rich their gold, and to put to death all barons and nobles. Being thus sworn,

Oberthal is ordered to march with the army against Munster, with purpose declared to seize and hang the rascal Count who dwells therein. All these pledges are confirmed by drinking wine together, but need yet remains that the stranger comrade shall show his face, that he may be known hereafter as a faithful soldier. Jonas strikes a light, and the instant it flares up the three Anabaptists recognize Oberthal, and with fury now unconfined they promise to punish him without mercy, and appoint a monk to attend him, that religious consolation may not be denied him in the last hour.

John, the accepted prophet, enters, in a pensive mood, as Oberthal is being conducted away, and is reverently hailed by Zacharias as the saviour of Germany. John expresses an intention to see his mother again, for whose safety he is deeply concerned, at which desire Zacharias affects angered astonishment, and reminds him that to seek his mother now will bring upon both him and her the vengeance of Heaven! To prevent John's purpose, Oberthal is led in, attended by a monk and by soldiers, who inform their prophet leader that the prisoner's death has been ordered. This usurpation of authority so incenses John that he threatens the three Anabaptists with death if they do not immediately release the prisoner, and commands all to leave his tent while he questions Oberthal. The Count being left with the man he has so basely wronged, cringes like a culprit brought to bar for his hellish deeds, admits that he deserves to die for his crimes, and with shame tells that Bertha, to preserve her honor from his lecherous assaults, threw herself into the river, but Heaven, in pity, caused her to be saved, and yesterday she was seen in Munster, whither he was journeying, to ask her pardon, when arrested. At this recital John is so rejoiced to know that Bertha lives, and has escaped a monster's designs, he orders that Oberthal be spared, and reserved for Bertha to decide what his fate shall be.

In the succeeding scene we are introduced to the camp of the Anabaptists, in which are many soldiers, greatly excited and angered at the Prophet (John), for sparing the life of Oberthal. Their distrust of him increases, and as each one in turn voices his opinion of John's treachery to the cause, they finally break forth in a demand that as a false prophet he shall perish by the axe, that is fitting punishment for traitors. John overhears these utterances of the conspirators, and turning fiercely upon the soldiers, demands to know who, without his orders, led them to battle? They all point to Matthias as their leader, but he, alarmed by the Prophet's anger, declares that it was Zacharias who assumed the leadership. Observing how completely they appreciate the insubordination of their acts, John denounces Matthias and Zacharias as instigators of sedition, who have invited the wrath of God, and will no doubt be made to answer their folly and crimes by a Heavenly chastisement. But magnanimously he offers to appeal to the Lord for mercy, and for renewal of the faith the traitors have forsworn. At his order all the Anabaptists fall upon their knees and in chorus send up their prayerful petitions for mercy and guidance. As the Anabaptists are at prayer, clarions and trumpets are heard in the distance, which John interprets as a challenge of the enemy, and he declares that Heaven urges the faithful to renew the battle on the morrow. Zacharias, humbled by John's reproof, calls him Great Prophet, Lord of the Holy Banners, and begs that he may join so divine a leader against the impious foe. Intense religious enthusiasm pervades the camp, under which John professes to behold a heavenly vision, prefigurement of his victory and elevation, and the act concludes with chants of a martial yet pious character as the soldiers begin their march on Munster.

Act IV.—The fourth act is played in the city of Munster, which has been captured by the revolutionary Anabaptists. The curtain rises upon a scene of the city square, upon the right of which is the palace, reached by imposing steps that are crowded with people ascending and descending, carrying bags of gold. The defeated nobles bewail their misfortunes, while the Anabaptist soldiers exult over their victory and praise the Prophet. Some of the noble class gather to themselves and discuss with tearful regret the fact that the Electors have been overthrown, and that this day the Anabaptist chiefs will proclaim their prophet leader Emperor of Germany. While the square is ringing with a chorus of "Long life to the Prophet," a beggar woman enters and seats herself on

"[illegible]"

the sidewalk curb, where she is approached by a citizen with request to know her troubles. The woman proves to be Fides, who, in a plaintively declamatory aria of great power, solicits alms:

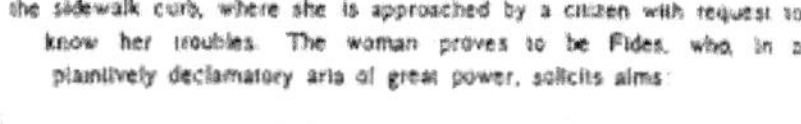

"Oh! give to save a suffering soul.
Oh! give! a wretched heart console.
Oh! give, I pray, to ease my woes.
For masses for my son's repose!"

This appeal induces several citizens to bestow pittances, after which they hurriedly pass out for fear of the soldiery, whereupon Bertha, in the disguise of a pilgrim, enters; she is immediately recognized by Fides, and the two affectionately embrace. Bertha at once describes the misadventure that has brought her to this place, in which she relates how, to escape the lecherous Oberthal, she sought death in the river, but was rescued by a fisherman, and then she fled to Munster to seek the protection of her grandfather, an old soldier, who is a guard at the palace. Passionately, Bertha pleads to be led to John and is transported by the hope of speedily seeing him, but Fides, trembling with grief, is compelled to destroy her happy anticipations by informing the poor girl that John is dead, murdered by the Prophet!

Unconscious that her son has been hailed as the chosen one of God to lead the Anabaptists, Fides wonders who this loudly-proclaimed Prophet may be, to which Bertha, equally ignorant of his identity, furiously replies that he is the monster tyrant who is drenching all Germany with blood! and forthwith conceives a purpose to secretly enter the palace and by God's help to kill him. Fides is too weak to offer assistance in this design for vengeance, but gives her prayers, and calling to the Holy Virgin for hope and comfort, the two pass out.

The scene next changes to the Cathedral of Munster, where the coronation is to take place. Guards of the Prophet are on duty when a great procession marches in, headed by Electors bearing the crown, sceptre, and other coronal paraphernalia. John next appears, bareheaded, robed in white, and proceeds towards the high altar, passing Fides, who is kneeling in prayer, and unmindful of all the pageantry attending the royal ceremony. During this pompous coronation march there is an accompaniment of clanging bells, solemn chants, organ peals, and choral rhythms of the most impressive character, furnishing a splendid and intensely dramatic prelude to the scene which is to follow. Suddenly, when the clarions and trumpets announce the coronation, Fides raises her head to call down the vengeance of Heaven upon the Prophet, that he may be cursed on earth and damned in the world to come, and then in a powerful aria of imprecation, she invokes the gods to make of Bertha a second Judith, by whose hand the base impostor king may meet a bloody death.

The organ rolls out a deep diapason, and a group of choristers enter, followed by the populace, who acclaim the Prophet King, the son of Heaven, a Messiah sent to redeem the land from oppressors. John now appears, robed in royal regalia, and immediately behind him come Jonas, Matthias and Zacharias, before whom the people prostrate themselves in adoration. John ascends the royal dais with a majestic demeanor, and placing his hand upon the crown, repeats the words: "I am the elect—the elect of Heaven!" Fides has risen and stands for a few moments intensely contemplating John, until convinced that she is not deceived in her first recognition, rushes forward and exclaims, "My son!" The people are appalled by this insult to their Prophet King, and express astonishment that she is not immediately dealt with for her audacity and sacrilege. John, moved by his love, is about to embrace his mother, when he is admonished by Matthias that recognition by word or act will be a mortal offence, to be punished by her death. Thus terrified, John masters his emotions and imperiously demands to know, "Who is this woman?" To which Fides, wrung by this, to her, cruel repudiation, answers that she is the poor woman who nourished him, watched over him with true maternal solicitude, rejoiced in his successes, wept for his misfortunes, loved him as a fond mother does upon her darling child, guided his youthful steps in honor, and sorrowfully she reproaches him for his ingratitude and shameful disrespect.

The people are astounded by the vehemence of Fides' protestations and wonder what mystery is this, which makes them half believe that John is more mortal than he has been represented. The three Anabaptists, perceiving the effect of her declarations, counteract it by pronouncing Fides to be a lying and deceitful wretch, whom the Son of God will not fail to punish as she deserves. John reinforces this harsh threat by assuring the people he cannot understand why this woman claims him as her son, or what her desire may be. Fides replies, that as a wretched mother she wishes most to forgive an ungrateful son, whom she had hoped to take to her heart as she has often done before. The Anabaptists pronounce her to be a blasphemer, and demand that the Prophet King shall atone her sinful words and guilty fancy with sentence of dire punishment. So declaring, the three Anabaptists threaten her with their daggers, but John interferes to prevent her murder by asserting that the poor woman is evidently mad and that only a miracle can restore her reason. So saying, he commands Fides to kneel, and supplicating Heaven to inspire him with a holy judgment, addresses her: "A son thou didst love; dispel every fear, and look upon me, and as thou seest the popular sword flourished to destroy, say if I am that son!" She fails as yet to understand that his own life is at stake in the answer, and exclaims, "O my son!" At this the people brandish their weapons more menacingly, and John turns to the Anabaptists begging if he has deceived the people they will kill him as an impostor, and exposes his breast to their swords. Perceiving now the cause of his repudiation, Fides declares to the people that her darkened eyes have failed her, for seeing now more clearly, she knows he is not her son! This denial of her previous asseveration convinces the populace that John is indeed the Messiah, who performs miracles by the great power of his voice. John gives secret orders to an officer and goes off; at the same instant Fides recognizes Bertha, who has come in to kill the Prophet, and to save her from committing the deed, leads her away. This intensely dramatic scene concludes the fourth act.

Act V.—The final act begins with a scene that represents a vaulted cavern in the palace at Munster, in which Matthias, Jonas and Zacharias appear in a conspiracy to deliver up John to the army of the Emperor of Germany, that they may thereby purchase immunity for themselves. Zacharias asks how they may escape when the Emperor reduces the place and makes the Anabaptists captives? which question Jonas answers by producing a paper from the King promising safe conduct out of the country, together with all their treasure, if they will deliver up the Prophet. This promise the three eagerly accept, and then pass out by the door on the right.

"[illegible]"

In the succeeding scene Fides appears in a narrow prison cell, to which she has been consigned by her son's orders, upon demand of the Anabaptists. She is distracted by conflicting emotions, one moment imprecating John as an ungrateful son, and the next beseeching Heaven to pity his unfaithfulness, and offering her life as a sacrifice if thereby his own may be preserved. In a little while an officer enters to announce to Fides the visit of the Prophet King, which news she receives with joyful manifestations, and gives expression to her transports in a passionate aria:

"Immortal grace, oh! conq'ring come,
His guilty conscience to reprove," etc.

John enters the prison, enveloped in a cloak, with a crown upon his head, and at a sign the officer withdraws. He greets his mother affectionately, but instead of returning his embrace, she commands him to fall upon his knees, before God, and prove to her that he is prophet and son of Heaven! Obediently he prostrates himself and entreats her to pardon a misguided son. To this she sternly replies, "My son! I no longer have one! The child for whom I lament—he was pure, innocent, and so devoted that hell nor heaven could make him deny his mother!" John acknowledges his shame and remorse, and pleads for the mercy of a mother's grace, but to his entreaties she answers with condemnation of his dastard deeds, his hands reeking with human blood, and his heart stained by a devil's passion. These reprovings, which he realizes are just, fill him with remorse, and in a powerful aria he describes the horror he feels for his misdeeds, but tries to justify his actions by a desire to avenge Bertha, and to punish the tyrants who have so long and grievously outraged the people. Fides declares that his guilt far transcends that of the oppressors, for no other has dared to challenge the wrath of God, thus adding the greatest sacrilege to his lesser crimes; but if he be sincerely penitent and truly desires a mother's love, she exhorts him to prove his integrity of purpose by renouncing at once the power that made him king; to abjure the claims of his unholy pretensions and confess the glory of God.

The demands of his mother seem hard for John to comply with, since to his selfish perception such renunciation means the relinquishment of the greatest earthly preferments, and a desertion of the comrades who exalted him, and who will call him coward and hypocrite. Fides is inexorable in her insistence, but consoles him for loss of power by assurance that true remorse can calm the anger of Heaven, and that through a mother's prayer a repentant son will find mercy. The counsel which she gives strikes deep into John's heart, making him conscious of his iniquity, and promising to be directed by her advisings, he beseeches his mother's blessing, which she joyfully bestows.

The interview between John and his mother, which has brought reconciliation and a heavenly peace, is interrupted by the appearance of an officer, who rushes in to apprise the Prophet that he has been betrayed and that the foe is upon them. Commanded to calm himself and explain, the intensely excited officer imparts the information that a scheme to sacrifice the Prophet was conceived even during the coronation feast, since which it has been discovered that a mad woman has planned to set the palace on fire that all may perish in the flames. The next moment soldiers descend the stairs with Bertha, whom they bring before John, as the culprit seized in the very act of applying the incendiary torch, and they entreat him to immediately order her execution. Bertha no sooner looks upon the Prophet than, with horrified astonishment, she recognizes him, even though he is robed and crowned as emperor, as John, her erstwhile lover; but her soul revolts at the crimes laid to his charge, and recoiling, she exclaims: "Begone! thy guilty hand dare not to fix on me; the axe has been thy sceptre! Thy laws were misdeeds! The blood which thou hast shed separates us forever!" Fides beseeches John to fly from this place at once, but his situation is so despairing he invites a doom that will end the torment that reigns in his heart. Conscience-stricken for his crimes, feeling that the hand of an avenging God is upon him, that Bertha despises him and prays for his punishment, he longs for death. Fides, with a mother's love, reconciled by his penitence, supplicates Bertha to show mercy to her remorseful son, but mercy has been driven from her heart by the murderous slaughter which John has instigated, and when he approaches her to implore forgiveness, she repels him furiously, and drawing a dagger she despairingly utters: "Yes, I loved thee once, thee whom I now curse! Perhaps I love thee still, and this shall be my recompense!" With these words spoken, she strikes the weapon into her breast and falls dead in the arms of Fides! The death of Bertha, who has been a sacrifice to his worldly ambitions, arouses the most uncontrollable

"Thou, tyrant, shalt perish with me.
Welcome, sacred flame! To yon celestial sphere
May our souls take flight!"

fury in John, and calling upon God to save his mother, he makes a vow to destroy the impostors who seduced him from home, mother, sweetheart, and peaceful content, by the allurements of a throne. His revenge, he swears, shall fall upon them; but realizing his own unworthiness to live, he resolves upon a plan whereby while bringing destruction upon the Anabaptist leaders, he will also perish with them, and therefore he instructs his officers: "When you see our foes come hither, close fast those gates upon this gulf, from which the sulphurous flame will soon arise to destroy all! From this accursed place you shall escape alone, my trusty friends, but I shall find my peace by dying with my enemies."

Having conceived his desperate purpose John invites the Anabaptists to the banqueting hall, where a revelry of good cheer is begun by a bacchanalian song which he sings with gusto, with choral refrain:

"Quaff, quaff, in joyous measure!
Breathe, breathe delirious pleasure,
Hail, hail the reign of pleasure.
Drink, drink to nectar's slave!
Hail, hail, this feast celestial!
Pledge triumphantly the brave
Comrades worthy of the Prophet.
Sweet recompense you'll soon receive.
All hail, all hail, all hail, all hail!"

As John finishes his song, doors open from the right and left, admitting to the hall the Bishop of Munster, Elector of Westphalia, and principal officers and nobles of the empire. After these come the Anabaptists who have betrayed the Prophet, headed by Zacharias, who insolently cry, "Death to the tyrant king!" John again gives orders to close the gates, that they may prove portals to the tombs of those herein; but this command the Anabaptists disregard, and rejoice that the Prophet has been given into their hands. Oberthal now steps forward, and laying his hand upon John, imperiously declares him a prisoner, as the leader of a murderous sedition which will speedily find a terrible and exemplary punishment. But exultantly John, in turn, announces that all are captives to a just fate, at which moment an awful explosion takes place, followed by falling walls and spreading flames, that cut off retreat. Triumphantly, John exclaims: "Tyrant, and traitors all, shall perish with me. I am the instrument as well as the object of Heaven's vengeance, that a deserving doom may atone our guilt." As he is speaking, a woman with disheveled hair rushes through the flames, into John's arms, whom he quickly recognizes as his mother, who has sought fire and falling walls that she may die with him. He embraces her tenderly, and she bestows her pardon for all past offences. Clasped in each other's arms they welcome the sacred flames that will bear their souls upward to the celestial sphere where peace and joy may be found to compensate for the strifes and sufferings of life, which touching scene completes the opera.

Lucrezia Borgia

(AFTER THE ORIGINAL PAINTING BY C. D. GRAVES)

LUCREZIA[?]: "Look you! at your feet!
Fate hath broken the magic dreaming;
(For thy head too surely vanquished
See her wrathful rival pour!"

LAST ACT, LAST SCENE

LUCREZIA BORGIA.

(LUCRETIA BORGIA.)

MUSIC BY DONIZETTI.——WORDS BY ROMANI.

LUCRETIA BORGIA is probably the greatest of Donizetti's several beautiful operas, notwithstanding it is sung less often than "Lucia." The subject which he has so admirably used, with the help of an able librettist, is borrowed from Victor Hugo's sublime tragedy of the same name, and the story of the novelist is followed as closely as lyric treatment will permit. Indeed, such free use was made of the original text that when the opera was produced in Paris, in 1840, Hugo secured an injunction against its further representation, upon the grounds of copyright infringement. The libretto was thereupon hastily rewritten, the characters considerably changed and a new title adopted, but subsequently, Hugo was pacified by a satisfactory payment, and Romani's text was used, as it continues to be. "Lucretia Borgia" was first produced in 1834, at the La Scala, Milan, where it had a long and successful run, but not until 1843 was the opera sung in English, in London, on which occasion it was enthusiastically received.

The story of "Lucretia Borgia" may be found in history, and is briefly told in all encyclopedias, so its recapitulation is not necessary here, save to remind the reader that she was the daughter of Rodrigo Borgia, afterwards Pope Alexander VI, and the sister of Cæsar Borgia, that one time remarkably successful Roman ruler, who after meeting with many misadventures was finally slain before Viano, 1507. Lucretia is charged with being at once a human vampire and succubus, but to speak the truth she was pious, prudent, highly educated, and a patron of learning. The story which Hugo tells imputes to her the most atrocious crimes and disreputable conduct, among other things representing that she was mother of an illegitimate son named Gennaro. To conceal his birth, Lucretia is said to have left him, an infant, with a fisherman, who adopted the child as his own, and gave him such advantages as his slender means afforded. Gennaro developed into a sturdy young man with an impetuous temperament, which led him to take service with the Venetian army, where, through the performance of many valorous deeds he rose to eminent rank. It is at this point of the story that the action of the opera begins, and is followed thus:

Lucretia Borgia, who at the time is wife of the Duke Alfonso d'Este, is about to start to Venice upon a secret mission, and coincidently an embassy from her husband's court is ready to proceed upon a similar purpose to Ferrara. Among the young cavaliers in the service of the Republic, and attached to d'Este's embassy, are Gennaro, and Maffio Orsini, who are inseparable friends, attached to one another by an oath to share each other's fortune, and a pledge to hate the Borgias. The two friends often discuss the crimes reputed to Lucretia, neither suspecting that she is mother to Gennaro, nor has she any information of her son since the day he was left an infant with the fisherman. An hour before the embassy is about to depart Gennaro, drowsy from the heat of the day, falls asleep on the terrace. While he is thus reposing, Lucretia comes upon him, and is so attracted by his comely appearance that she pauses, with womanly curiosity, to contemplate his person, and to wonder who he may be. While she is admiring the handsome captain, Gennaro awakens, and seeing Lucretia betraying an interest in him he addresses her after the manner of gallants of the time, and the two at once engage in earnest conversation that

PALACE OF THE CÆSAR BORGIA.

leads quickly to mutual infatuation. Asked by Lucretia to relate to her something of his adventurous life, Gennaro tells of his unknown parentage, and longings to discover his mother. Having spoken freely of his own life, Gennaro in turn requests that she reveal her name and inform him whence she comes, but she modestly refuses, giving many excuses; and while the two are thus conversing, Orsini and four companions come upon the scene, who immediately recognizing Lucretia, denounce her to Gennaro as the crime-laden woman he has been taught to despise.

In the next scene, the Embassy, to which Gennaro is an attaché, has arrived at Ferrara, and as they stroll about the city, he comes to the Ducal Palace of the Borgias. So stung is he by the disgrace he feels for having indulged in an amorous interview with the Duchess (Lucretia), that in a fit of passion he defaces the ducal arms above the palace entrance, for which iconoclasm he is arrested and brought before the Duke, Lucretia's husband, for punishment. By a strange chance it happens that the Duke is cognizant of the secret attachment that Lucretia formed for the young captain, and his jealousy aroused, he has placed a watch upon her actions. Lucretia does not know who destroyed the royal insignia, and is so indignant at the act of vandalism that she extorts an oath from the Duke to punish with death the culprit when he is found. The Duke and Duchess sit in judgment when the offender is brought in, and as he enters, Lucretia discovers, to her horror, that the prisoner is the young soldier in whom she took such a vivid interest that love for him was excited. The now wretched woman beseeches the Duke to disregard her merciless request, made in the heat of an insane anger, and to show compassion, but the Duke is inexorable, and in a jealous rage he accuses her of being Gennaro's wicked paramour. Death he pronounces upon the offender, but to Lucretia he permits the dread alternative of seeing Gennaro perish by the executioner's sword, or administering to him by her own hand a draught of the deadly Borgia wine, such as she has secretly given to so many of her victims, and which has made her name dreaded.

Lucretia is driven to despair by the cruel order of her husband, but as his commands must be obeyed, she accepts the poor alternative of presenting the poison cup. Gennaro has been kept in a side room during this tragic proceeding, but he is now brought forth and reintroduced under the pretence of acquittal and friendship, and the wine is prepared and offered to him as a friendly drink with the Duke. The moment the cup is drained, the Duke retires from the room, congratulating himself upon the accomplishment of his design to lead his wife and her paramour into a fatal snare. Lucretia is overwhelmed by her despair, but suddenly remembers that she possesses an antidote, which she quickly produces, and forcing Gennaro to swallow it, she then shows him a means of escape from the Palace, and entreats him to flee without delay from the Duke's anger.

Gennaro, restored to health, hastens to quit the city, but when upon the point of departing, he meets Orsini, who persuades him to forego his resolution for a day to attend a fête to be given that evening by the Princess Negroni. During the festivities a quarrel takes place between Orsini and Gubetta, a Spaniard, who belongs to Lucretia's retinue. Knives are drawn, and great excitement ensues, but order is presently restored, and the hilarity resumed. Suddenly, the lights begin to pale, and a moment later a procession of Capuchin Monks, dismal and dolorous, appear, as attendants to Lucretia. As she appears within the door of the banquet room, she declares she has come to repay the insult that Orsini and his companions gave her: that "for their ball in Venice she has returned them a supper in Ferrara, for all are poisoned!" The Monks now draw aside, and five coffins are shown, for the bodies of Orsini and his four companions. To the amazement of Lucretia, Gennaro, whom she had supposed was gone to Venice, steps forth and asks that a sixth be provided, for he too has partaken of the wine. All now go out save Gennaro and Lucretia, and she implores him to receive from her hands the antidote that will save his life. He takes the saving cup, but finding that he cannot divide its contents with his friends, he manfully determines to share their fate, but first bids her prepare for death at his own hands. Lucretia, horror-stricken and remorseful, warns him that he is about to commit an awful crime, for that he also is a—Borgia! The poison has already begun its deadly work, and Gennaro, with feeble breath, exhorts her to disclose the secret which her words imply. To his entreaty, Lucretia tells him that he is her—son! This revelation breaks the thread of his life, and Gennaro expires in his mother's arms. At this moment the Duke appears looking for his victims, but he finds only his anguished wife, who, after disclosing her secret, falls dead upon the body of her son.

Prologue.—The opening scene is a beautiful one, representing the terrace of the Grimani Palace in Venice, during a night festival. At the back a glimpse of the Grand Canal is had, with graceful gondolas gliding over its surface, and beyond lies the city bathed in glorious moonlight. Several persons enter and sing the praise of Venice, birthplace and home of pleasure. Gubetta observes that splendid as the palace of Grimani appears, more gorgeous is the Court of Don Alfonso, the brave Duke of Ferrara, and the Duchess, Lucretia Borgia. Orsini reproaches Gubetta for daring to speak the name of this most infamous of criminals in the presence of this company, a sentiment which his four companions heartily endorse. Orsini, to illustrate the courage of Gennaro, proceeds to tell a tale, but Gennaro, having heard it often spoken, has no patience to listen to its repetition, and wrapping his mantle about him says he will sleep until the story is ended. Orsini now relates to the four others that on the blood-red field of Rimini he was wounded nigh to death, and lay smothering in his gore, while the trampling hoofs of a thousand cavalry bore swiftly down upon him, sweeping the embattled plain like a destroying besom. Even there when danger breathed its horrent flames, Gennaro, though till then a stranger, rushed forth and out of the very jaws of death bore him to a convent near by and nursed him back to health, nor asked other reward for his daring service than that of friendship. For this noble deed there is no prize that can requite, but a pledge he gave and swore they together thenceforth to share each other's fate. Orsini also tells that while they were exchanging vows, a gigantic phantom, shrouded in black, uprose before them and with forceful voice warned them against the Borgia, whose dwelling place and odious presence alike breed destruction and ruin. This recital serves to impress more deeply upon Orsini's companions the duty of despising Lucretia Borgia, and of opposing her whenever opportunity offers. After this prelude to the dramatic action that is to follow, Orsini and his four companions quietly steal away, leaving Gennaro soundly sleeping on the terrace, wrapped in his martial cloak.

In the succeeding scene a gondola glides by to a landing, and from it steps a masked lady, who proves to be Lucretia Borgia attended by Gubetta, a Spaniard in her service. She quickly perceives the sleeping captain, Gennaro, and commanding Gubetta to retire, she advances cautiously and gazing with pleasurable interest upon the stranger, sings a brilliant aria, "Holy beauty, child of nature," etc. Her admiration so increases that she removes her mask and draws still nearer the sleeping soldier:

"To call but a kiss the dearest,
Laden with holy affection
Yielding him more protection
Reposing on my heart."

The Duke Alfonso, her husband, has become possessed of a jealousy, and following upon her track, with a companion, they come upon Lucretia as she removes her mask to kiss Gennaro's hand, but wisely keep themselves concealed from her view to better discover the issue of this new infatuation of the fickle Duchess. The affectionate demonstrations of Lucretia arouse Gennaro, who seizes her hand and detains her to express much gallant sentiment in praise of her charms, and soon vows his love. She presses for a proof of his sincerity and he declares that no love has he ever known before except for his mother, whose face, alas, through evil fortune, he has never been permitted to behold. Her curiosity excited, she entreats him to tell of his adventures, and how it came to pass that he has never known his mother? It is a strange tale, and no less mournful, he replies, and then proceeds to relate the story of his life in an exquisite romanza, the wondrous beauty of which makes it one of the most charming airs in Italian opera:

"Deemed of a fisher's lowly race,
Where the wide beach and wild-wood
Echoing smiles from Naples' sun,
Witnessed my humble childhood.
One day there sought me an unknown Knight,
Breaking the spell that charmed me,
Who having horsed and well armed me,
A writing then bade me scan
Penned by a mother, ah! misery -
Each word the scroll was bearing,
Told how a wretch seduced a breast
For me, its child sore fearing,
Hushed in my heart, I guard her will."

Lucretia is enthralled by Gennaro's melancholy story, and asks him if he still retains the letter that proves his unhappy lot? Appreciating her sympathy, and pleased by her manner, Gennaro draws it forth from a place near his heart, and permits her to read it. By this evidence she discovers that the handsome captain is no other than her illegitimate son, who was left an infant with a fisherman to conceal her disgrace. She exhorts him to ever adore his mother, and to pray every day that she may welcome him back again, to which he declares his purpose never to rest until he finds her. While the two are thus conversing, several persons, in masks, approach from different parts of the stage. Among these are Orsini, and his companions, who drawing near recognize Lucretia as she is trying to release herself from Gennaro, who detains her to learn her name. Lucretia covers her face with her mask, from the angered gaze of Orsini, but he exposes her, regardless of the threats of Gennaro, and in a concerted number, of intensely dramatic power, reveals that she poisoned his brother; that she stabbed his aunt to possess herself of his birthright; that she lured Appiano's young nephew to a fatal banquet, and to Gennaro he exclaims, "Since our names are familiar to you, know then that this wanton, this incestuous night-loving betrayer, is—'Lucretia Borgia!'" A cry of horror escapes from her lips at this exposure of her crimes, and she falls fainting, which intensely dramatic scene furnishes conclusion for the prologue to the first act.

Act I.—When the curtain rises again there is shown a public square in Ferrara, on the right of which is a palace with a marble escutcheon over the main entrance on which the name "Borgia" appears. The time is night, and on the right is a small house, through the windows of which lights are seen. The Duke and Rustighello enter, covered with long mantles, and pausing before the house the Duke asks his companion if he has followed the footsteps of the villain near to the Ducal Palace, whither Lucretia invited him? Rustighello, proud of his spying and detective abilities, answers in a spirit manifesting his satisfaction, that he has traced him to Cubetta's house, where night after night Gennaro is entertained by his comrades with much wine-drinking and revelry, often continuing until the dawn. The house to which Gennaro has been tracked is opposite, and making sure that he is now within, the Duke threatens that this night shall be the last the paramour will spend in drinking bouts with his vile companions, and in a passionate aria vows his vengeance: "Haste then to glut a vengeance," etc. The Duke hears the sound of voices drawing nearer, the lights are extinguished, and he retires with Rustighello to await events. In the succeeding scene, Gennaro, Orsini and four friends appear, all in a convivial mood except Gennaro, whose dejection is marked. They try to revive his spirits by telling him of a banquet to be given this night by the Princess Negroni, to which they have been invited and urge him to join them, but he refuses, and so nurses his grief, with sighs and misgivings, that Liverotto makes bold to charge that he is in love with the Borgia. This accusation rouses Gennaro to great anger, and declaring that no man on earth abhors the female fiend more than he, admonishes his companions that they must answer him with their swords if her name be thus associated again with his own. Petrucci warns him to speak in lower tones, for yonder is her dwelling place! Gennaro looks towards the palace, and seeing the ducal coat of arms, with the word "Borgia" engraved above the door, he draws his dagger, and mounting a flight of stairs leading to the escutcheon, defaces the hated sign by striking off the letter "B." Two men habited in black come upon Gennaro while he is committing this vandalism, and somewhat fiercely demand to know what feeling prompts him to such a deed. To their questioning he boastfully replies that if the offender be demanded he will gladly answer to the charge. The others, somewhat alarmed at the bold act, retreat and Gennaro withdraws into his dwelling.

In the next scene, Rustighello, serving the Duke, and Astolfo, who is in the service of Lucretia, appear on opposite sides of the street. The former demands to know the purpose of Astolfo, loitering about the palace at such an hour, to which answer is made that it is to save a Venetian youth, who lodges somewhere near, from danger. Being more particularly interrogated, Astolfo confesses that he has been requested to conduct the stranger unto the Duchess. Having gained a knowledge of the designs of Astolfo, Rustighello makes a signal, which is responded to by a body of armed men rushing upon the stage, who by his directions steal into Gennaro's dwelling and arrest him regardless of Astolfo's warning.

In Scene IV there is shown a saloon in the Ducal Palace, from a recess in the left of which ascends a spiral staircase. The Duke, Rustighello, and an usher enter to prepare for the business they now have in hand. Being assured that the prisoner is safe within their power, the Duke gives Rustighello a key and commands him to ascend the stairs, and to bring to him from "Numa's chamber" two goblets which will be found there, one of gold and one of silver, but to beware that he tastes not of the wine that is in the golden cup, for it is a deadly potion. These he is ordered to hold in readiness behind a screen, and to be also armed with a sword, to answer a call according to such signal as he may make. As Rustighello goes for the fatal cup, the usher announces the Duchess, who immediately comes in manifesting the greatest indignation, and to the Duke she addresses her complaint:

"Though the fourth of my husbands, ye know it, Don Alfonso, too slowly I assure ye!"

> "To you I look for vengeance!
> Since there is lately committed
> Crime of the blackest nature! One in Ferrara
> Holdeth your spouse so lightly; in actual daylight
> He doth assault her, and mutilate her 'scutcheon."

The Duke, with much sang-froid, tells her this information is not new to him, and asks her pleasure? "It is my will," she answers, "whatever his guilty reason, be who he may be, that the vile wretch quit not this room living!" The Duke promises that her wishes shall be obeyed, and at once orders the prisoner to be admitted. Gennaro is quickly brought in by armed guards, and the Duke, smiling, asks if she knows the culprit? At sight of Gennaro Lucretia almost faints from terror, understanding the dreadful situation in which her son is placed through her own ill-timed request. Gennaro, losing none of his courageous spirit, addresses the Duke to know for what transgression he has been dragged from his home by armed minions. The Duke, still smiling, replies that some vicious varlet has travestied the mighty title of Borgia by defacing the coat of arms, and that now they seek the culprit. Lucretia interposes to express her conviction that the prisoner is not guilty, and would defend him against the charge, but Gennaro, placed upon honor to speak truthfully, frankly confesses the deed. In an undertone, the Duke reminds Lucretia that he has promised to punish the offender according to the harshness of her own request, whereupon, praying the support of Heaven, she beseeches that this serious matter be given a closer examination. At a signal from the Duke, Gennaro is taken away, and the two being now alone, Lucretia humbling herself before him, beseeches her husband to spare the youth, a favor so trifling that she bespeaks his mercy to please her, for mercy, she reminds, is the brightest jewel that may be worn in princely coronet. The Duke hears her patiently, but declares that his decrees are irrevocable, and that his promise to her is inviolable; but more than his regard for promises is his desire of vengeance upon the prisoner who has been proved to be her paramour! Terribly shocked by the Duke's charges, Lucretia is unable to refute his accusation, for circumstances, she realizes, seem to confirm all suspicion; in agony and helplessness of grief, she rises to a pitch of despair, and admonishes.

"Aye, though the fourth of my husbands, ye lord it,
Don Alfonso, too sternly, I assure ye!
They who have wronged me have ever deplored it!
They who slight me cannot shun my fury.
All thy malice I scorn with derision.
Know thou hast with the Borgia to deal!"

These words of menace fail of their purpose to drive the Duke from his resolution to punish Gennaro, as Lucretia's paramour, and reminding her that in Ferrara his power is absolute, he will grant no other concession than to permit her to choose whether his death shall be by poison or the sword. This she cannot, on the moment, make up her mind to do; with a show of impatience at her indecision, the Duke starts to quit the room, when she implores him to remain an instant longer, to listen to her beseechings, and in God's name refrain from this horrible murder. Finding the Duke firmly obdurate, and more deeply angered by her pleadings, Lucretia has strength only to request that if Gennaro is thus to perish it may not be by the bloody sword, and having so spoken she sinks on a seat. The Duke makes a sign to the guards, at which they bring Gennaro into the room. The prisoner is graciously accosted, and informed by the Duke that through the intercessions of the Duchess it has been decided his life shall be spared, for that he has ever been accounted a valiant man, towards whom Ferrara would appear magnanimous. Lucretia well understands how the Duke's words conceal a murderous design, but Gennaro is unconscious of the perfidious purpose, and thanks the Duke for his merciful decision. To prove his deserving, Gennaro now reveals that once when the Duke's father was beset by numerous foes, a poor youth did lend such timely assistance as to preserve his life. The Duke, with much surprise, asks if he is that same youth? To which question Gennaro modestly replies that it was he who gave this helpful succor, nor thought it more than duty. Lucretia's hopes are excited that the Duke will requite Gennaro's brave deed by granting him a full pardon, but this joyful belief is quickly dispelled when the Duke, in a loud voice, asks Gennaro if he will serve beneath the banner of the Borgia? The young captive answers that he owes allegiance to Venice, to which having sworn loyalty, his oath is too sacred for him to violate for any cause. The Duke then tries to bribe him with a purse of gold, but this Gennaro likewise refuses, whereupon, under a pretence of friendship, the Duke invites him to drink with him a last farewell in a generous beaker of wine, and asks Lucretia to

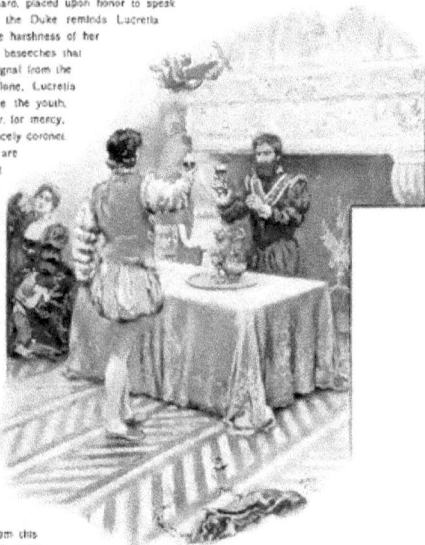

forthwith bring in the flagons. A moment later Rustighello enters with two flagons, one of gold and the other of silver, which he places on a table with two cups. The Duke now turns to Lucretia and taking her hand with positiveness cautions her against betraying any emotion that might excite Gennaro's suspicion, for it were meet that the deed should be done quickly, that the poisoned wine be drunk freely, and without lack of confidence. Lucretia is horrified by these preparations for the deed to which she must be an unwilling accessory, but her helplessness compels obedience to the merciless Duke. Gennaro, rejoicing in the belief of his deliverance, expresses his gratitude in a tender air:

"Grace so benignant favor,
Scarce had I hoped as my guerdon;
But here to find a pardon,
Must seem a dream alway.
Mother, thou art my saviour,
For thy son's weal ye pray!"

The Duke commands Lucretia to help Gennaro to the wine, while he fills his own cup out of the silver flagon, and the two cups being thus filled, the Duke wishes him long life, and the men salute and drink together with mutual expressions of good fortune. The poison having now been drained, the Duke (aside) scoffs at Lucretia for having tricked *her* paramour, and then retires with Rustighello.

When they are left alone, Gennaro approaches Lucretia, and bowing low, he acknowledges his gratitude for her merciful intercession, and confesses that he is overpowered by her goodness, to which she replies in a magnificent aria, revealing to him the poison that lurked in the cup that he drained, and imploring him, in mercy to her, to take the antidote which alone can save him:

"Hapless victim from the poison he gave thee,
This one antidote only can save ye;
Take it! drink it, but a drop from the phial,
Precious life is thine! Then again,
Drink and fly hence! I brook no denial,
O'er thee angels forever more reign."

Gennaro refuses to accept from her hand the proffered draught, for in her revelation he sees again the curse that follows her ministration, the death that she distributes, that has made the name Borgia a dreadful thing to utter, and as a vile fiend he will not trust her. But Lucretia begs so passionately, as a mother, that Gennaro is finally persuaded to drink the antidote, and by her urgings he then escapes by a secret door as the Duke and Rustighello appear at the back of the stage, and Lucretia shrieks and sinks on a seat. This dramatic scene concludes the first act.

"[illegible]
[illegible]"

Act II.—When the curtain rises again, it is to reveal a night scene, and there is shown a small court adjoining the dwelling of Gennaro, and one window lighted. Rustighello enters with a band of bravoes, who with a purpose to seize Gennaro, approach the house, but take alarm at some noises and retire to await his appearance, when they hope to ambush him. Orsini now comes on and raps at Gennaro's door, and being admitted, he explains that the Princess Negroni has this night spread a great supper, to which his friends have been invited, and he requests Gennaro to join him. The young captain, greatly troubled, begs to be excused, for that a matter of great moment compels him to depart for Venice in an hour. Orsini will not accept this as a satisfactory excuse, and reminds Gennaro of their oath to share together cloud and sunshine, even life and death, and asks why he would treat him with so much unkindness. Gennaro cannot resist this importuning, and after pleading in vain to be excused, he frankly tells Orsini that this banquet rouses his worst suspicions, but that since his friend does urge it, he promises to attend, though "death impends with fatal power." Orsini dismisses these fears as sad vexations, and bids him take courage, and to think rather of the favor in which all women hold him. The two render a duet, deeply expressive, "Thinking love must pay such kindness," etc., following which they exchange instructions as to where they shall meet, and what they shall do. Before parting they reaffirm the pledge of their changeless devotion in a melodious duet: "O thy fortune, whatever it may be, shall be mine again, I swear it," etc.

The two withdraw together as Rustighello and his ruffians come in, who, while in hiding, have overheard the arrangement made by Orsini and Gennaro to attend the supper of Princess Negroni. After singing in chorus of their design to apprehend Gennaro, the bravoes pass out and the succeeding scene introduces the saloon of the Negroni Palace, which is beautifully decorated and brilliantly illuminated. On one side of a large table, which is spread with luxuries and flowers, the Princess and her ladies of honor are seated, and on the opposite side are Orsini, Liverotto, Vitellozzo, Gazella and Petrucci, each with a lady beside him, and at the two ends are Gubetta and Gennaro. The supper begins with toasts to wine, each gentleman praising his preference, and all drink together when the name of Venus is proposed. Gennaro, whose mind is still upon the adventures of yesterday, soon shows weariness, and rises as if about to go, but Orsini restrains him, by requesting him to hear an effusion composed by himself the other morning. At this proposal of Orsini to turn poet, the company laugh heartily and offer him such taunts that he resents it by drawing a knife and would attack Gubetta but for the protests of the ladies, who declare the row will scandalize all present and hastily make their exeunt. When the ladies go out, Liverotto begs that peace may be observed, and Vitellozzo admonishes the disputants that to-morrow is a better time to cut each other's throat like butchers. By this means a reconciliation is effected, and the company make apology for all rude manners shown, and offer to renew friendships in a glass of wine. A cupbearer, clad in black, now enters, who carries around a flask, and offers to each person a draught of Syracuse wine, which all receive with pleasurable manifestations. All drink except Gubetta, who empties his goblet over his shoulder, an action that Gennaro observes, but Orsini excuses it by declaring that the Spaniard already has his fill until he is reeling. Gubetta is not yet too drunk to make the most of his evil designs, and he calls on Orsini to favor them with the verses, not doubting that such wine and the inspiration of good company will make him a great bard. The others join in the request, to which Orsini responds by rendering: "Oh, the secret of bliss in perfection, is to never raise any objection," etc.

This drinking song of Orsini's is interrupted by the distant sound of a funeral bell, and by voices chanting the Catholic funeral service. Gennaro, in deep surprise, wonders what these sounds signify, which Orsini explains by supposing it is a service over the body of some old monk being taken to his grave, and continuing his levity, he offers a toast to death in this wise:

"On the spring tide of life lusty flowing,
On the ripe sun of youth gaily glowing,
Death may gloat with his blear eye so yellow
Here's a health for the jolly old fellow!"

A body of penitents file slowly into the room, and arranging themselves on two sides of the banquet chamber, they continue their doleful chant, until one by one the lights go out, leaving the saloon in darkness. The gay revelers are sobered by this ominous sign, and they attempt to flee the place, but discover, to their intense dismay, that all the exits have been barred, and conclude that a demon, fell and powerful, must be among them. The central door now slowly opens, and Lucretia appears, attended by armed men, at sight of whom the revelers recoil with horror. She advances to the centre of the room and utters, strangely:

"See, 'tis the Borgia! how lately a sorry ball
All here did give me in Venice,
I now in turn bid you sup in Ferrara!
Ye thought to pass unpunished,
Yet thought so vainly. Great as was your insult,
My vengeance is as great; five narrow coffins
Now are waiting to receive your bodies;
For one and all have taken poison!"

Gennaro thereupon reveals himself, and approaching Lucretia he tells her that five coffins will not suffice, for a sixth is needed, to house his own body, since he will not

"The beginning of wisdom is the fear of the Lord."

desert his comrades even in death. Lucretia is astonished to find him here, thinking he had gone to Venice, and her despair is greater than ever, realizing how a second time she has compassed his destruction. But hoping to save him again, she orders removal of all the others from the room, and then closing the doors against his exit, she exhorts him to drink the antidote quickly. He shows her the phial which she gave him as a protection against poison, but resolutely declares that he will not swallow one drop till all his comrades have first partaken. She informs him that all the contents will scarce suffice to save one life, and beseeches him to swallow it without delay, or else the poison, which is even now swiftly coursing through his veins, will bring him to a terrible death. Coolly he asks her if she has no more of the antidote, to divide with his friends, and when she answers him nay, he takes a knife from the table and orders her to prepare to meet her doom. She cowers before him, and begs for mercy, but he seizes her savagely, and reminding her how inexorable has been her hate, how unrelenting her murderous malevolence, in killing his friends, he will make her a victim of her own attempts at vengeance. Gennaro lifts the knife to requite her crime, at sight of which Lucretia utters a shriek, and to stay his hand she tremblingly reveals that he is a Borgia! that she is his mother! Overwhelmed by remorse, she sings a despairing aria:

"Spurn, aye, spurn me, I do implore thee
Not to spurn my life's blighted blossom!
Night and day, too, in mourning o'er thee
A thousand deaths do rack this bosom.
Drink, ah! drink then! the poison to prevent,
Oh yield, I pray thee, ere death shall win," etc.

As Lucretia concludes her song, the voice of Orsini is heard from within, and report is made of the death of his companions, one after another. Lucretia continues to beseech Gennaro to save himself, but he is even less disposed to do so since learning that he is son to such a monster, and reproaching her for her crimes, that bring disgrace upon him, he dies in her arms. She is for the moment stupefied by this tragic result of her perfidious and miserable life, and contemplates with shame and penitence her criminal career, that has culminated in the death of her own child. Awakened conscience causes her to cry for help, for succor, and throwing herself upon the body of Gennaro, she prays that her sins may be expiated by the remorse she feels, and the life which she now willingly surrenders. Lucretia's shouts for assistance have been heard by the people in the adjoining saloon, and in response thereto the Duke comes running in, with Rustighello and guards. Scarcely noticing the prostrate woman, for whom his concern is smallest, he fiercely demands to know where Gennaro can be found, to which Lucretia, feebly raising her head and pointing to the body, replies:

"Ungrateful one!
By thy hand, too, must I die!"

"Look you at your feet!
Fate hath broken the magic dreaming,
O'er this head too surely vanquish'd
See her wrathful vial pour now!"

Lucretia sinks back and expires on the body of Gennaro, and the chorus intone, "Wretched offspring, more wretched mother," which tragic scene furnishes a fitting conclusion for an opera that is intensely gloomy throughout.

A SKETCH OF ROSSINI.

GIOACCHINO ANTONIO ROSSINI, one of the greatest of the modern school of Italian composers, was a native of the very ancient town of Pesaro, on the Adriatic Sea, where he was born February 29, 1792. His parentage was an obscure one, for his father held the little honorable dual post of town-trumpeter, or crier, and inspector of slaughter houses, and his mother was a poor baker's daughter, though she had some musical talent and a good voice, which she turned to some account. Young Gioacchino's early education was slight, but he showed such inclination for music that Prinetti gave him lessons on the harpsichord for three years, and would no doubt have continued his unrewarded instruction, but for his pupil's propensity for making sport of his bald head and big spectacles. As a punishment for the boy's fun-making, his father apprenticed him to a silversmith, but shortly after secured his release and placed him under the care of Angelo Tesei, who taught him singing and harmony. His progress was amazingly rapid, so that at the age of ten he was able to read music at sight and to play piano accompaniments, while his voice was so good that he sang the part of Adolfo in "Camilla," but it was the only time he ever appeared on the stage as a singer, though he sang often in church. After studying three years under Tesei, Gioacchino applied himself to counterpoint at the Bologna Conservatory, and then took up the violoncello with Cavedagni. About the same time he began composing, but though his creations were highly praised, he became so disgusted with his teacher, Mattei, that he quit the school.

Rossini's musical education was less than half completed when he began himself to give lessons and assumed the directorship of the Bologna Academy, during which time he composed his first cantata, "Death of Orpheus," which was performed August 8, 1808, and won for him the first prize over many competitors. In 1810 he wrote his first opera, a one act comedietta for a Venice theatre, which had a pronounced success. In the following year he produced a two act opera buffa, for, a Bologna theatre, which was received with equal favor. So greatly encouraged was he by these two initial successes, that he began now to compose operas with remarkable rapidity, many of which were well received, but not a few brought him much disappointment, nor was it until "Tancredo" was produced and given at a Venetian carnival, in 1813, that he won permanent fame. His "Sigismond," in 1815, was a lamentable failure, and he was so disgusted by the inappreciation of the Venice public that he returned to Bologna, where he met Barbaja, and accepted from him an offer of $175 per month, and a share of the proceeds of the gaming table, for his services as musical director of the San Carlo Theatre at Naples. He went to Rome in 1815 to direct the production of his new opera, "The Barber of Seville," which, however, was hissed on its first representation. Between 1815 and 1823 Rossini wrote twenty operas, some of which were very successful, and in the last year named he went to London, where several of his operas were sung, and proved so popular that at the end of five months he found that his profits exceeded $50,000. His next removal was to Paris, where he became musical director of the Theatre Italien, but after serving two years he was deposed and then accepted the dual post of first-composer to the King, and inspector-general of singing in France, with an income of $4000 per annum. In 1829 he composed "William Tell," his masterpiece, and though it was the greatest of his many pronounced successes, and his age was only thirty-seven, it was practically his last musical composition, for he seems to have fallen into a lassitude which he either could not or had no desire to throw off. Thereafter, for a period of nearly forty years, he did little, except to compose his celebrated Stabat Mater, in 1832, and the Petite Solennelle, in 1864, but his interest in the theatre continued, and in 1851 he established the Rossini Theatre in his native town, Pesaro, which, however, failed of support and is now a ruin. On the other hand, the Rossini Conservatory, which was founded directly after his death, is still a flourishing school, and at the present writing is directed by Mascagni. Rossini was a thrifty man and left a large fortune at his death, which occurred at Passy, near Paris, November 13, 1868. His funeral, which took place from the Trinite, on the 21st, was most imposing, being attended by a great number of the most famous persons of Europe. He was married twice, first to Isabella Colbran, the singer, in 1822, afterwards to Olympe Pelissier, in 1847, who survived him. The complete list of his works comprises fifty operas, and twice as many oratorios, cantatas, vocal pieces, sacred music, instrumental, etc. He was many times decorated, and at the time of his death he was grand officer of the Legion of Honor, foreign associate of the Institut, honorary member of nearly all the European academies, and commander in many orders.

Gioacchino Antonio Rossini

William Tell

(AFTER THE ORIGINAL PAINTING BY WILLIAM DE LEFTWICH DODGE)

GESSLER.—"*Why had you this other arrow?*"
TELL.—"*For you, had I slain my child.*"

ACT III. SCENE III.

WILLIAM TELL.

MUSIC BY ROSSINI — WORDS BY JOUY AND BIS.

ILLIAM TELL is almost universally considered to be Rossini's greatest composition, although it has been said he spent only thirteen days upon the score, a claim, however, that has never been confirmed by unquestioned authority. Rossini was remarkably popular all over Europe, but especially so in Paris, notwithstanding he had not a little opposition. Upon retiring from the position of Inspector of Singing, in 1828, he signed a contract with the Government of Charles X to furnish five operas in ten years for the Paris Academy of Music, for which he was to receive $3,000 for each opera. It was in pursuance of this agreement that "William Tell" was written, which was produced at the Academy, August 3, 1829, where the music was warmly applauded, but the drama was openly condemned. Directly after the staging of the opera, Rossini paid a visit to Bologna, where he was staying when the news of the July revolution of 1830 first reached him. He returned to Paris in the following November, when to his chagrin he found his contract, made with Charles X, repudiated by Louis Philippe's government that had succeeded meantime, through the fortunes of revolution, and the courts to which he appealed could give him no redress. It is due to his disappointment and embitterment over this incident, no doubt, that Rossini refused to further devote his splendid genius to operatic creations, and thereafter his life was given up largely to indulgences that somewhat clouded his otherwise glorious reputation.

The drama of "William Tell" closely follows Schiller's story, especially the most stirring episodes, but the original librettio has undergone several changes, at Rossini's suggestions, and is the work of many hands. The opera had fifty-nine representations as first written, but thereafter it was reduced from five to three acts, and the whole was revised no less than four times. The scene of the opera is laid in Switzerland, and the story relates the adventures of William Tell, a distinguished revolutionist, who delivered the Swiss Cantons from the German yoke in 1207. The narrative recites the disaffection and hostility of the Swiss peasantry against their oppressors, which culminates in revolt when one of Gessler's officers commits an outrage upon the only daughter of a herdsman, Leutold, who avenges the crime by slaying the perpetrator. For this act of a just vengeance, Leutold is pursued by Gessler's officers, and being pressed closely, he takes refuge with Tell, who rows him across Lake Lucerne when the waves are so tempestuous that no other boatman will undertake a crossing, and thereby places the fugitive beyond danger. At the same time, Melchtal, the village patriarch, incites the people to insubordination, for which Gessler orders his arrest and prompt execution. The situation is complicated, but made more interesting by the introduction of a love adventure, wherein Arnold, who is son of the executed Melchtal, is enamored of Matilda, Gessler's daughter, and upon him devolves the duty of avenging his father's death. For a while Arnold hesitates between love and obligation, but finally he is persuaded to join his comrades under Tell, who is leading an insurrection, and swears fealty to the cause of revolution and death to the tyrant. To discover the chiefs of the revolt, Gessler orders a pole to be set up in the market square of Altorf, upon the top of which he causes his hat to be fixed and orders every one, under pain of death, to pay homage to it, an act which the semi-slavish peasantry perform without protest, but Tell heroically refuses to pay such degrading genuflexion to a despot, whereupon he is seized and condemned. His death sentence is, however, commuted to a trial exhibition of his great skill as an archer, and he is promised his freedom if he will shoot an apple from the head of his little son. This he successfully accomplishes, but at the moment the people are praising the feat, Gessler perceives another arrow in Tell's quiver, and being suspicious, asks how he had designed to use it. The inflexible hero courageously confesses that it was to kill the tyrant had he slain his son. For this bold utterance, Gessler orders Tell thrown into prison, where he languishes for a season, but meantime Matilda renounces her father and lends her efforts to the liberation of Tell. Through her incitement, Arnold recruits a band of brave followers, and by a desperate expedient rescues Tell, who soon afterwards kills the tyrant, and the affair happily concludes with the freedom of Switzerland declared, and the marriage of Arnold and Matilda consummated.

The overture to "William Tell" is one of the greatest, aye, sublime, compositions ever written, which describes with melodious vividness the grandeur of the Alps in their majestic stillness, succeeded by an imitation of a terrific storm that sweeps the mountain peaks and dashes furiously into the valleys; then sounds the Alpine horn in the stirring "*Ranz des Vaches*," and the trumpet call to freedom, that enthuses and prepares the audience for the exciting scenes that follow.

Act I.—When the curtain goes up, it is to reveal a village nestling in a valley bounded by towering mountains, with a rushing torrent on one side, and William Tell's house on the other, and three huts in the foreground, near a lake. Tell is discovered leaning on his hoe, while Edwige, his wife, and Jemmy, his son, are busy with their work, and a single fisherman is in a boat repairing his net. The action begins with a stirring Alpine chorus:

"Fair is the morn, fair shines upon the mountains
Light from the eastern skies, joy from above
From cliffs rebounding, sweet echo sounding
Joyful repeats our song fervent and pure and strong," etc.,

which is followed by a quartet, in which the fisherman sings of his lady love, whose presence he sighs for, and tells of his country in the grip of a tyrant, while Edwige and Jemmy extol the courage of the father, whom neither tempest nor adverse fate can inspire with fear. The song is interrupted by sounds of rejoicing heard in the distance, in which is distinguished the Alpine horns of the cow-herds calling the kine, to which a quartet of voices respond with happy anticipations of an approaching festival that the trumpets announce.

In the next scene Melchtal enters, followed by Arnold, and Swiss peasants, escorting two brides and bridegrooms, who are received by Edwige, with hospitable welcome and good wishes, that the rites may be renewed that bring reward of fidelity and love. She requests Melchtal to perform the nuptials of the peasants, that their happiness may be complete, to which, after some reluctance, he yields when solicited by the shepherds. After celebrating the day with joyous song to Hymen and love, and executing a merry dance, the chorus *exeunt*, and Tell invites the others to share the shelter of his lonely habitation, where long his ancestors have had their abode, and where concealed he lives without fear of foes, happy for being father of a noble boy, whom he now embraces. Melchtal, turning to Arnold, admonishes him of the joy that a son brings to Tell, and asks if his own old age is to be similarly blessed, reminding him that though this festival is consecrated by a double hymeneal vow, he has not heard that Arnold has yet pledged his hand. Having thus intimated his desire that his son shall soon marry, Melchtal passes out, followed by all the others, except Arnold, who being now alone, gives utterance to his conflicting emotions in a pathetic solo in which he tells of his passionate love for Matilda, daughter of the tyrant Gessler, for whom he has neglected honor, country and father. He deplores his sad fortune, and bewails that, snatching her from a deadly avalanche and thereby saving her life at risk of his own, he is doomed to lose her by a cruel fate that yields her to another.

While Arnold is soliloquizing of his unrequited love, the sound of a horn is heard, which he interprets as an announcement of the approach of Gessler, and that Matilda accompanies him. His infatuation is so overmastering that his patriotic instincts are for the time repressed, and he resolves to brave every peril to see her once more. As Arnold is about to go out to meet the tyrant and his daughter, Tell enters, and perceiving his agitation, entreats him to remain and confide the cause of his distress. Arnold dissembles, by declaring that his grief is great to know that the tyrant's yoke continues, and other miseries await them. Tell is not to be thus deceived, and charges him to speak boldly, nor longer to conceal the true reason for his trembling and pale countenance. Thus pressed for a confession, Arnold is induced to declare his love for Matilda, but fortified by the presence of the patriot leader, he promises to pluck his passion from his heart, and thus make the sacrifice that his honor and country demand. Tell accepts the pledge, and though he now knows that Arnold has served the tyrant, the grief he manifested is proof of sincere repentance, and their comradeship is cemented. While Arnold's love of country is strengthened to make the greatest of sacrifices, he is doubtful of the ability of the patriots to resist the power of Gessler, whose cruelty would be expended in shocking vengeance should the revolution fail. Tell declares if their valor desert them not, the tyrant shall surely fall, but that if conquered the tomb shall be his refuge and Heaven his avenger. While the two are thus conversing of their country's need, a horn is heard, at which sound Tell turns suddenly, and after a moment's pause bids Arnold not forget that his father, Melchtal, is persecuted by Gessler, and asks if he would, coward-like, bend to supplicate the tyrant's scornful favor. Stung by these words, Arnold threatens to immediately cross and bid defiance to Gessler; but Tell advises that nothing be done rashly; rather wait until Melchtal be made safe, and then strike boldly for the freedom of Switzerland. Arnold is distracted by his griefs, by the impulses that struggle within him, the love of his country and affection for his imperilled father opposing his infatuation for Matilda, daughter of the oppressor; but his patriotism triumphs, and he determines to join the revolt and cast in his fortunes with Tell until Gessler is dethroned and the land made free. Tell is rejoiced by this loyal decision, but he cautions Arnold to give no intimation of his purpose, and to do naught that might mar the shepherds' pleasure on this day of festival.

"Be it beyond the depth of danger! [illegible] to Heaven [illegible]!"

The interview between Tell and Arnold is interrupted by the entrance of Jemmy, Edwige, Fisherman, and Melchtal, who precede peasants and two brides and bridegrooms. The two couples take their positions before Melchtal, the patriarch, who bestows a blessing upon them as the villagers sing in chorus:

"Oh, Heaven! The source of blissful love
Their vows propitious deign to bind;
Pure as the celestial light above,
May they true joy forever find."

Melchtal addresses the bridegrooms, exhorting them to emulate the examples of their ancestors, and impressing that it is to such as they that their country looks for protectors; the brides he counsels to imbue their offspring with worthy sentiments, keeping ever in mind that upon these Helvetia must depend for succor when tyrants oppress the land. This ceremony of blessing and exhortation is arrested by sounds of the chase, at which Arnold, believing that Gessler is near, suddenly quits the place. Edwige observes a troubled expression on her husband's face, and anxiously inquires the cause of his seeming anger. Unwilling to disclose his designs to her, Tell makes an excuse to follow Arnold, but he requests her to see that the party continue their merriment during his absence, promising to return soon, admonishing:

"Thus may the roar of the coming tempest
In sounds of revelry be masked;
Such sounds shall our tyrant's ears assail
When we our liberties have gained!"

As Tell departs, the festival of hymeneal rejoicing begins with a chorus, in which, however, Jemmy nor his mother take any part, for serious thoughts have been aroused in their minds by Tell's action, which they try in vain to understand. While standing aside by themselves, Jemmy perceives a trembling shepherd approaching, whose strength is barely able to support him. When he draws nearer, the Fisherman discovers that it is Leutold, a poor but honest man, who carries a hatchet reeking with blood, and implores protection and vengeance! When he has recovered sufficiently to explain the misfortune that has befallen him, to the eager questionings of Edwige he relates: "Of all my once large family, an only daughter heaven had spared me; one of the minions of the governor (Gessler) did try by force to steal her from my bosom, and with hellish lust to rob her of honor. But by this weapon he has fallen, and behold! here streams the wretch's blood! Bear me, I entreat you, to yonder shore, where I shall find a safe asylum from my pursuers." The Fisherman pities the misery of Leutold, and would gladly save him, but he fears the torrent and the rocks, and declares it impossible to reach the shore and that such an effort would bring certain death. Leutold still beseeches, but his prayerful entreaties are vain, until Tell returns, to whom the desperate man addresses his importunity to save him from the monsters now upon his trail, to whom he must fall a prey, unless passage to the opposite shore can be quickly obtained. Tell turns, scowling, upon the coward fisherman, and fiercely demands to know if he refuses to render aid to a despairing countryman, to save him from the vengeance of a bloody-minded tyrant? The cowering poltroon still protests against encountering the perils of a passage, and while he is picturing the deadly dangers of the boisterous lake, voices of pursuers are heard without, crying for the blood of Leutold. The imminent jeopardy of the poor shepherd appeals so strongly to Tell's pity that he bids him take to the boat quickly, and that he will himself row him across. Edwige begs Tell not to thus rush to his death, but he assures her that sure protection is given to those who put their trust in Heaven, and brooking no further delay, he springs into the boat and rows off with Leutold.

After Tell's departure, Rodolf, a captain of the guards, comes in hastily, with a squad of soldiers, shouting for vengeance against the murderer, but Jemmy exultantly informs him that the man they seek is now beyond the reach of danger. Rodolf is furious at being thwarted in his efforts to arrest Leutold, and though the roaring thunder portends a coming storm, he commands Edwige, Melchtal and Jemmy, and the peasants to remain and disclose who has saved the assassin, under pain of death if they refuse. The frightened shepherds surround the three and implore them to tell who it was that aided the escape of Leutold, reminding how cruel is the despot Gessler, who will certainly let his wrath fall upon them, but Melchtal, nothing daunted, advances to Rodolf and tells him that what the father has done, in defending the honor of his daughter, is to be commended, and that threats of punishment cannot avail to make him a treacherous informer. Angered to a desperate pitch of passion by what he considers is a defiance of his commands, Rodolf orders his soldiers to seize Melchtal and take him before Gessler for judgment, and that everything belonging to these peasants be put to the torch, that by fire and slaughter they may be taught to respect the authority of their lord. Jemmy warns the captain that an avenging God will not forget this infamy, and that justice may one day overtake the tyrant through the trusty bow of his father. Disregarding the brave words of Jemmy, the soldiers promptly obey Rodolf by seizing and binding Melchtal, whom they hurry away, which dramatic finale ends the first act.

Between the first and second acts the orchestra performs a stirring gallopade, repeated from the overture, which is effective in preparing for the succeeding scenes.

Act II.—The rising curtain shows a charming mountain landscape, with a glimpse of the lake of the Four Cantons on the left. Shepherds are seen in the background dressing recently slain animals, when a party of huntsmen appear, and a grand double chorus is rendered, which is one of the sublime melodic features of the opera. As the huntsmen and shepherds leave the stage, Matilda timidly enters, and first looking furtively about to assure herself that she is alone, gives expression to her anxieties and emotions for Arnold, for whom she confesses a passionate love, and an intense desire to see him. After thus soliloquizing, and declaring her devotion, she sings a charming romanza that expresses the longings of her heart:

"Oh, wild shady wood, whose shadows surround me,
Thee I more prize than the pomp of a throne;
Here, 'midst the storm that beats wildly around me,
With him I love would I make thee my home.
Echo, echo, alone thou hearest!" etc.

As Matilda concludes her beautiful song, Arnold appears, as if responsive to her love-call, but not sure how she will receive him, he apologizes for the intrusion. She inspires him with hope by telling that he has been expected, to which he answers joyously that her commands it will

give him happiness to obey, even if it be to abandon Helvetia, and a father dear, to wander in a strange land, where ignoble death and a nameless grave may be his doom. These rueful thoughts she dismisses by confessing that her love for him is pure and changeless, exacting no sacrifices, and halting at no differences of social station, trusting in Heaven to favor their attachment and to bless their union. His heart is suffused with delight by these sweet avowals, and he is ready to follow her desires wherever they may lead him. Their vows of devotion being thus exchanged, Matilda bids Arnold to now return to the field of glory, there to win fresh laurels, and when victorious he comes to her again, she will reward him with her hand, which is followed by a passionate duet between the two. They are warned by the sound of footsteps that some one is drawing near, and hastily prepare to part. She tells him to meet her at the earliest dawn of to-morrow in the ancient tabernacle, there in the Almighty presence to receive her last adieu. Arnold kneels at Matilda's feet, and tenderly kisses her hand, after which token she departs, and Tell and Walter, a young peasant, come in, who notice Arnold's flushed manners, and banter him with having been entertaining some agreeable company. Arnold tells them they have no need to explain their intrusion, but Walter protests that it were better he should ask the purpose of their visit. Tell interposes, with a remark that their designs can scarcely concern Arnold, since he has abandoned his friends to serve the cause of the tyrant secretly. Arnold, with show of temper, demands to know upon what grounds he bases such a charge, to which Tell answers that Matilda's flight and his confusion plainly indicate the direction of his aspirations, and further explains that suspicion, aroused by his action the previous night, has caused him to be watched, that his loyalty might be determined. Arnold cowers before his accusers, and pathetically asks if love for Matilda and her promise of fidelity be not a sufficient defence for his actions? Tell denies that love for a bitter enemy to his country's freedom can be excused, and puts to him the question, "Do you, truthfully, still love Helvetia?" To this Arnold replies that Helvetia no longer exists, save as a land where hatred, discord, and cowardice abide, a country which has become so odious that he has resolved to leave it in response to honor's call, in foreign parts, since valor and love his heart divide. Tell betrays great grief at this decision, and to persuade Arnold that it ill becomes a Swiss to abandon his country when it most needs his services, appeals to his patriotism, but this proving unavailing, he gradually breaks to him the news that by Gessler's orders Melchtal, the aged patriarch, the resolute patriot, the noble father, has been put to death, and that he expired weeping for his son. Thus informed of the death of his father, Arnold is overwhelmed by a torrent of grief, to which he gives expression by heaping censure upon himself for designing the betrayal of Helvetia, and permitting his sword to repose in its scabbard while his father's blood is crying to him for vengeance. In despair he asks what he can do to release himself from the shackles of a mad love, and to redeem his honor, as a worthy son. Tell assures him that no other service than his duty can be required by Heaven or his country. Thus reminded, Arnold impetuously swears that his own hand and none other shall punish the tyrant, which he would attempt forthwith, in the hot haste of his eager vengeance, but Tell exhorts him to be prudent, and be content to render loyal aid to the revolution that the true friends of Helvetia are about to foment. Further informing, Tell advises Arnold that this very night there will be an assembling of patriots in this valley, who have wrought their ploughshares and scythes into spears and swords, with which arms they are resolved to destroy the tyrant and free the country, or perish in the attempt. Their plans and purposes determined, the three render an inspiring trio, pledging union, and inviting Heaven's aid in their efforts to redeem the land from oppression, and to expiate the martyrdom of Melchtal.

Following the magnificent and powerful terzetto is the splendid spectacle of the gathering of the inhabitants of the Unterwald, which is perhaps the supreme glory of the opera. The peasants in great number, bearing weapons of many kinds, pour into the darkened valley, and being cordially received by Tell, Arnold and Walter, they break forth in a mighty chorus of courageous stimulation, vowing their ardor and longings for death or victory. While the assemblage is singing, a trumpet blast is heard, the significance of which the peasants well understand, but which they now regard as an inspiration, and the signal of Helvetia's uprising. At this juncture another body of Swiss inhabitants come to swell the assemblage of patriots, who are jubilantly welcomed by Tell, and these in turn are followed by a crowd of settlers from Uri and the lake, all brave men, who in a grand chorus acclaim Tell as their wise counselor and noble leader. A compact by oath is now formed by the peasant warriors from the three cantons, and measures are concerted for the morrow. The oath which Tell administers is of the most vehement character, binding with inviolable sacredness all who take it, to redeem Helvetia and destroy the oppressor, and calling down a swift and awful punishment from Heaven upon any who shall prove recreant to their vows and traitors to their country. The day is now breaking, and the watchword of party is given: "To arms!" which thrilling scene forms a dramatic climax to the second act.

Act III.—The third act opens with a mountain scene, and a valley where, in the great tabernacle of nature, appointment has been made by Matilda to meet Arnold, and speed him with tender farewell, upon his quest for glory. The two enter together, and Matilda expresses surprise to observe her lover so excited, which she, however, attributes to his grief at parting, and therefore tries to console him with the hope that he may shortly return to her a victor to receive the reward of her hand. Dejectedly, despairingly, he tells her he must forego his former intent, and even decline her proffered hand, since honor and duty alike now call him from thoughts of love to avenge his father's death:

"For blood and vengeance, the only passion
Which now my heart may occupy
All glory I renounce—hope of honor—
Love—even thee, Matilda!"

When she asks him for further explanation, he makes bold to inform her that his father has been cruelly murdered by order of Gessler, and that she being daughter of the cruel despot, he must reject the love which once it was his heart's ambition to gain. His words burn into her very soul, and in the agony of her grief she piteously bewails her sad lot, which must henceforth be peaceless, the misery that falls to unrequited affection. But though sorrowing that the angry shade of his murdered sire has interdicted their ill-assorted love, she encourages him to obey the call of stern duty, promising that even while he is seeking revenge against her father, she will bear his image upon her heart, and think of him as that noble one who saved her life, and to whom she gave the love that time nor circumstance can destroy. While Matilda and Arnold are bidding farewell, a parting of sorrowing lovers, a tumult is heard which she explains is the joyous announcement of an approaching military pageant, but suspecting that it is Gessler on one of his spectacular marches, and fearing for Arnold's safety, she beseeches him to flee quickly, assuring him that wherever his steps may wander, thither will her anxieties for his welfare also follow. He refuses to leave, declaring that these cries serve to increase his fury, and his eagerness to glut his rancor upon the head of the foul slayer of his father, but Matilda pleads so tearfully that she at length induces him, for her sake, to seek safety, and he goes out with Matilda, saying:

"What conflict within my bosom rages!
Ne'er can I my fond love forget
To my thoughts thou'lt ever be present!"

Scene II of Act III represents the grand square of Altorf, bordered with apple and lime trees, and in the centre a pole is set up surmounted by a cap to which the peasants are required to bow in servile homage. In the background is the castle of Gessler, on one side of which is a throne for the haughty and cruel governor. A large gathering of people, including Gessler, Rodolf, guards, soldiers and populace appear, who sing a chorus of laudation to the tyrant, which he answers insolently by extolling his power, and commanding that while upon his throne every subject, of whatever grade, shall bow reverently to the cap, which is the symbol of his authority; and after thus pledging their allegiance the assembled peasants may pass the day in merry sports. Having heard this expression of their oppressor's will, the multitude, male and female, render a charming tyrolese chorus, accompanied by dancing:

"With dance and song pass time along,—
To music's sound our hearts rebound,
O'er hill, o'er mountain,
Through bower, round fountain,
Sweet sounds are mounting
From valley and dale."

While the crowd are enjoying themselves, the pleasant scene is suddenly interrupted by Rodolf and soldiers dragging forward Tell and his son, who are commanded to bow to the cap. Tell defiantly replies that the tyrant's armed power enables him to perpetrate his oppressions upon the weakness of the people, who are in awe of his cruelty. "You make them fear, but not me; the base order I despise, as I hate all that can a man debase." Gessler, in a rage, asks who is this audacious man? and when told that he is William Tell, that miscreant who aided Leutold to escape, orders are given to seize him and take his bow and arrows, which the soldiers promptly execute, while in chorus they praise the good fortune that has placed in their hands unarmed, the archer feared by all, and the boldest swimmer in all Helvetia. Gessler promises that an example shall be made of this contumacious rebel, for whom no mercy must be shewn. Scornfully, Tell expresses the wish that it might be his lot to be the last victim of the tyrant's malice, and then in a low tone he bids Jemmy to run quickly to his mother and tell her to raise a lighted torch on the top of a lofty mountain, where it may be a war-signal to the three cantons. Jemmy is about to go out, when Gessler commands him to stay, incensed the more by the tenderness displayed by Tell, and when to questioning he is told that the lad is Tell's only son, he asks the bold patriot if he would save him? To this inquiry Tell marvels what wrong the boy has done, and protests that himself being the offender, punishment should be inflicted on no other. Despotically, Gessler declares that the wrong of the lad is in being son of such a rebel, in whose footsteps he may be prone to follow.

[illegible]

"Of his fate the arbiter you shall be.
The most able archer you are reckoned,
Amongst all your countrymen.
On the head of your son this apple place,
And with an arrow, before mine eyes,
You shall strike it off.—"

The strong, courageous man trembles at this horrible decree. Loving Jemmy better than life itself, Tell's soul cries out in agony at the prospect of being made the executioner of his own son, and refusing to humble himself to avoid the punishment for his own deeds, he is willing to make any renouncement, to render any servile homage, to perform any obsequious act, if thereby he may save his only son from peril. But Gessler refuses his appeals, and orders that the alternative shall be sentence of death upon the lad. The tears fall fast from Tell's eyes, and his frame shakes with terror, observing which Jemmy encourages his father by reminder of his matchless skill, and saying, "Give me your hand—upon my heart place it; listen, not with terror, but with love it throbs." The heroism of his child brings fresh resolution to Tell, who bids paternal love be silent, and reasserting his will, he calls for his bow and arrows. In compliance with this request, his bow and a bundle of arrows are restored. He receives them fondly, like old friends, and emptying the quiver upon the ground, he selects two arrows, one of which he hides in his bosom.

When Tell announces his readiness for the ordeal, Gessler commands that the son be bound and placed, to which order Jemmy protests, as an indignity upon his free-born nature, asking that he may unshackled die if it be fate's decree, and promising to submit himself dauntlessly, without trembling, to his father's aim. The heroism of the boy excites great pity among the Swiss, who in chorus beseech that innocence like this may mitigate Gessler's fury, but it fails to move the despot's heart to mercy. Jemmy's request to be left unbound is granted, and as he goes to take his place against a tree, he exhorts, "Have courage, my dearest father!" at which words Tell's hands tremble so that he can scarcely hold the weapon, while his eyes become dim from weeping. Begging the last privilege to embrace his son, Tell hugs Jemmy with the passion of despair, but after holding him to his bosom for a moment, the loving father, tenderly addressing, admonishes Jemmy that there is One above who forgets not the innocent, and entreats him to put his trust in Heaven, and thinking of his mother, that these will sustain and defend him. During this pathetic interview, Jemmy exhibits the greatest boldness, confident of his father's skill, and when directed he bravely takes the place assigned to him, by a tree, and receives the apple upon his head. Tell looks fiercely at Gessler as he feels for the concealed arrow, and then adjusts the other in his bow as the boy stands rigidly against the tree, determined that no movement, however slight, shall divert his father's aim. Tell nerves himself for the ordeal, as if given new strength from Heaven, and sweeping the tears from his eyes, he quickly adjusts his bow and in a moment the arrow flies straight to its mark, splitting the apple in half, and embedding itself deeply in the tree. At this happy deliverance, the Swiss peasants shout with exultation, and Jemmy runs to embrace his father, who, from the very excess of his joy, faints, and in doing so lets fall the arrow that had been concealed upon his person. Gessler is in dreadful rage at the prospect of Tell escaping his vengeance, and seeing the extra arrow, he fiercely demands to know why it has been retained. Recovering himself, Tell courageously answers, "It was for you had I slain my child!" These threatening words bring upon him again the peril from which he has escaped, for the moment, for in murderous anger Gessler orders his soldiers to seize and bind both Tell and his son, who are to remain in chains until the hour of their approaching death, which shall be before another day.

Matilda, Rodolf and attendants enter while Tell is being bound. Looking with horror upon the cruel show of a tyrant's rage, Matilda implores Gessler, her father, to recall his dreadful sentence, and when he refuses, she resolutely defies him, and declares that while life is spared her, she will defend the boy by appealing to her sovereign, and demands that, no culprit he, the lad be at once released. In an undertone Rodolf advises Gessler to give up the boy, since the father still remains, upon whom vengeance may be sated. The people murmur, and protest so vigorously that the despot yields the boy, but retains Tell, and orders that he shall be taken across the lake to Kusnacht, hoping he may perish in the passage, but if not, that he shall be left upon the island, to become a prey to hunger or fall a victim to voracious beasts. Moved by pity the Swiss implore Gessler to show mercy, but the bloody despot disdains their appeals, declaring that his rage cannot be appeased except by the death of the traitor. Matilda is terrified by these awful words, but secretly she vows that through her efforts both father and son shall yet be saved. The peasants continue their importunities for mercy, until with show of intense impatience Gessler orders them to depart forthwith, threatening, if they longer remain, harassing him with their beseeching, to put Tell and his son to death without further delay. At this the people disperse, calling Heaven to punish the tyrant, and the soldiers drag Tell away, followed by Gessler and Rodolf, which affecting scene closes the third act.

Act IV.—The final act opens with an exterior view of a rustic habitation, before which Arnold is discovered, alone, in sorrowful meditation over the wrongs his countrymen have suffered, and his own affliction, through the execution of a beloved father by the cruel tyrant. He starts to enter the house, which was once his home, but misgivings arise that cause him to pause and ask himself if he is really worthy to cross the sacred threshold before his father's death is avenged. He advances some steps towards an adjoining room, and then stops suddenly again, beholding many memorials of his honored sire, and confesses, despite his boasted resolution, that he cannot enter until vengeance is accomplished upon the despot and murderer. Sadly he sings:

"Oh! bless'd abode, within whose walls
Mine eyes first saw the light,
Once so belov'd, yet now thy halls
Bring misery to my sight." etc.

His reflections are broken in upon by a chorus of voices from within calling for vengeance, which is at once followed by the appearance of a crowd of armed Swiss who declare their purpose to rescue Tell, and ask Arnold to lead them in the desperate enterprise. With great resolution he responds to their appeals, and records a vow to kill Gessler by his own hands or perish in the attempt. His rashness the Swiss confederates disapprove, warning if caution be not observed that his own life will surely pay the forfeit, but Arnold cannot be restrained in the resolve which he has made, and that Tell may be rescued promptly he urges that the tyrant be boldly attacked at once, offering to lead them forward this moment to liberty or death, exclaiming:

"Yes, come: delusive is all hope
Of justice from the tyrant vile.
Glory, honor, vengeance, alike demand
That by our prowess Tell be saved."

Inspired by Arnold's utterances the Swiss shout for revenge, and with rattling of arms they follow their leader as he rushes impetuously off the stage.

The succeeding scene represents a house on the bank of the Lake of the Four Cantons, the waters of which are becoming agitated by an approaching storm. A party of Swiss are with Edwige, whom they invite to rest a while, for to proceed would mean certain death from the gathering tempest. She refuses their hospitality, urging that her desire is to encounter Gessler alone. When warned that such defiance can only result in her own destruction, she despairingly declares that it is death she seeks, since all that is dear to her has been lost a husband beloved and a treasured son. At this juncture Matilda appears, and the voice of Jemmy is heard from within calling "mother," followed quickly by his entrance upon the scene. At sight of her boy, Edwige utters a cry of joy, but instantly noting the absence of Tell, she eagerly asks: "But your father—why is he not with you?" Jemmy assures his mother that the protecting care of Matilda is about him, and that very soon she will free his father from captivity. Matilda now finds voice to console Edwige, that as the son has returned saved from a frightful storm, so will the father be restored, through Arnold and his patriot followers, which performance ending their grief a hope ariseth that cheers her own heart with love's fulfillment.

While Edwige, Matilda and Jemmy are rejoicing over their pleasant prospects, shouts of "Victory and liberty!" are heard, and a moment later Tell and Arnold come in. Edwige rushes into the arms of her hero husband, who first embracing her warmly, joyously announces:

> "Gessler hath fallen at last. The arrow behold
> With which his heart I've pierced; and the lake
> His burying place hath prov'd!"

Arnold now perceives Matilda, whose affection for him he cannot doubt, but he has fears that the death of her father, accomplished by an uprising in which he was himself a leader, may arouse her hate. He therefore addresses her somewhat indifferently, "You here, Matilda?" to which, however, she responds warmly, with assurance of her love. Exhorted by her to seek the field of glory, and returning thence victorious to receive her hand as a reward, he has fulfilled her request; therefore, though her father has fallen, it is less the kinship than the tyrant's death she remembers, and henceforth to her Arnold shall be the hero-lover. This happy termination, the freedom of Switzerland from a despot, the restoration of Tell and his son, and the consummation of the aspirations of Arnold and Matilda, is celebrated by a hymn of freedom, and the crowning with laurel of Tell and Arnold by Swiss women, which scene and exultant chorus concludes the opera.

Death of Tell, who yet Lives in the Hearts of his Countrymen.

Robert the Devil

AFTER THE ORIGINAL PAINTING BY H. T. CARISS

ROBERT—"*Ah! I see, now, the branch —*
symbol high — the dark and potent spell,
Which gives the hand that boldly grasps it
Unearthly power and immortal state."

ACT III. SCENE III.

ROBERT THE DEVIL

MUSIC BY MEYERBEER——WORDS BY SCRIBE AND DELAVIGNE

ROBERT THE DEVIL is the most spectacular of Meyerbeer's works, and though it has always been immensely popular, especially in France and England, it is very inferior, from a musical view-point, to "The Huguenots," "The Prophet," and "The African." The libretto, too, has fewer excellences than Scribe is to be credited with in other of his dramas, the objections being found in his sensational treatment that often, for the sake of effect, approaches dangerously near the ludicrously absurd. Notwithstanding the strange conceits that mar the dramatic story, it has been said the original was more grotesquely disfigured by the introduction of uncouth forms, such as sea-nymphs and goblins, which Meyerbeer wisely insisted should be banished. A marked substitution was made in the temptation scene, by introducing a bevy of profligate nuns, in place of enchanting naiads, as Scribe had originally designed. The change, it must be confessed, is small improvement, besides being almost sacrilegious, and in the first year of the opera the scene was made the subject of endless ridicule by both the critics and the public.

"Robert the Devil" was first represented at the Paris Academie, November 21, 1831, where it had a glorious reception. The following year two imperfect translations were brought out at rival London theatres, Covent Garden and Drury Lane, when at one the opera was called "The Demon; or, the Mystic Branch," and at the other, "The Fiend Father; or, Robert of Normandy." In June, 1832, the original (French) version was given at the King's Theatre, London, and met with the most extraordinary approval. It was not until May, 1847, that the opera was produced in the Italian, when it was put on the boards of Her Majesty's Theatre, London, with Jenny Lind in the principal rôle. It is truly a remarkable commentary on the capricious nature of amusement devotees, that what had delighted them very much for several years, with inferior singers in the cast, should suddenly, with the début of the most exquisite voice of the period, give them the greatest displeasure. Describing that first night, when "Robert the Devil" was sung in Italian, the biographer of Meyerbeer (Grunelsen) writes: "The night was rendered memorable not only by the début of Mlle. Lind, but also by a disgraceful exhibition such as was never before witnessed on the operatic stage. Mendelssohn was sitting in the stalls, and at the end of the third act, unable to bear any longer the executive infliction, he left the theatre." It is to be presumed that a great part of the audience followed him, for the engagement proved to be a failure, though a subsequent revival was a conspicuous success, and the opera still retains its very pronounced popularity.

The story upon which the opera is based runs as follows: Robert, Duke of Normandy, is the illegitimate son of Duchess Bertha, by a fiend who assumed the shape of a cavalier to the better prosecute his amours. This unnatural son, inheriting some of the diabolical characteristics of his father, is guilty of so many gallantries and crimes that he becomes known as "The Devil," and is banished from Normandy by his own subjects. Seeking new lands in which to give exercise to his evil propensities, he arrives in Sicily with the intention of participating in a tournament given by the Duke of Messina, in which the prize is to be the hand of Princess Isabella. Directly after his arrival in Italy, while carousing with his knights, Rambaldo, a minstrel, sings of the misdeeds of Robert, who is so offended by this insolence that he is about to avenge the insult when Alice, his foster-sister, and the betrothed of Rambaldo, intercedes. So passionately does the poor girl plead for mercy, and so prayerfully does she exhort him to abandon his sinful ways, that Robert's heart is touched, and in the interview he confides to Alice his love for Isabella. Their conversation is interrupted by the entrance of Bertram, Robert's fiend-father, at sight of whom Alice shrinks back affrighted, recognizing in him the evil spirit that holds mastery over Robert. She cannot remain in his presence, and after she departs Bertram entices his son, Robert, to the gaming table, where he soon loses in succession all his money, sword, horses and armor. Being thus reduced to beggary, Robert is unable to attend the tournament, by which failure his knightly honor is sacrificed.

The spell of mystery and diabolism has full effect in the opening of the second act, when an orgy of damned spirits takes place in the doleful cave of Saint Irene. Bertram is one of the company, and during the revels he makes a compact with the spirits whereby they are to release Robert from their influence and give him wholly into his (Bertram's) hands. Alice, who acts the part of good angel to Robert, has had an appointment with her lover, Rambaldo, in the cave, and overhearing the agreement between the evil spirits and Bertram, she forms a resolve to save Robert, if her power be equal to her desire. Soon thereafter Bertram meets Robert and promises to relieve his melancholy and retrieve his losses if he will visit the old Abbey of Saint Rosalie at midnight and carry away a mystic cypress branch which will be found growing at the head of the marble effigy of his dead mother. Robert consents to perform this task, under assurances from his fiend-father that the branch gives to its possessor powers of invisibility, riches, happiness, and immortality. Robert penetrates the gloomy ruins of the abbey, and when he arrives at the crypt Bertram appears, and pronounces an incantation that summons from their graves the spirits of a host of nuns. Among these ghostly shades is the spirit of Helen, former abbess of the cloister, who gives Robert courage to disregard the horrors of the place, and leaves him subject to the fascinations of the nuns. These charm him for the moment, but perceiving the mystic branch, he seizes and bears it away. The immediate effect is to give him a demoniacal nature, and possessed by a fell design he hurries to Messina and penetrates the chamber of Princess Isabella. The power of the talisman is at once exerted to put the attendants of the Princess into a profound sleep, which advantage Robert uses to carry off the Princess. Her entreaties to be spared and her appeals to his better nature prevail upon him at length to break the magic branch, which at once destroys its charm. At this the attendants of the Princess awake and rush forward to seize Robert, but he is saved by the timely help of Bertram, who blinds the eyes of the soldiers and bears him away. Robert tries to resist the fatal influence that pursues him, but is constantly constrained by Bertram, who tries to compel him, by stress of misfortune, to sign a compact that will bind him to evil for all eternity. Robert is induced by the fiend-father to meet the Prince of Grenada in deadly combat, but is overthrown, which so humiliates him that he seeks Bertram for advice, and is about to sign the compact that will restore his power and prestige, when the sound of sacred music falls on his ears, which calls up pious recollections of his mother, and he begins to weep. Bertram counteracts these sacred feelings by revealing the shame and mystery of his origin, whereupon Robert is again about to sign, when suddenly Alice appears, to announce the glad news that the Princess Isabella awaits him at the altar. Robert rejoices and would fly to his love, but the evil influence of his demon-father restrains him and would force him downward; a great struggle between the good and bad ensues, which continues until the clock strikes the fatal hour that dissolves the spell. Bertram's power is broken and the earth opens to engulf him, nor can cries for mercy avert his doom. Relieved of the incubus of evil disposition, Robert is conducted by Alice to the cathedral, where Isabella awaits him in nuptial robes, and Alice is rewarded by the hand of Rambaldo.

Act I.—When the curtain rises upon the first act of the opera, a view of Palermo is shown, with tents under shade trees, by one of which Robert and Bertram are seated at a table, attended by esquires. On the left is another table, around which several knights are gathered drinking wine. The action begins with a bacchanalian chorus of a truly brilliant character: "We'll live for pleasure only in woman, wine and play." When the song concludes, some envious knights express surprise at the attendants, splendid arms, and rich samite tent of the stranger, and wonder who he may be. They do not doubt, however, that he is a prodigal knight come to Messina, like themselves, to do battle in the tourney for Isabella's hand. Judging by their actions that the knights are making him the subject of their conversation, Robert salutes them and drinks to their good fortune, which courtesy calls forth a repetition of the chorus. At this point Rambaldo is introduced by Alberti as a strolling minstrel from Normandy, whom he recommends as an excellent singer. Robert generously bestows a purse upon the pilgrim and asks him to sing, to which request the minstrel promises to describe in song the deeds of a young duke who is called, for his profligacy and cruelty, "Robert the Devil," a veritable son of Lucifer, that has been banished from his native land. Robert handles his dagger menacingly, having a mind to avenge the insult, but he is restrained by Bertram, and Rambaldo now sings, with choral accompaniment, of the Duke begotten

"Knights, valets and esquires,
In this wine I, one and all, salute you!"

in guilty amour by a prince of demons, who, with face and heart like his sire, and a power derived from compact with Satan, uses his baneful influence to inspire wives and girls with fatal passion in order to accomplish their ruin.

Unable longer to curb his anger aroused by these exposures, Robert reveals his personality and orders his soldier attendants to arrest the minstrel. Rambaldo is terrified by the offence which he has unconsciously committed, and falling upon his knees before Robert, beseeches for pardon, but is answered that within an hour he shall hang for his insult. Rambaldo entreats that he has been sent with his intended bride upon a holy commission, to search for one Robert of Normandy, whom he had not known and therefore least suspected that he was the noble lord of whom he had just sung. This appeal for mercy fails to move Robert, but mention of an intended bride excites his sensual interest, and he promises Rambaldo to spare his life if he will bring this girl to him, warning, however, that she shall be no bride of a minstrel. Rambaldo shows his grief, which Robert spurns, and commands that the girl be quickly brought in.

While the roisterous knights are singing "We'll live for pleasure only," Alice, Rambaldo's affianced, is dragged in, crying for pity, but she is jeered at as a helpless beauty, who may save her lover's life by conforming to what may be required of her. Robert turns to face her and is horrified to discover that it is his dear foster-sister. She throws herself at his feet begging for protection, which he instantly grants by threatening to kill anyone who attempts to harm her. The other knights offer objection, but Robert menaces them with his sword and compels them to draw aside while he calms her fears by begging she will call him brother, though he is an exile driven often to despair and little deserving. Asked what purpose has brought her to Palermo, Alice tells him it was to fulfill a sacred duty, that she has put off her marriage for a season and come hither with her affianced husband to be bearer of sorrowful news. Urged to speak, she tells Robert that his blessed mother he will behold never again, and that she brings to him that mother's dying message, the last utterances of a devotion divine in its loving attachment, which she delivers in a tender aria

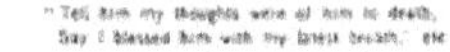
"Tell him my thoughts were of him in death,
Say I blessed him with my latest breath," etc.

and warning him of the fatal power urging him to ruin, she exhorted Alice to be his guardian angel to draw his feet into paths of virtue. This message touches the heart of Robert deeply, and he bewails the ill fortune that not only robbed him of a mother, but denied him the solace of being present to receive her last blessings. Alice, perceiving him to be receptive to holy influences, confides that one day his mother entrusted a precious paper to her keeping, with instructions to deliver it to him whenever he shall be worthy to receive it, and thereupon Alice, kneeling, presents to Robert his mother's will. He shrinks back, confessing that the time has not yet arrived when he may worthily receive so valued a token, and requests Alice to retain it. Opening his heart to his foster-sister, Robert dwells upon his misfortunes, greatest of which he esteems his failure to win the hand of Princess Isabella, which he sought to gain against her father's consent, but was set upon by her protecting attendants, and would have perished at their hands had not a friendly knight, Bertram, defended him from their savage onslaughts. Alice suggests that he write a note to the Princess asking if she is still faithful to the affection she once pledged him, and offers to be herself bearer of the message. Robert is overjoyed by this pleasing prospect of communicating with the woman who possesses his heart, and calling his secretary, dictates a note, which he seals with the hilt of his sword, at the same time declaring that Alice is indeed his guardian angel, whose proof of friendship he can never fully repay. Archly, she reminds him that she, too, is in love, and that the debt which he confesses may be discharged

Oh, good my Lord,
[illegible]

this day by permitting her to be wed to Rambaldo. He promises his consent, and then handing the note to Alice bids her bear it quickly to the Princess. Bertram now comes in, at sight of whom Alice is much frightened, which causes Robert to show some concern, and to assuage her fears he introduces the new arrival as his valiant friend Bertram, of whom he has just spoken. Alice explains her misgivings of the stranger because he bears such a striking likeness to Satan as he is represented in a painting that hangs in the village church. Robert laughs at her fears, and kissing her hand in token of his gratitude, he tells her to go at once to the princess. Bertram approaches Robert and sardonically asks if gratitude is becoming to one in his service—if it is not indeed the sign of unthankfulness to him? Robert commands him to be silent, and frankly confesses that he is in dread of the fatal influence he exerts, which is always enticing to evil. At this language the fiendish Bertram pretends to weep, as if grieving that Robert should doubt his affection. When Robert insists that he shall hereafter withhold his advice, Bertram obsequiously promises to offend no more, and invites his son to rejoin the cavaliers and try his luck at gaming. At this moment several knights enter, with Alberti, and immediately Robert challenges them to meet him in a game at dice, which they promptly accept. A table being set in the centre of the stage, several knights crowd about it and the play begins. Bertram, by his magic arts, has set a spell of misfortune upon Robert, who loses time and again, but is encouraged by the fiend to continue the game, until he hazards successively all his money, his jewelry, horses, arms, and armor, thus stripping himself of all means for entering the tourney. The act concludes with a strong concerted number, Robert cursing his ill luck, the knights making sport of his despair, and Bertram exulting over the prospective success of his fell designs.

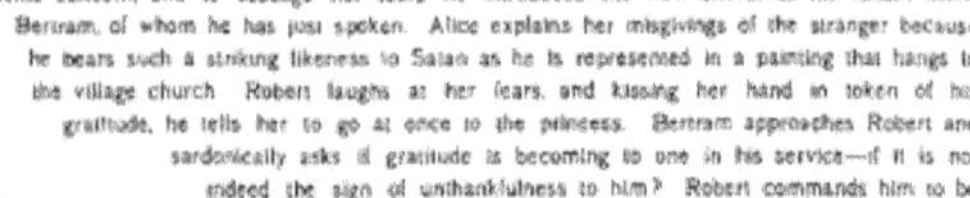

Act II.—The second act opens with a scene showing an apartment in the ducal palace of Sicily, in which Isabella appears alone. In a pathetic aria she expresses her grief at being abandoned by Robert, who taught her first to love:

> "Ah! hope deserts me, dark seems the future!
> Gone now the visions of youthful love," etc.

[illegible]

In the scene that follows, a company of young girls enter, bearing a petition which they present to Princess Isabella as Alice comes in. The latter trembles with timidity in the presence of royalty, but she presently summons courage to hand Robert's letter to the Princess. The latter takes it eagerly, and perceiving at once who is the writer, she gives expression to her joy and prays that Robert may fly to her quickly, never again to part. As Alice and Isabella now pass out, Bertram enters, followed by a herald-at-arms, as Robert appears passing along the gallery, concerting means how he may overcome his rival for Isabella's hand. Bertram approaches his son, and in an undertone tells him his aims may now be accomplished. The herald hands Robert a cartel challenging him to deadly combat with the Prince of Grenada, who awaits an answer in a neighboring wood. This defiance is eagerly accepted by Robert, who desires to meet his adversary without delay, and the three thereupon pass out, as the stage is filled again by the entrance of Isabella, conducted by her father, followed by Bertram, Alice, Rambaldo, lords, ladies, esquires and people, accompanying six young couples who are about to be married. The action is renewed by a chorus, succeeded by a ballet divertissement, after which a herald-at-arms enters and addresses the Princess: "When all the noble champions come here to-day to prove their valor, the Prince of Grenada, in pledge of his faith, the honor requests of being armed by you." Isabella hesitates, which her father observing, directs her to make a prompt reply, as the Prince of Grenada enters the hall and goes directly to the Princess. Bertram chuckles with fiendish satisfaction at the progress of his plans, for Robert has, by a ruse, been lured away into the woods in a vain quest for an adversary, thus giving opportunity to the Prince to reach the Princess without the embarrassment of a rival's presence. The esquires, in a chorus, sing praises of their noble leader, while Isabella, obeying the urgings of her father, timidly and reluctantly invests the Prince with arms and armor for the tournament for her hand.

Alice marks with great anxiety the absence of Robert, and marvels what can have detained him, but Rambaldo bids her not be alarmed, for that he will certainly arrive before the lists are closed, to enter for the tourney and to bless their union at the altar, which is now prepared. Bertram, however, congratulates himself upon his successful artifice to keep Robert from the meeting. The chorus now call for the assembling of all valiant knights who desire to do battle for a princess' hand, after which announcement a trumpet sounds, and at a signal Isabella descends from the throne and addresses the cavaliers in an aria:

"Hark! the trumpet's glad summons sound on the ear,
It becomes the gallant warrior now to conquer or to die," etc.

A procession of knights, ladies and esquires move across the stage, followed by Isabella and her father. Bertram remains on the opposite side of the stage in a state of exultation, gloating over the painful anxiety manifested by Alice, which scene concludes the second act.

Act III.—The first scene of Act III represents the mountain of Saint Irene, appalling in its gloomy isolation and gray grandeur. In the foreground are the ruins of an ancient temple, marked on the left by a cross, and on the right is an entrance to the underground caverns. Bertram and Rambaldo enter, the latter by appointment to meet Alice here, and the former to prosecute his evil designs. To the inquiries addressed to him by Bertram, Rambaldo acknowledges his extreme poverty, which condition causes him the greatest unhappiness, for he is unable to conceive how he shall care for Alice in a manner befitting her station. Bertram is quick to profit by his advantage, and to gain a new victim he gives Rambaldo a purse filled with gold, the sight of which so delights the poor lover-minstrel that he cannot convince himself it is not a dream, which scene is embellished with a splendid duet, "O Generous Master." Having gained Rambaldo's confidence and gratitude, Bertram begins to sow seeds of dissatisfaction in his mind by reminding that so much gold makes him rich, and that as wealth is the supreme attraction of mortals, he may, by seeking, obtain a wife of fairer face than Alice wears. Rambaldo gives an attentive ear to Bertram's fatal flatteries, and seems to be entirely persuaded to adopt his advice. When the minstrel goes out, debating the matter in his mind, Bertram, left alone, begins preparing materials for incantation. While thus engaged he felicitates himself upon having made another conquest, of a soul that will soon be joyfully welcomed by the legions of hell, though while giving expression to his satisfaction he cannot dismiss from his mind the dreadful fate that must be his own when at last his lease of life and his iniquitous career is ended. He hears the noise of infernal jubilation, to mitigate which he sings, accompanied by a demon chorus:

"A robe for your highness, [illegible]
[illegible]"

"Ye spirits of evil, think not of the light,
But join the mad revel of darkness and night!"

And is answered by demons declaring that brighter star has never fallen, and greater master the world diabolic has never known. These praises by the impish chorus serve to arouse the faint fire of conscience that still smoulders in his heart, and he resolves to obtain through his son, even by sacrifice, a remission of his crimes, or by graver deeds of infernality win a crown in hell. After soliloquizing in this manner of his life and doubtful prospects, Bertram disappears within the cavern, his presence among the demons being welcomed by a burst of flames and groaning acclaims.

Alice is now seen slowly descending the mountain, calling the name of Rambaldo, but receiving no answer, she expresses her fears of the dangers that seem to lurk in such a lonesome place, to which nothing but love for her betrothed could lure her. In great sadness of heart she sings a plaintive cavatina that is one of the sublime beauties of the opera:

"When I left my Norman valleys,
Said to me a holy hermit,
You shall one day be united
To a faithful, loving heart." etc.

As she draws near the mouth of the cavern the sun becomes darkened and strange voices fall upon her ears, which excite her fears, but these are quickly dismissed by thoughts of the loved one whom she is coming here to meet, and she moves forward confidently, praying the Holy Virgin to protect a virgin's love. The noises increase and the earth begins to tremble, which fill her with fresh alarm, and she is about to flee when a chorus from beneath shout the name of "Robert!" Thinking some danger threatens him, she resolves to brave all the perils, but to hide herself that in case of need she may be near, to give him such help as her feeble strength will permit. Again she moves a few steps towards the cavern mouth, and presently takes courage to peer in, at which moment "Robert!" is shouted in her ears, which so frightens the poor girl that she rushes for refuge to a cross close by, and embracing it falls in a faint at its foot.

Bertram emerges from the cavern, pale and agitated, bewailing the prospect of losing his son, irrevocable judgment having been pronounced by the evil spirits that if Robert does not yield this night to the wicked influence, he shall be released from the spell. Alice overhears the conditions of this compact and determines to save Robert, but when Bertram discovers her she dissembles, and professing extreme weakness, to his questioning, if she heard his remarks, declares that she has neither heard nor seen anything. Bertram manifests a savage joy that his designs are unknown to her, and in his heart he conceives a purpose to beguile the innocent girl that she also may become his prey. With this object he practices his arts of flattery, but she shrinks back, and for protection clasps the holy cross. Her rejection of his overtures causes him to believe that she has discovered his plans for winning Robert into his power, and he tries to intimidate her by declaring that her eyes have penetrated a mystery forbidden to mortals, and threatens that if but a single sound escapes her lips her life will pay the penalty, and the forfeit will also include the lives of all her kindred. At this moment Robert approaches, mourning over his losses of worldly goods and honor, at sight of whom Bertram admonishes her of the doom that will be brought upon her if she reveals what she has seen or heard.

[illegible]

The appearance of Robert is followed by an intensely dramatic trio, in which Bertram, Robert and Alice express their respective sentiments, at the close of which Bertram, by a signal, orders Alice to retire. She obeys reluctantly, but after retiring a few paces she rushes back again, and defying death she beseeches Robert to listen! Bertram glares at her with Satanic threatening, and tells her to speak out, in the name of father, kindred, and betrothed, which admonition compels her to hesitate, and she gives Robert no better excuse for her action than that she dare not speak! Alice now passes out, and the two being alone, Robert appeals to Bertram to extend the help that he has promised, an aid that will free him from the spell of misfortune which has cost him so dearly. Bertram is exultant at finding Robert so amenable to his will, and tells him that the calamities so recently sustained have been brought upon him by a demon agent of his rival, whose power for harm cannot be broken save by acts of sacrilege such as the fiend himself has practiced by which to obtain that power. Robert is deeply anxious to be instructed in the mystic duties that will avert the spell, and is thus informed by Bertram: "Thou must have heard of that awful spot where lie entombed those all-daring women who followed here on earth the magic art. In that mysterious place there stand the desolated cloisters, and the tomb of Bertha, thy mother. If thou wishest to live, thou must not speak with those spirits departed whose doom is connected with that abode of death. Into that place where none can enter but at the risk of life, wilt thou have courage to enter?"

Robert, possessed of a stout heart and most eager to redeem his honor, willingly braves all the terrors that Bertram pictures, and the next scene discloses the mysterious vaults. Bertram enters alone, and while the orchestra renders music that is fearsomely suggestive of diablerie, he discourses of the cloisters dedicated to Saint Rosalie, which have since been profaned and made a haunted spot of vice by offerings of incense to evil deities. He calls up the spirits of sacrilegious nuns, in the name of Beelzebub, during which address and invocation sulphurous flames are to be seen playing along the deserted aisles and issuing through crevices of the tombs of the nuns. Slowly the stone slabs are displaced and there rise out of the sepulchres the forms of shrouded females that glide in a procession of ghostly figures to Saint Rosalie's effigy, which, however, they are unable to pass. The stage gradually becomes lighted by a strange halo, and as the spirits group themselves before Bertram, he thus addresses them:

"Ye daughters once of heaven, but now of hell,
All obey the will of your master!
Behold! There hither comes a knight
To pluck the mystic cypress branch.
But if his heart shall fail him through fear;
Lest my purpose be defeated,
By your charms thou must seduce him."

The nuns signify their assent by bowing, and the moment Bertram withdraws they are animated by the passions they had felt while in the flesh. Helen, their superior, invites them to profit by their short release from their narrow tombs and yield themselves to pleasure. Joyfully adopting this advice, the ghosts take goblets and dice from their graves and begin an orgy of drinking and gambling. Some make offerings to an idol, others crown their heads with cypress, and when these diversions are exhausted they throw off their cerements and indulge in a bacchanalian dance. When their revelry is at its height, a quick change in the diablerie music announces the slow approach of Robert, whereupon the ghostly nuns leave off their saturnalia and conceal themselves behind the columns to await the entrance of their victim, whom they are resolved to entice from every sense of virtue by practice of their infernal arts.

Robert enters the desolate cloisters, and advancing with hesitation and misgiving, he is almost persuaded, by the awesomeness of the dark abode and ghostly tombs, to relinquish his desperate purpose, until his eyes suddenly catch sight of the mystic branch, whose potent spell gives supernatural power and immortality to the hand that grasps it. His first impulse is to seize the mysterious symbol and hurry from the place, but a dread steals over him that some infernal art may be laid to punish, and he is about to flee from the terror-inspiring spot when he suddenly finds himself surrounded by the nuns. One offers him a cup of wine, but he refuses to accept it, whereupon Helen, more fascinating than her spectral sisters, proffers a goblet, with such witchery of beguilement that Robert is unable to resist the temptation, and he takes the wine. Being susceptible to her power, Helen leads him to the tomb of Saint Rosalie, by which grows the magic branch, but instead of plucking it he draws back in alarm, whereupon the nuns offer him dice, which he is about to accept, when again some force which he does not understand causes him to recoil. Helen now renews her blandishments and leads him a second time to the tomb, caressing him passionately the while she points to the branch in such an alluring manner that he hesitates no longer, and grasping it as the most precious of prizes he waves it aloft and makes his way out of the cloisters. As Robert exits the nuns gradually sink down by their respective tombs, from each of which a demon springs out and secures his prey. The act ends with a devils' chorus, exulting at the fall of Robert.

Act IV.—The rising of the curtain reveals the apartments of Isabella, Princess of Sicily. Several female attendants are removing her bridal ornaments and distributing them among the six brides of the morning, which is performed while the chorus render a joyful air: "Wreathe now your hair." Albert, a Sicilian knight, who is a contestant for Isabella's hand, enters, bringing precious presents for the Princess, ante-nuptial gifts of pearls, diamonds, and tokens of his love, which he offers and then retires a pace, as Robert descends the staircase. He advances towards the Princess, who is seated, carrying the magic branch before him, the potency of which renders the Princess, Albert and the attendants immovable in a death-like slumber. Observing the Princess, so beauteous in her sudden repose, he contemplates her with the greatest admiration and confirms his purpose to possess her even at the cost of forcing her to follow him, should a rival possess her heart. All conditions favoring his designs, and conscious of the power the talisman gives him, he exclaims, "Isabella! for thee the spell is broken which has lulled to sleep thy senses." Relieved, she wakens, and opening her eyes, is astounded by sight of Robert standing before her. She realizes that she is the victim of some strange illusion and implores his protection, to which replying he manifests a savage satisfaction in finding her so distressed, the punishment that he would inflict for her surrender to a rival lover. She shudders at his Satanic countenance, and wonders what awful influence swerves him from his honor. He admits that his power is derived from spirits infernal which will be exerted remorselessly for the destruction of the hated one who would displace him in her affections. Surprised by these words, Isabella asks, if his love for her is so strong, why he did not appear in the lists to-day when to the victor her hand was to be the prize? This question serves rather to enrage him the more, since it so forcibly brings to his mind and taunts him with the malevolent fortune that dispossessed him of money, weapons and horse; therefore he fiercely answers her: "Do not urge my passion to despair! Here I command; all here obey my power; nothing can break the chain by magic spread. Thou must yield at once! my bride or victim!"

Isabella, terrified by Robert's manner, lifts her voice in supplication that he may be released from the evil power that holds him a slave to dishonor, and in mercy's name she beseeches him to quit the place, for vain are all his wishes. He declares that no appeal can alter his resolution to compel her to follow him, which cruel intent she pleadingly responds to in a world-famous air, the sweetest of the opera:

"Robert, dearest, who deemed me once so fair
Behold me kneeling in thy great despair
Mercy for thyself, I humbly pray thee,
Mercy in Heaven's name please to show me."

These tender accents and prayerful tears subdue Robert's purpose; against them he can no longer resist, for they have conquered the demonic spirit that possessed him through the baneful arts of Bertram, but in renouncing his design his heart grieves for the feeling that he has lost her forever, that the prize which he had hoped to possess must be abandoned, and that life no longer contains any charms for him, since no means are left by which he may contest at the tournament, ill fortune having robbed him of horse, weapons and armor. Isabella tries to console him, but hope is fled, and he declares, if his rival's sword shall triumph in the tourney, that he will slay himself at her feet. Having thus uttered his despair, Robert breaks the magic branch, thereby destroying all its mystic power, and immediately the large doors in the rear of the stage unfold, revealing the entire court attendants and knights asleep. They wake, one after another, and come hurriedly forward singing in chorus of the strange occurrence of overpowering sleep that seems to portend a death within the hall.

Albert, rousing himself, perceives Robert, and orders the knights to seize him, a man whom he pronounces bold in peace, but a craven in battle, whose punishment for daring to enter the princess' chamber shall be executed without mercy before the

[illegible]

morning's dawn. As the knights move towards him, Robert defies heaven and earth alike, indifferent now of his life, and invites them to spend their vengeance upon him. Isabella implores Alberti's pity, for she has no power herself to save, and despairingly repeats, "He must die before to-morrow's dawn!" Alice grieves that she can offer no assistance, and Rambaldo likewise bewails his helplessness. The knights rush on Robert and bear him away unresisting, as Isabella sinks in a swoon, and Alice falls upon her knees to offer up a prayer for Robert, which situation furnishes a dramatic climax for the fourth act.

Act V.—The concluding act opens with a scene of the cloisters, and a chorus of monks singing, "Men of sin or of misfortune," etc. Robert enters, conducting Bertram to this holy place of refuge. Bertram has, by exercise of his magic powers, delivered Robert from his enemies, by blinding their eyes, after which he provided the means for him to meet his rival, the Prince of Grenada, in combat. Robert now enters to tell Bertram of the issue of the fight, which has been against him, and his sword deceiving him he was defeated by Alberti, who to complete his humiliation, after vanquishing him, spared his life, that he might live in detestation. Bertram professes great regret and sympathizes with Robert in his misfortunes, but reminds him that he forfeited hope of victory by recklessly breaking the enchanted branch, thereby losing his loved one to a rival. Robert appeals to know if some art may not yet avail him to gain the Princess, promising that for power to satisfy his vengeance he will submit to any ordeal or condition. Bertram thereupon produces a scroll and pen and pledges Robert assurance of the success of all his wishes if he will sign a compact plighting faith. Eagerly Robert seizes the pen and paper, but at this instant sacred music is heard, at the solemn sounds of which he pauses suddenly and turns amazed to Bertram, saying: "To such songs I listened in happy days of boyhood, when prayers to Heaven my dear mother offered for me." At this sacred remembrance Robert weeps, and as the music continues he interprets it as the voice of his blessed mother calling her son to repentance.

Bertram clearly foresees that the pious recollections stirred in Robert will soon destroy the Satanic influence if it be not quickly counteracted by reviving his revengeful feelings, to accomplish which the artful designer pretends to applaud the sentiment aroused by the celestial music, but tells him it is a heavenly admonition to avenge himself upon his boastful rival, who even now may be leading Isabella to the altar. Robert is stung by these words into uncontrollable passion, but his misfortunes and despairing condition he attributes to Bertram, who he believes is leagued against him, and bids him begone! Pretending amazement, the crafty dissembler tries hard to disabuse Robert's suspicion, by proffering the sincerest love and fatherly interest in all his affairs, and thereupon he discloses the mystery of Robert's origin. Assuming the disguise of a fair lover through the power given him by a compact made with the Prince of Darkness, Bertram tells how he beguiled an innocent maid with soft speech, and the issue of that wrong was a son, who ever since has been a source of contention between the powers of good and evil, which must finally be determined this very night. Urged to speak more plainly Bertram confesses that this son, conceived through infernal artifice, is—Robert! Further explanation the arch hypocrite vouchsafes, that, to make his influence supreme, a fiend took on the likeness of Alberti, and by hellish arts overcame Robert in battle, but that he may this same fiend vanquish by signing the compact that is proffered, whereby as son he will be restored to his father. Bertram warns that if the contract be not signed before midnight, Robert will be lost to him forever, for that the dread powers have so ordained, wherefore, as both their fates are now depending, he entreats him as a dear son, his only joy, the object of his dearest ambition as a devoted father, to hesitate no longer to perform an act so necessary, and to sign at once ere they be separated to meet never again.

The appeal of Bertram persuades Robert, and confessing that hell is strongest, he declares his intention of being faithful to him, but at this instant Alice enters, who, having overheard Robert's last words, brings the joyful message that the noble Princess, Isabella, now waits him at the altar. Bertram resents this interference, and with a show of impatience tries to lead Robert away. The evil spell is still upon him, which he is as yet powerless to resist. His mind is possessed by Bertram, while his heart yearns for the Princess, and it is with these conflicting emotions that he violently contends. Bertram renews his efforts to force him away and is succeeding, to the horror of Alice, who appeals to Robert to obey the holier impulse, to regard his oath, to listen to the monitor of honor, to think of the beautiful Princess who is waiting at the altar for his coming. In turn Bertram beseeches him to follow him, to be a comfort to a doting father, and to urge more persuasively, he takes a parchment from his bosom and tells him to read it carefully, by which he may be induced to perform a duty. Robert glances at the scroll and seeing that it is the compact to which he has given assent, he answers, "Yes, to thee, oh, my father, I yield my sad heart." Alice continues her entreaties which Robert resists with the reply that he is bound by a power more potent than his oath. Finding her beseechings are without avail Alice rushes between Bertram and Robert, at the same time drawing from her bosom the will of Robert's mother, which he is requested to carefully peruse, and thereby sound the depths of his ungratefulness. He takes the paper and reads:

"My love, oh, son, will follow to protect thee,
Beyond the grave in world above I'll watch thee.
Beware the devil's words that have thy heart dismayed,
Think of thy mother, who was by his arts betrayed."

Robert's hands tremble so violently that in his intense agitation he drops the scroll, which Alice picks up quickly. Faltering between opposing influences Robert is undecided what to do, whereupon Bertram renews his entreaties, and upon his knees he implores Robert to ease his torturing anguish by consent to follow him. Robert pleads for pity, while Alice implores him in the name of his mother, and Bertram beseeches that as a dutiful son he will save a wretched father from endless torment. While the two are struggling to gain ascendency over Robert, the clock strikes twelve, at which solemn sound Alice lifts her eyes to heaven to thank the Holy Power that has saved Robert, and Bertram, vanquished, sinks from sight, claimed by the fiends of evil. Robert falls insensible at the feet of Alice, who strives to revive him. A rolling of thunder is heard, succeeded by sacred music, and the scene changes to the country near Palermo, where a cathedral is shown and a chorus of invisibles is heard, "Robert is to heaven faithful, and for him its gates unclose." Alice conducts Robert into the cathedral, where he meets Princess Isabella, and a double wedding, between Robert and Isabella, and Rambaldo and Alice, closes the opera. The finale terzetto, between Robert, Bertram and Alice, is at once the most dramatic as it is the most tuneful number that Meyerbeer ever wrote.

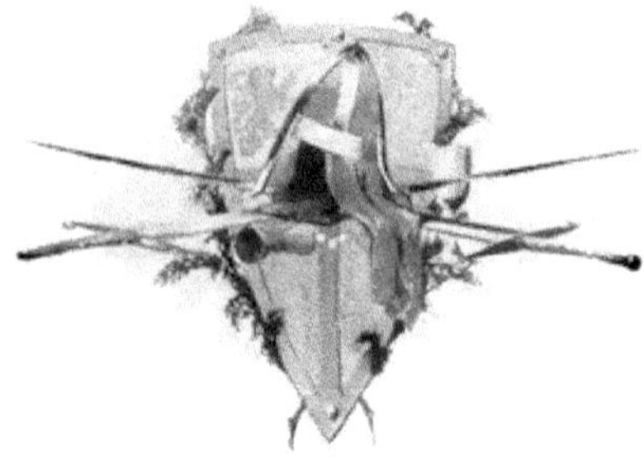

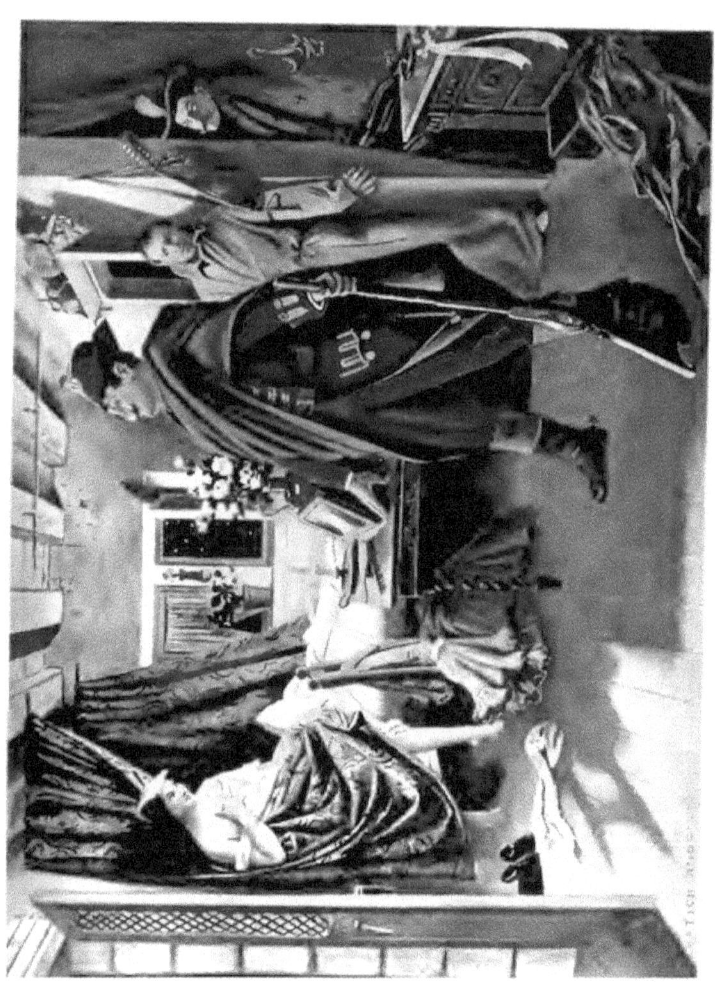

Fra Diavolo

AFTER THE ORIGINAL PAINTING BY WILLIAM DE LEFTWICH DODGE

ZERLINA.—"*Fie, sir!—You shouldn't bolt into people's rooms in this manner.*"

LORENZO.—"*Forgive me, and affect not such coyness. You are ever beautiful in any guise.*"

ACT II.—SCENE III.

FRA DIAVOLO.

MUSIC BY AUBER —— WORDS BY SCRIBE

FRA DIAVOLO, although belonging to the opera comique, is entitled to a place in this work, chiefly devoted to legends of the Grand Operas, because of its unique position as the greatest of its class, and the association to which it is universally admitted as one of the most melodramatic, spirited, and melodious of operatic creations. The story was originally treated by Lesueur in "La Caverne" (the den), which was afterwards rearranged as a spectacular pantomime, when it bore the title, "The Robber of Abruzzi." The original has been changed greatly by Scribe to adapt it to caricature of modern rich travelers, in which attempt he was remarkably successful, while the music shows throughout the highest genius of the humorist and the composer. As the story recites: The scene is laid in and near a village inn of Italy, which is kept by Matteo, whose daughter, Zerlina, is loved by Lorenzo, a brave young soldier, who distinguishes himself as a resolute pursuer of Fra Diavolo, a brigand chief. When the action begins, an English nobleman, Lord Allcash, and his wife, Pamela, conventional tourists, appear before the inn of Terracina greatly agitated, having just been robbed of a part of their valuables by a band of highwaymen. The two appeal for help to recover their stolen property, and Lorenzo promising to give them the needed assistance, sets off in pursuit of the robbers. After plundering his victims, Fra Diavolo disguises himself as a marquis, and adopting the title of the Lord of San Marco, he repairs to the inn, where he exhibits so much courtly grace as to speedily gain the admiration of Lady Allcash (Pamela). This is less difficult to do because of the unmatched conditions of the English Lord and his wife, the former being old and rich, while the latter is young and coquettish. The attentions of the Marquis are so well directed that he speedily obtains the confidence of the susceptible lady, and so flatters her with praises of her rare beauty and charming accomplishments, that he secures, by her half-consenting, a richly-jeweled locket that contains her portrait. Lord Allcash discovers his wife's infatuation, and makes a noisy protest, and a quarrel ensues, but the Marquis, by cajoleries, of which he is a master, presently mollifies his lordship's jealousy, and even gains his confidence so completely as to hear from his lips how he foiled the robbers by anticipating an attack and secreting his money in the lining of his wife's dress. Being now possessed of the information he has sought, Fra Diavolo sets his plans to secure the hidden wealth. He turns his attention for the while to Zerlina, chambermaid of the inn, who has also general care of travelers, and she, believing him to be really a marquis, is much pleased by his flatteries, tells him, among other things, the story of Fra Diavolo, and of the fear in which the bandit is held, as well also the secret admiration felt for the daring rover by sentimental girls who are always looking for bold lovers.

Learning from Zerlina what room has been assigned to Lord and Lady Allcash, Fra Diavolo renews his tender devotions to the Lady and completely fascinates her by singing an exquisite barcarolle with mandolin accompaniment. This pleasant engagement is rudely interrupted by the return of Lorenzo and his carbineers, who report that they came up with the band of robbers, and in a fight killed twenty of the marauders, besides recovering much of the stolen jewels, but that the chief escaped. Fra Diavolo thereupon hastily retires a little way before his identity can be discovered. The excitement is great following Lorenzo's statement, but Lady Allcash is saved from hysteria by a return to her of her jewels, and as the night is now far advanced, preparations are made for retiring. Zerlina lights Lord and Lady Allcash to their room, and then repairs to her own chamber. But in the meantime Fra Diavolo and two of his companions have returned and secreted themselves in a closet of Zerlina's room. After she has retired, and the coast is believed to be clear, the three robbers issue from their hiding place to accomplish their designs, but in crossing the room they make a noise that partially arouses Zerlina. One of them raises his dagger to stab her, but he is awe-stricken by a prayer which the still sleeping girl murmurs, and at the same time the voices of carbineers on the outside admonish the robbers to return to the closet. Zerlina, disturbed, rises and dresses herself, and the house being set in an uproar, Lord and Lady Allcash, *en déshabillé*, come rushing into Zerlina's room to learn the cause. Lorenzo also enters to lend assistance, if it be needed, and hearing a noise in the closet, he proceeds to investigate. Fra Diavolo boldly steps forth, and to preserve his personation of a marquis, declares that he is there to keep an appointment with Zerlina. Lorenzo promptly challenges him for this aspersion of his fiancé's character, which Fra Diavolo accepts for the morning, thereby being able to retire, and his companions manage to get out of the house without being seen.

Fra Diavolo, after his cunning escape from the inn, flees to the mountains and resumes his watch of the highway, hoping always to meet Lord and Lady Allcash, to his better profit than his last adventure. His course as a brigand, however, is to terminate soon, for he is lured to attend a marriage ceremony in a near-by village, where he is taken unawares and captured by Lorenzo's carbineers.

Act I.—The opening scene of the opera shows an Italian inn, upon the porch of which, gathered about a table, is a party of carbineers drinking, and singing of love and wine, the twin joys of a soldier's life. Lorenzo presently enters, with Zerlina, and announces a reward of twenty thousand crowns for the arrest of Fra Diavolo, besides which promise of gain is the honor and glory that the capture will bring. The carbineers express their pleasure at the prospect of winning so much money, and order more wine, which Matteo brings, but as he passes the bottle he notices that Lorenzo has no glass, and that he refuses to drink when one is handed him. He also observes the troubled look upon Lorenzo's face, and divining the cause, tells the company that Zerlina is to marry Francesco, the rich farmer, on the morrow. As Matteo goes for wine, Zerlina, with a show of anxiety, asks Lorenzo if he is going in quest of Fra Diavolo, to which he mournfully replies that this is his intent, and that perhaps he will be killed, but that his death matters little to her, since she is soon to become the bride of another, thus leaving him naught to do but die. A picturesque duet follows, in which Zerlina begs Lorenzo to remain, to be her comfort, for her heart is ever with him, but he persists in his intention to go away and be killed.

At the close of the duet a carriage drives up, with postilions and liveried servants, and from it issue Lord and Lady Allcash, who cry out in great distress of mind, and betray so much fright that for some minutes they cannot explain the particulars of their mishap on the highway. When at length Lady Allcash, known as Pamela, manages to recover her breath, she relates the particulars of their distressing adventure in a catchy cavatina:

"What a country this for strangers
Assailed by many dangers,
Infested by a robber band,
No one secure in all the land.
Alas, the contents of my casket—
My jewelry and my laces,
Of these, alack! there are no traces
Taken were they by a fierce brigand."

Discouraged by their misadventure, in being robbed on the highway, Lord Allcash and Pamela declare their intension to return home at once and travel no more, but the carbineers afford them some small consolation by promising to go at once to capture the robber and his band. At this outburst of courage, Lord Allcash advances towards Lorenzo, and addressing him as Signor Brigadier, entreats him to redress the outrage he has just suffered in this country, explaining that his lady (Pamela) has done him the honor and the pleasure to marry him of her own free will, even though the ceremony was performed at Gretna Green, that for her generous act he consented to travel in Italy, and that while peaceably and delightfully enjoying their honeymoon in their carriage, on the highway, a bold robber band attacked them, and forcibly took all their fine diamonds, besides many fine laces of great value. Therefore, Lord Allcash beseeches Lorenzo to hazard his life in an effort to apprehend the brigands and restore the precious jewels.

Lorenzo, being made acquainted with the details of the robbery, expresses the opinion that it has been committed by Fra Diavolo's band, and learning which direction the bold brigand took, he proposes to go in pursuit at once. Before taking his departure, with the soldiers, however, Lorenzo calls for wine, and while Matteo is serving it, Zerlina once more appeals to him, but despite her protestations of devotion to him alone, Lorenzo still believes, as her father has just told, that her hand is promised to a rich farmer. In a desperate frame of mind, stung by jealousy, he calls his carbineers, and giving a hasty farewell to Zerlina and the two travelers, he marches away to the pursuit with his company of soldiers.

Lord Allcash has not failed to notice the gloom on Lorenzo's face, and thinks it may be fear of Fra Diavolo, who among the common people is superstitiously regarded as being invulnerable, but Matteo disabuses this suspicion by pronouncing Lorenzo to be one of the bravest of men, and excellent in every way, save for his poverty, and in being an aspirant for Zerlina's hand, when she deserves a husband who is better able to support her. This explanation of the situation serves to arouse Lord Allcash's interest in the love affair of the poor young officer, and with the hope of mending Lorenzo's fortune, he calls for pen and paper, and asks Matteo to write, as he dictates, a reward of three thousand francs to any one who shall recover the stolen jewels. Pamela interposes with a request that the reward be increased to ten thousand, since the jewels cost at least a hundred thousand, and rails at her husband for being the cause of their misfortune, through insisting on following the by-road. He impatiently reminds her that he did so to escape that elegant cavalier who has been tracking them from place to place, and giving her attentions that it ill becomes an honest wife to receive. She ventures to defend her conduct by declaring that it was the cavalier's music that pleased her, but Lord Allcash objects emphatically to music when it is made a vehicle for coquetry, whereupon a particularly pleasing duet is sung by the two: "I don't object; I do object." Lord Allcash ends the domestic altercation by setting it down against all his wife's objecting that she shall not see this Neapolitan Marquis again. Scarcely has the irate Englishman expressed this determination when a carriage rolls up before the door of the inn, and to the consternation of Lord Allcash the same Marquis (who is Fra Diavolo in disguise) steps out and greets Pamela affectionately as his "charming lady." The English lord is astounded by this familiarity, and so expresses himself, but Pamela, flattered, as a woman may always be, is unable to decide within her own mind whether the attentions are impertinent or agreeable.

Zerlina and Matteo look on the meeting between the guests with pleased surprise, and having no doubt that the Marquis will imburse them well for his entertainment, they give him particular attention. Lord Allcash warns his wife against the flatteries of this persuasive stranger, but she protests that it is no fault of hers if the Marquis thinks her divine and falls in love. A quintet follows, "Oh, rapture unbounded," which is universally regarded as being the most effective of the many harmonized ensembles that Auber, prince of his class, ever wrote. The Englishman is so angered by the manifest disposition of Pamela to encourage the stranger, that he forces her into the inn, but in going she bows most graciously to the Marquis. When Lord and Lady Allcash leave the stage, Fra Diavolo, masquerading, questions Matteo of his daughter, and of the guests in the house, and remarks that the Englishman is evidently a victim of spleen. "Aye, and with good cause," replies the inn-keeper, "for he has just been attacked and robbed in the mountains." The Marquis, eating rapidly the while, affects to discredit the report of robbers as a tale to alarm travelers, for passing night and day over the mountains, he has never himself once been attacked. Matteo assures him it was only by the most excellent good fortune that he has so long escaped, for this Fra Diavolo— The Marquis stops him abruptly to ask "Who is this Fra Diavolo of whom every one appears in dread?" which question Zerlina answers in an exquisite romanza:

"On yonder rock reclining,
That fierce and swarthy form behold!
Fast his hands his carbine hold,
'Tis his best friend of old," etc.

When Zerlina has sung of the fierceness with which Fra Diavolo fights, the terror that his name inspires, and of his gallantry to maidens, the Marquis rises suddenly and sings the concluding verse, in which he asks that justice be shown to one who shares his prizes, and thus often provides the means to rustic beaux with which to win and care for brides. When Zerlina's beautiful air is ended, Beppo and Giacomo, two of Fra Diavolo's robber companions, enter so softly and present such a ragged appearance, that Zerlina's fears are excited, and Matteo answers their craving for hospitality by bluntly telling them he does not entertain vagabonds. The Marquis, to the more perfectly preserve his disguise, gives a piece of money to the two, in the name of Zerlina, and magnanimously offers to pay for their accommodations for the night. This proposal pleases Matteo, and he goes out, with Zerlina, to prepare supper for the new arrivals. The three being now left alone, Fra Diavolo sits down at one end of the table and begins to pick his teeth, affecting a contented air, as Beppo, first looking cautiously about, takes up the bottle and pouring out a glass of wine, offers to drink his health. Fra Diavolo is indignant at this impertinent familiarity, but Giacomo begs him to abate his anger, since Beppo is a new recruit of excellent promise who has not yet learned the respect due his superior, and in a low voice tells Beppo to remove his hat. Fra Diavolo is not entirely satisfied with the excuse, and calling for water, as he washes his hands he warns Beppo that if he repeats his familiarity his life will pay the penalty. As if disregarding this threat, Beppo informs the brigand chief that the English Lord was stopped on the highway, and that a rich booty of jewels rewarded their enterprise. Fra Diavolo replies that this is no information, but asks if the casket containing five hundred thousand francs was found and appropriated? Sorrowfully the two robbers have to admit that they were unable to find the money. This report angers the robber captain again, for he counts as lost the precious three days he has spent singing barcarolles to Lady Allcash, trying to discover the secret hiding place of her vast store of money; but taking fresh courage, he resolves to renew his flatteries, hoping yet to gain her confidence, and her wealth as well. He now dismisses the two fellow brigands, and a moment later Lady Pamela comes in to order a punch for her Lord, when she is at once accosted by the Marquis as a charming creature. Pamela, greatly startled, cautions him to beware, for her husband is in the next apartment, and is as jealous as Othello! The Marquis, most cordially affable, reassures her of his honorable purpose, and suggests that they sing a duet together, at the same time taking up a mandolin that Zerlina has left on the table. Thereupon he sweeps his fingers across the strings, and renders a graceful love ballad, "The Gondolier, Fond Passion's Slave." When he finishes his song the Marquis gazes fondly into Pamela's eyes and tenderly asks, "Must your heart, then, forever remain insensible to the flame that consumes me?" Moved by his speech, the vain woman makes a false show of trying to evade him, but it is that he may increase his ardor, which the disguised brigand does not fail to do, by confessing that his soul is a slave to her unequaled charms, her classic features, graceful form, glorious eyes, and all the accomplishments that bespeak a perfect mind, in a heavenly tenement, and—his eyes suddenly falling upon a medallion of diamonds worn by Pamela—those precious adornments that so becomingly grace her person. Completely charmed by his honeyed speech, Pamela becomes tractable to his persuasions, and with growing confidence she tells him this piece of jewelry was all that escaped the robbers; that she managed to hide it carefully, not more for its great value, but quite as much because the medallion is really a locket made for her husband, and contains her portrait. Her vanity is so excited that she opens and shows it to him, at which the Marquis betrays the most extravagant admiration, and concludes his apostrophe to her unrivaled charms by putting the locket in his pocket, dissembling rage at the thought of his rival, even though he be husband, wearing it. Pamela, frightened, tries to regain the medallion, and protests vigorously, but the Marquis declares he will never suffer it to be taken from him, but will wear it forever, next to his heart. During the struggle, Lord Allcash enters, at which interruption the Marquis quickly seizes the mandolin and resumes his song. Pamela, smiling, speaks tenderly to her husband, whose jealousy is only intensified thereby, and a terzetto expressing conflicting emotions follows, which is a remarkably beautiful melody.

"Ah, madam, my soul is a slave to your unequaled charms!"

Servants enter and take off the tables, and the three being again alone, the Marquis sets about the task of reconciling Lord Allcash and gaining his confidence as he has that of Lady Pamela. The subject of the robbery is introduced, and the Marquis, in a voice that indicates compassion, expresses the hope that his Lordship has not lost the five hundred thousand francs drawn from the bank at Livourne. "Oh, no," answers Lord Allcash, "I saved them by a stratagem which I must not divulge." But after some chaffing the Lord and his Lady reveal that it was by changing the gold into bank notes, and then sewing the bills in his lordship's coat and her ladyship's crinoline. The Marquis laughs sincerely as he feels the dress, and expresses his surprise that such lovely material could hide so much wealth. At this juncture music is heard, and as Lord and Lady Allcash go to the back to look whence proceed the sounds, Beppo and Giacomo mysteriously enter, and in an undertone inform the Marquis that a brigadier with some soldiers is advancing. Fra Diavolo is too courageous to retreat, with danger of betraying his identity, and remains when Lorenzo and his carbineers return, singing a triumphal chorus, "Victoria! Victoria!" When they come into the inn, Zerlina greets Lorenzo joyfully, and hears from his lips report of how he pursued the robbers so resolutely that they were brought to bay, and in the hard-fought battle that followed, his brave soldiers killed no less than twenty of the brigands, upon the body of one of whom was found a casket, which he produces, and triumphantly shows to Lord Allcash. Pamela cries out in the exuberance of her joy at the recovery, "Ah, 'tis mine! How fortunate!" for it is the box that contains her jewels.

The Marquis can ill conceal his wrathful feelings, and pledges to take a terrible revenge, but he watches every movement of the soldiers, careful of his disguise. Lorenzo exultantly tells Lord Allcash that he defeated the brigands by courageously fighting, but that the robber chief contrived to escape, though his capture is certain since the course of his retreat is known. Lorenzo is all eagerness to depart and resume the pursuit, but Pamela detains him, and requesting the loan of Lord Allcash's pocket book, she takes therefrom ten thousand francs and tenders the money to Lorenzo as his reward in fulfilment of the advertisement. Lorenzo at first refuses to be thus compensated for his duty, but Pamela presses him to receive the sum as Zerlina's fortune, which may lead him to another. At these words Zerlina takes the bank notes herself, joyously exclaiming, "I accept them for him. Thank Heaven, Lorenzo is now as rich as his rival!" which so delights her lover that he promises to ask consent of her father to-morrow to bless their union. Lorenzo now departs with his soldiers in pursuit of the robber chieftain, leaving Fra Diavolo and his two comrades to complete their plans for robbing Lord and Lady Allcash of their bank notes and jewelry, which scene closes the first act.

Act II.—When the curtain rises, it is to show a chamber of the inn, on the left a bed and toilet table, on the right a door leading to an inner apartment, and at the back a passage conducting to the street. Zerlina, with a light in her hand, is about to retire, but she answers the call of Lord Allcash, to tell him that his bed will presently be prepared, after which she petulantly complains of her multifarious duties, and of the confusion that sets her head to swimming, but in a pretty aria she congratulates herself that very soon she will be freed from these annoyances, to be the bride of the dearest man in the whole world. While she is thus felicitating herself, Lord and Lady Allcash enter, the former yawning and entreating his wife to retire, for early on the morrow they must resume their journey. Pamela has no desire to rush off to bed, and is so unkind to his lordship as to call to his mind the time when he was willing to sit up to the latest hours, provided she would keep him company. The two fall to quarreling, during which Pamela declares her resolve to stay at the inn to be a witness to Zerlina's wedding, and also insists on acquainting the maid with the eccentricities of husbands. By much coaxing, Lord Allcash at length induces his wife to retire to her room, but as they are going out, he suddenly discovers that the locket which she invariably wore is now missing, and demands to know what has been done with it. Pamela is thrown into confusion by this request, to escape which she quickly changes her demeanor, and tenderly persuading, but without explaining, she leads him to his room, preceded by Zerlina lighting the way.

As Zerlina, Lord and Lady Allcash go out, Fra Diavolo comes in, trying to locate his lordship's room, but is somewhat confused, by the directions given him, as to which is really the first room at the end of the corridor, for he finds so many trunks, chairs and boxes as cause him to believe that this is a lumber-room. He finally concludes that he has properly located the Englishman's bed-chamber, and is about to apprise his comrades, Beppo and Giacomo, when he perceives a mandolin that hangs near the window and, regardless of his situation, he takes it down and accompanies himself in a beautiful serenade.

Beppo and Giacomo appear at the open window, and are cautioned by Fra Diavolo against making any noise, for his lordship's chamber, and all his wealth of bank notes and jewelry, is near by, which may be gained only by the exercise of great stealth. Beppo and Giacomo are so anxious that they would proceed at once, but their chief bids them wait until Zerlina, who has lighted his lordship to his room, returns. A moment later the maid's footsteps are heard, after she has spoken good night to her guests, at the sound of which the three brigands hurriedly conceal themselves in a closet. Scarcely are they hidden when Zerlina enters, carrying a candle, which she sets upon a table, and prepares her bed for the night, speaking to herself all the while of the happiness that is in store for her and which is very soon to be realized. When after much preparation she has made her bed ready, and begins to disrobe, her joyful heart prompts her to sing a charming cavatina: "To-morrow, aye, to-morrow, I shall be a happy wife," etc.

While taking out the pins from her dress, one of them pricks her finger, which causes her to stop and imprecate the cause of her pain. This so increases the curiosity of Beppo that he peeps through the cabinet, and is charmed by the sight of so much loveliness. Fra Diavolo also becomes likewise interested in the disrobing act, and pushes Beppo away that he himself may witness the pleasing spectacle. Zerlina, unconscious of being observed, proceeds with her preparations for bed, taking off in succession apron, corsets, petticoat, admiring her figure in the glass meanwhile, as she sings of the bliss that will be hers when she is Lorenzo's wife. The three robbers in the closet are unable to wholly restrain their mirth at such a beauteous sight, and their half-suppressed laughter falls on Zerlina's ears, but hearing nothing more, she thinks the sound must have come from Lord Allcash's room, and being now in her white night-dress, she kneels by her couch and addresses a prayer to the Holy Virgin. After performing her devotions, Zerlina throws herself upon the bed, and is soon asleep. Finding their opportunity at hand, the brigands come out of the closet, and blowing out the light, cautiously advance towards the chamber of Lord and Lady Allcash, Giacomo carrying his dagger open, to be ready for any emergency. Beppo suggests that their enterprise may have more certain favor if the girl be first dispatched, which Fra Diavolo opposes, but being accused of faint-heartedness, he gives his dagger to Beppo and tells him to do the deed. With the weapon upraised, Beppo goes behind the couch to strike the fatal blow, but at this instant Zerlina, in her sleep, repeats her petition to the Holy Virgin, which, for the moment, disarms his resolution. Recovering his courage, Beppo is again about to stab the girl, when a loud knocking is heard at the door of the inn. This alarms the robbers, and they quickly retreat to the closet, as Zerlina, awakened by the noise, sits up in bed, half afraid to seek the cause of alarm. She is soon reassured by the voice of Lorenzo, who calls from without to give entrance to himself and carbineers. Zerlina, in a flurry of pleasurable excitement, hastily grasps her clothes and flies to the window to see if it be indeed Lorenzo, and finding him impatient at the delay, she throws him the key to the kitchen and begs that he will give her time to dress. A moment later loud knocking is heard on Lord Allcash's door, and he, thinking it is Zerlina, entreats her to be calm until he can investigate. Lorenzo, by his lordship's voice, has learned his mistake in knocking at the wrong door, and he now enters Zerlina's room through a door on the right. Frightened by his sudden intrusion, and abashed by her déshabillé, she pulls the curtains about her, and complains of his boldness in bolting into her room in such a manner. It is his ardent love that has made him so impetuous, but realizing now his rudeness, he addresses her coaxingly. "Forgive me, my dear Zerlina, and affect not so much coyness. You are ever beautiful, whatever your guise."

Lord Allcash, hearing a tumult in Zerlina's room, rushes in, only partially appareled, but seeing Lorenzo he is doubly surprised, and eagerly asks the cause of all the noise. The exultant and happy young officer joyously supplies the information by telling that he has been put upon the track of Fra Diavolo, whose haunt has been revealed by an honest miller, and his capture is certain before another sunset. While Lorenzo is thus pleasantly engaged, telling his exploits to Lord Allcash, and flattering Zerlina, his carbineers, who have remained without, clamor for something to eat, whereupon to satisfy their hunger Zerlina runs out to prepare breakfast, for it is now nearly daylight. In her absence his lordship and Lorenzo fall into conversation about nervous women, who are frightened by the smallest sounds, and while they are thus talking and the Englishman is vaunting his own great courage, the two are startled by the falling of a chair, in the closet, which Beppo, by an awkward movement, has overturned. After much bantering as to who shall make an investigation, Lorenzo starts towards the closet, but Fra Diavolo, seeing that he must be discovered, bids his companions to remain concealed, and boldly steps out of his hiding place. Lorenzo at once demands that he shall explain the cause of his presence in Zerlina's room at such an hour! Taking his lordship aside, the robber chief shows him the locket which he holds as an endearing pledge of Pamela's love, at which Lord Allcash sputters with indignation, and threatens to meet him later, a challenge that Fra Diavolo accepts in a low voice, and with marked coolness. The audacious brigand next turns his attention to Lorenzo, and drawing him apart, tells him that it were better had his shame been kept unknown to the Englishman, but since he is so imprudent as to demand explanation of the intrusion, let the truth be known, that it was to meet Zerlina. Lorenzo, in shame and horror, declares that he has been betrayed by her, whereupon, with mock chivalry, Fra Diavolo resents impeachment of her character, and offers to oppose his rage against her. This serves to increase Lorenzo's anger, who has no doubt now that he is face to face, by accident, with Zerlina's secret lover, and accordingly he demands satisfaction, which Fra Diavolo promises to grant him, with swords, at an appointed rendezvous at seven o'clock. This arrangement not only gives Fra Diavolo opportunity to escape detection of his identity as a burglarious brigand but also the chance of avenging himself upon Lorenzo, for it is his purpose to have his comrades concealed near the place appointed, and to assassinate the young officer when he approaches.

After a musical quintet, by the five on the stage, Lady Pamela enters from her chamber on the left, and simultaneously Zerlina comes running in from the right to announce that breakfast is ready for the carbineers. She immediately notices the gloom on Lorenzo's face, and at the same moment Pamela discovers the melancholy on her husband's features. To requests to know their cause of grief, Lord Allcash and Lorenzo abuse the two women as the most perfidious of wretches, and refuse to make any explanation of their sudden show of anger. Lorenzo bids Zerlina begone, and reminding Fra Diavolo of their engagement to meet at the Black Rocks at seven, he starts to go out. Lord Allcash at the same time starts towards his room, at which movement Zerlina seizes Lorenzo to hold him back, while Pamela hangs desperately upon her husband, each petitioning, by prayerful entreaty, for explanation of their cruel conduct, this scene closing the second act.

Act III.—When the play is resumed, a pretty landscape of mountain scenery is shown, with an inn in the foreground, on the right of which is an arbor containing a table and rustic seats. On the summit of a mountain, in the distance, is a hermitage-chapel, with belfry, from which Fra Diavolo is seen descending by a winding pathway. In a recitative he congratulates himself upon the plans he has perfected for executing a revenge upon Lorenzo, and felicitates himself upon his happy station in a vigorous aria, in which he recounts his acts of prowess as a bandit king who levies tribute upon wealthy travelers. This he follows with a cavatina, "We never demand aught from the fair," and a rondeau: "Since life speeds swiftly away, let us enjoy it while we may," etc. After giving expression to his feelings in songs of self-congratulations, Fra Diavolo soliloquizes of his perfected purpose to ambush Lorenzo at the Black Rocks, where several brigands have been posted, who will take great pleasure in shooting the officer that pursues them. Having this matter arranged to his liking, he takes counsel with himself as to how he may gain possession of Lord Allcash's bank notes. The plan soon suggests itself. When the wedding procession is marching to the chapel, and the soldiers are away, he considers it an easy thing to do to plunder his lordship of the bank

notes and jewelry, after which he will invite Lady Pamela to spend a vacation with him in the mountains. The idea pleases Fra Diavolo immensely, for he has not the slightest doubt of his success, and is tickled very much by thinking of how London society will discuss the lady's adventure with a brigand, and how envious all will be of the very romantic experience.

Delighted, as he affects to be, by the prospects that lie so close before him, Fra Diavolo is still somewhat concerned about Beppo and Giacomo, whom he left behind as trusted spies, and has not since seen. Afraid to return to the inn, he decides to communicate with them by means of a note which he will leave in a decayed tree-trunk, as agreed upon, and thereupon he sits down to write a line on a tablet. Scarcely is the note finished and deposited, when the sounds of approaching footsteps admonish him to take refuge in concealment behind the arbor. Directly enter Matteo, Francesco, and many villagers, wearing green branches on their heads in honor of the wedding ceremonies about to be performed. These sing an Easter chorus of welcome to a group of young peasants who descend the mountain carrying flowers and announcing the coming of the bridegroom. On the side are seen Beppo and Giacomo, who keep hidden from the villagers, and watch from behind the arbor the festivities, deeply impressed by the sacred observance of Easter Day, for though professional brigands, hesitating at no crime, they maintain a show of pious zeal upon all holy days. Matteo takes Francesco's hand, and kneels with him at a shrine to offer up a prayer of thanks for Heaven's blessings, which action is imitated by all the female peasants as they sing in chorus praises of the Holy Virgin. These devotional services finished, Matteo, by signs, invites the wedding train to enter the inn, whereupon all exeunt except Beppo and Giacomo. The two robbers now sit down at the foot of a hollow tree and discuss the probability of their meeting Fra Diavolo, when suddenly Beppo remembers the chief's instructions, that in case of his failure to appear at the rendezvous he would leave his orders in a note which would be found in this same hollow tree. Thereupon, looking for the paper, he finds it and reads, "As soon as Lorenzo shall have departed for the Black Rocks, where my comrades will be in ambush, and the people for the wedding, do not fail to give me warning by ringing the bell of the hermitage. I will then hurry with others of our band to the inn and possess ourselves of the wealth of Lord and Lady Allcash. You must wait for me." These instructions are clear, and the two brigands set to watch, particularly for the carbineers, who are expected to leave in a little while in pursuit of the robbers. While the two are keeping a sharp lookout, Beppo suddenly remembers that this is Sunday, and he is at once horrified by his chief's proposal to murder Lord Allcash on a holy day. Giacomo somewhat less pious, dismisses these scruples of conscience as ill-becoming to a stout heart; besides, the intended victim is an Englishman, and the killing will therefore bring good luck the rest of the year. This argument quite satisfies Beppo, and he calls Heaven to assist their purposes.

While Beppo and Giacomo are keeping watch near the arbor, Lorenzo appears, on his way to the Black Rocks to keep his engagement to fight Fra Diavolo. He is extremely melancholy, with the belief that Zerlina has been false, and expresses his grief in a tearful air, "But, love, farewell!" and then in a recitative he tries to console himself by appealing to his courage to bear the loss: "I have the power to tax her with her guilt, and proclaim her shame before all, but I will not thus dishonor the girl I have so fondly loved. It is better, because more honorable, that I should be silent: let her marry, if she can, some one who may make her happy. My lips shall utter neither complaint nor reproach. The hour of my appointment is at hand; bravely I will go to my death for her, which shall be my only revenge." Before he departs, Matteo, Zerlina, and servants from the inn, enter. At the master's bidding, tables are set, and wine served for the thirsty soldiers, and while this is being done, Zerlina timidly approaches Lorenzo to tell him that her father has promised her hand to Francesco, and that he is now preparing for the wedding which will take place within an hour unless explanation be quickly given of his strange conduct. Lorenzo haughtily answers that her marriage does not now concern him, at which she beseeches him to tell her why his love has so suddenly changed, but he remains imperturbable and she is compelled to go away, in response to her father's call, distracted in mind over Lorenzo's unaccountable coldness.

Beppo and Giacomo enter from the right and take seats at opposite ends of a table, in the arbor, where they may better watch all the proceedings, and loudly call for wine. Zerlina re-enters now, but instead of serving the robbers she turns again to Lorenzo and implores him to give her some explanation. The impatience of Beppo and Giacomo to be served, prompts Zerlina to call Roberto to wait upon them, and she renews her entreaties, but at this moment the carbineers appear, and in chorus admonish Lorenzo that the time for their departure has arrived. Lorenzo startles, for he is thus made to realize that the hour appointed for his duel with Fra Diavolo is at hand. Hastily he instructs a subaltern to post his soldiers at a point near the Black Rocks, and to there wait half an hour, when if he does not join them, to guide the men to their prey. Beppo hesitates to allow Lorenzo to rush upon certain death, and has a mind to warn him of the ambush, but Giacomo interposes. Zerlina, distracted with her grief, makes an effort to restrain her lover, but at this instant Francesco, accompanied by friends invited to the wedding, intercepts her, as villagers, with crowns of flowers, raise their voices in a choral invocation to Hymen. Matteo now advances, and joining the hands of Francesco and Zerlina, pronounces his blessings. Seeing Lorenzo departing, she implores him to relieve her tortured heart, which he is at last induced to regard by telling her that last night he found concealed in her room a secret lover, but he refuses to speak further, and rushes off to join his soldiers, who stand at the back of the stage.

Beppo and Giacomo pound the table and call for more wine, but perceiving Zerlina standing alone, an impersonation of grief, Beppo asks his companion if she is not the identical girl, of charming figure, that they saw last night at her toilet, at the same time imitating Zerlina's postures, and repeating her words before the glass. Zerlina does not fail to notice their strange actions, and instinctively believes that some plot is designed. She therefore rushes after Lorenzo, and seizing his hand, addresses him, with much emotion, "I am ignorant of the cause of your suspicion, and I have tried in vain to discover the mystery, but this I know, and want you to believe me, last night I was alone in my chamber. While alone I spoke words concerning one most dear to me, and believed no mortal ear save mine own could hear them, yet within this minute those words were repeated by those two men [pointing to Beppo and Giacomo] who must have been concealed in my room without my knowledge." At this information Lorenzo is astounded, but believing her words he orders his soldiers to seize the two brigands. This command is promptly obeyed, and a search of the prisoners discloses weapons, and also the note written by Fra Diavolo. Thus convinced of their character, Lorenzo orders that Giacomo be conducted to the hermitage and there be compelled to ring the bell, while Beppo is placed under surveillance in the centre of the stage. All the wedding guests, including Lord and Lady Allcash, Matteo, Francesco and Zerlina, are asked to conceal themselves behind the arbor. In a few minutes the bell begins to ring, Fra Diavolo appears, and seeing no one but Beppo he calls to him. Lorenzo, from his hiding place, points a gun at Beppo, and admonishes him how to answer. Thinking the way clear, Fra Diavolo signals to his three companions to advance, and the four now come forward with confidence, but in the next moment a peasant recognizes the captain as Fra Diavolo, the brigand chief, and Lord Allcash exclaims, "It is the Marquis!" Fra Diavolo greets Beppo, and exults over the prospects of soon acquiring the bank notes, the jewelry, and the wife of his lordship, but on the next instant the stage swarms with carbineers, who quickly disarm Fra Diavolo and bind him fast, and his companions are similarly made prisoners. The opera closes with a quintet of voices singing the last verse of Zerlina's romanza, and the cry, "Victoria! Victoria!"

A SKETCH OF AUBER.

DANIEL FRANÇOIS ESPRIT AUBER was a native of Caen, Normandy, where he was born January 29, 1784. His father was the King's forester, therefore a man of much leisure, if not of great means, who so improved his time that he became an amateur musician of considerable note, and often amused Louis XV, the profligate, and also Louis XVI, the unfortunate. Young Auber had many advantages, for his uncle was the court painter, and the family received many marks of royal favor, which meant generous pensions that enabled the recipients to live in semi-grandeur. His father designed that Daniel should adopt a commercial calling, to which end he sent him to London, where he held a position with a business house for a short while, but the place was so uncongenial that he gave it up, and turned his attention to music, for which he had a strong inclination. After taking pianoforte lessons for a year with Ladurner, young Auber was seized of a passion for chamber music, and he composed several pieces which were so well received that he soon became a favorite in London and Paris drawing-rooms. It was not, however, until after he had passed the age of twenty that he attempted serious compositions for public performance. His first dramatic work was re-writing an old comic opera called "Julia," for which he scored the orchestral part, and followed this with another similar creation, but neither was ever performed outside of private circles. After these initial attempts at composition, Auber studied hard under Cherubini for quite two years, when he came before the public in 1813 with a comic opera called "The Soldier at Home," which was well received, but his next dramatic work, "The Testament," or "Love Letter," was not represented until 1819. Both of these two early compositions were of a simple character, but in 1820 he essayed to write a three-act comic opera, to which he gave the title, "The Castle Shepherdess." This very meritorious work was produced at the Opera Comique (Faydeau) the same year, and in the second year succeeding was performed, at the Comique also, his "The Court Concert," which gave him a large reputation as a composer of light and tuneful music. Then followed in succession, "The Mason," "Masaniello" (1828), "Fra Diavolo" (1830), "The Bronze Horse" (1835), "The Black Domino" (1837), "The Crown of Diamonds" (1841), "Zerline" (1851), and "Emma," or "The Promise" (1853).

Auber reached the apogee of his fame with the production of "Fra Diavolo" and "Masaniello," which was probably more firmly established by his remarkably brilliant "Crown of Diamonds," three operas that will be favorites, especially in France, for a long while to come, if indeed they be not imperishable. Later he wrote "The Devil's Portion," "The Siren," and "Haydée," but these had an ephemeral run, and are almost forgotten now. It is not exceeding the limits of impartial judgment to represent Auber as the greatest of opera comique composers, a position that is almost universally accorded him by critics of all nationalities. It is a noteworthy fact, too, that while his music bears the stamp of inspiration, his compositions were really the result of much labor, for he was so conscientious that no piece left his hand before it had received the fullest benefit of his care. The passion that was manifested early in life remained with him to the very last years of his career, and though his great genius showed symptoms of decay after he reached his seventieth year, his last opera, "Dreams of Love," was written when he was eighty-five, an example of sustained power and creative intellect that has few compeers, and of the famous composers Verdi alone may be cited as his equal in this respect. Altogether, Auber wrote forty-two operas, besides several others in collaboration, all but three of which were brought out at the Paris Opera Comique. That his countrymen appreciated his distinguished talent, is attested by the great honors that were heaped upon him. In 1825 he was made a chevalier of the Legion of Honor, and in 1829 he was admitted as a member of the Institute and Academy of Fine Arts, besides being decorated with insignia of many orders, scientific as well as musical. His death occurred in Paris, May 12, 1871.

DANIEL FRANÇOIS ESPRIT AUBER

The Barber of Seville

(AFTER THE ORIGINAL PAINTING BY WINFIELD S. LUKENS)

COUNT ALMAVIVA.—"O, go to the devil, [knocking the parchment from his hand]—Silence!
Mr. Doctor Lawman, my lodging is fixed here, and here I will remain."

ACT I.—SCENE X.

THE BARBER OF SEVILLE

MUSIC BY ROSSINI——WORDS BY STERBINI

The Barber of Seville, though it is not the greatest of Rossini's operas, has the distinction of costing him the least labor, and probably of bringing the largest reward. The story of its composition and first production, which was at Rome, February 5, 1816, is extremely interesting, and has the further merit of being brief. Rossini, sometimes known as the "Swan of Pesaro," was engaged to write two operas for a Roman carnival, and to carry out his contract, which was near expiration, he secured permission to make use of Beaumarchais' "Barber of Seville," regarding it as suitable material for his purpose. He had also the courtesy to prefer a like request to Paisiello, who had written an opera thirty-five years before, based on the same subject, and bearing an identical title. Consent being obtained from both, Rossini applied to Sterbini, who at the time occupied a room in the composer's house, and had some reputation as a contributor, to write the libretto. As a help to the librettist, Rossini hummed the tunes that came into his head, which enabled Sterbini to catch the spirit of the action, and as fast as he completed the verses Rossini set them to music. The two worked harmoniously and diligently together, so completely absorbed with the matter in hand that they ate and slept little for an interval of thirteen days, at the end of which time the opera was completed. "The Barber of Seville" was mounted and produced at the Argentina Theatre four weeks after Rossini began work on the score. There was a feeling of hostility manifested towards the composer, which was intensified by a series of mishaps so ludicrous that it is almost a wonder the opera survived them. Garcia, who was the tenor, insisted on accompanying himself in the serenade, and when in the most effective passages a string on his guitar broke and the song was interrupted until a new string could be supplied and tuned. This was vexatious, but not so much as a misfortune that soon followed, for Don Basilio tripped on a trap-door and fell on his nose so hard that he had to finish "Calumnia," a bass solo, with a handkerchief over his face to hide the blood. Worse than either of these was the extremely ludicrous misadventure that occurred in the very midst of a splendid finale, when a stray cat ran on to the stage and had to be chased hither and thither before it was finally driven into the wings. The audience naturally went into an hysteria of laughter, which continued to the close of the performance. At the end of the first act Rossini, thinking more of his music than of his situation, had the ill judgment to applaud, which so angered the audience that he was greeted with a storm of hisses, under which he quitted the theatre, and hied himself home to bed in the deepest mortification. Notwithstanding the mishaps and condemnations of the first night, the second performance, which Rossini refused to attend, was cordially received, and the enthusiasm became so great that nearly the entire audience repaired in a body to the composer's home, where they gave him an ovation.

Some necessary changes were made in the music of the opera after it had run a week at the Argentina, one of which was the writing of a new overture. The scene beneath Rosina's balcony, which at first introduced a Spanish air, was afterwards changed so as to substitute the Count's beautiful solo, "Lo! smiling in the orient sky," borrowed from the opening chorus. The subject of the most effective trio, "Steps as soft as zephyrs dying," was taken from Haydn's "Seasons." Rossini wrote a trio for the music-lesson scene, but through some strange misfortune this little gem was lost, wherefore it has ever since been the fashion of Rosinas to interpolate any air their fancy may please.

"The Barber of Seville" is a comic opera in two acts, the scene being laid in the Spanish city of Seville, and the plot is as follows: Count Almaviva is deeply in love with Rosina, who is the ward of Doctor Bartolo. His affairs might proceed satisfactorily but for the opposing fact that the Doctor wishes to marry her himself, and herein lies the complication. Almaviva is known to Rosina as Count Lindor, who starts his wooing with a serenade, but not knowing a ready means for meeting the lady of his heart, he confesses his love to Figaro, a barber and factotum of the city, whose aid he solicits in securing an interview. Rosina's guardian, however, is very watchful, and induces Don Basilio, her music-teacher, to help his schemes and assist his vigilance. Despite their spying, Rosina contrives, through a secret letter, to inform the Count that his passion is reciprocated, and requests to know his name. With Figaro's help the Count manages to enter Rosina's house disguised as an intoxicated officer, but he is apprehended by the guard, and placed under arrest. Gaining his liberty the Count manages to again invade Doctor Bartolo's house, this time hiding his identity under the disguise of a music-teacher, pretending that Don Basilio is ill and that he has been sent to take the instructor's place. To secure Bartolo's confidence the Count produces Rosina's letter, to himself, and declares to the Doctor that it was given him by Almaviva's mistress. He promises to use the letter if Bartolo will permit an interview, to create jealousy in Rosina, which he assures will cause a rupture between Rosina and her secret lover.

By the Count's cunning strategy he obtains an interview with Rosina, which progresses so favorably that an elopement and marriage is planned. Figaro, as a trusty aid to the scheme, obtains the keys to a door that leads to the balcony, to assist in the escapade that is to take place at midnight. During the arrangement of these plans Don Basilio suddenly puts in an appearance and the disconcerted Count, unable to make prompt explanation, is compelled to flee.

Doctor Bartolo now shows to Rosina her letter, accompanying it with the Count's false explanation, by which means he succeeds in arousing her jealousy, under stress of which she discloses the plan of elopement and agrees to marry her guardian. At the time fixed for the flight, the Count and Figaro make their appearance at the house, and contrive to see Rosina while Bartolo is gone in quest of an officer. A reconciliation is, of course, quickly effected, and as a notary is at hand, the marriage promptly takes place, the affair thus ending happily for all except the discomfited Doctor.

Act I.—The opening scene of the opera shows a street of Seville at early dawn. Fiorello, a servant, with lantern in hand, introduces several hired musicians, followed by Count Almaviva, wrapt in a mantle, who has come to serenade Rosina. Fiorello and the musicians render in chorus a short serenade, and then the latter tune their instruments to accompany the Count in a beautiful song indited to the dear mistress of his heart and fortune:

"Lo! smiling in the orient sky,
Morn in her beauty breaking,
Canst thou, my love, inactive lie—
My life, art thou not waking?" etc.

The aria begins with a sweetly expressive largo and concludes with a florid allegro, but its charming sentiment and melody fail to bring Rosina to the balcony, though a fair face shines at the window. Feeling that his efforts to beguile Rosina are vain, he gives a purse to Fiorello, who distributes the money therein among the musicians. Their thankfulness is so effusive that the Count fears they will wake the neighbors by their noise and orders them to disperse. All go out save the Count, who pensively paces up and down before Doctor Bartolo's house, waiting the appearance of Rosina, whose habit it is to come out upon the balcony at early dawn to breathe the fresh air. While the Count is thus exercising his patience, Figaro, with a guitar slung over his shoulder, comes upon the scene, merrily trolling his celebrated buffo aria:

"Room for the city's factotum here,
I must be off to my shop, for the dawn is near;
What a merry life, what pleasure gay,
Awaits a barber of quality." etc.

In the song he describes jauntily his busy life and the skill that has made his services in demand by both men and women, not omitting to praise his graces as a beau. Suddenly he becomes aware of Count Almaviva's presence and changes his vaunting tone to obsequious manners, but the Count is too deeply concerned in Rosina to give attention to flattery, and commanding Figaro to make less noise, confesses that he is in love with the ward of a silly old physician, and under the name of Lindor he seeks an interview with the beauteous lady. Figaro spares no words in assuring the Count that as barber, surgeon, botanist, apothecary, veterinary, major-domo, and all the other professions, he can afford him much assistance. This promise of aid gives the Count great happiness; a moment later the balcony door opens and Rosina steps forth, and looks anxiously up and down the street, wondering why her lover has not come yet, a gallant knight pictured in her dreams, who she fondly hopes will soon deliver her from the

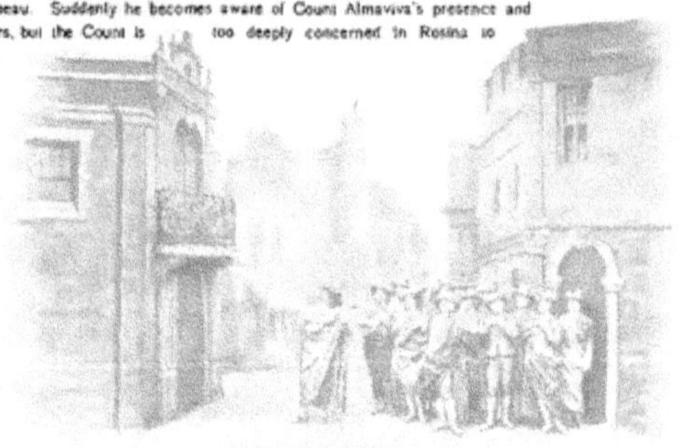

"Lo! smiling in the orient sky,
Morn in her beauty breaking!"

embarrassaments of an overwatchful guardian. As the romantic girl appears upon the balcony, Almaviva is enraptured by her as a sweet vision inviting him to realms of bliss, and in transports of happy anticipation he softly exclaims:

"Oh, my life! My angel! My treasure!
At length do I behold you, at length!"

But his rhapsodizing is cut short by Rosina, who, not yet discovering her lover, in the dim light of early morning, murmurs to herself: "How very provoking; I wished to give him this note." The Count is about to reveal himself and declare his passion, but is restrained by the sudden appearance of Doctor Bartolo, who, always dogging her steps, has sought Rosina on the veranda, and seeing a letter in her hand demands, with jealous curiosity, to know to whom she is writing? Having to make a quick explanation she tells Bartolo that she has been waiting with much impatience the coming of her music-teacher, desiring to deliver to him the words of a newly composed song entitled "Useless Precaution." On the instant, perceiving Almaviva, she lets the letter fall from her hand, and it flutters to the ground. With great show of anxiety she requests the Doctor to go quickly and recover it, which he proceeds to do, but is anticipated by Figaro, who leaves his place of concealment an instant to secure it, then retires again. The old Doctor searches diligently, but unable to find the note, he believes Rosina has tricked him, and angrily orders her into the house, threatening to wall up the balcony. When the Doctor retires, Figaro reads as follows:

"Your assiduous attentions have excited my curiosity. My guardian is shortly going out; as soon as you perceive him quit the house, devise some ingenious method of acquainting me with your name, circumstances, and intentions. I can never appear at the balcony without being haunted by the inseparable attendance of my tyrant. Be assured, that entirely and most eagerly disposed to break her chains is the very unhappy ROSINA."

"Oh, my life! My angel! My treasure!
At length do I behold you!"

The Count's sympathies now act as reinforcements to his love, and declaring Rosina shall be freed, he asks Figaro to tell him what character of man is this wicked guardian. The barber answers the question by picturing the Doctor as a very demon—avaricious, suspicious, and a terrible blusterer. At this instant the door opens and Doctor Bartolo appears, and speaking to some one on the inside, promises to be back in a few minutes, but in the meantime orders that no person be admitted during his absence, not even Don Basilio, should he come. He shuts the door carefully and in an aside mutters, "I wish to hurry on my marriage with her. Yes, this very day I am going to conclude the affair." Doctor Bartolo now exits, and the Count resumes his conversation with Figaro by asking who is Don Basilio? the barber answers that he is an intriguing match-maker; a hypocrite, with never a farthing in his pocket, who has lately turned music-teacher to instruct Rosina. This information satisfies the Count, and he promises to reward Figaro handsomely for all his services; aye, even with gold in quantity to his heart's content. These promises of generous pay for assistance that is of a kind he is specially delighted to render, fill the greedy heart of Figaro with a great joy, and his sympathies are now firmly bound by golden ties to the prodigal Count, to whom he pledges the most assiduous and effective services. Under the inspiration of his good fortune, Figaro renders a gay air:

"Mighty Jove, in golden shower
Once, who fell on Danae's breast,
Give to me the dazzling power
Every maid to make me blest."

At the conclusion of this florid song, Figaro, ambitious to earn the promised reward, suggests to the Count that he may gain Rosina's presence by disguising himself in the uniform of a colonel and pretending drunkenness. The suggestion meets the Count's instant approval, and he declares that no time shall be lost in putting it into execution, but before going about this very particular business he has Figaro accurately describe the location of his barber shop, so that he may be quickly found when needed. This light and lively duet leads up to a sprightly melody sung with much spirit by the two:

Count.—"When song is flowing, when love is glowing
O'er fancy throwing her light divine!
Thoughts bright and beaming, as sunbeams streaming,
O'er maidens dreaming, then, then are mine."

Figaro. "When cups are clinking, when gold is chinking,
Those to my thinking are more divine!
Thoughts bright and beaming, as guineas streaming,
O'er misers dreaming, then, then are mine."

Upon finishing the song, Figaro enters Doctor Bartolo's house and the Count goes off in a gleeful mood of expectation.

The succeeding scene reveals a chamber in Doctor Bartolo's dwelling. Rosina has discovered that her lover's name is Lindor, and she now appears, with a letter, which she has just written, in her hand, and wonders how she may send it. Remembering that she saw Figaro in earnest conversation with the Count, she resolves, but with some timid doubts, to entrust it to him to deliver. She now renders an exquisite aria, which is one of the rarest jewels in the lyric casket, so melodious that it is frequently heard on the concert stage, where it rarely fails of an encore:

"A little voice I heard just now
Oh, it has thrilled my very heart!
I feel that I am wounded sore,
And Lindor 'twas who hurled the dart.
My guardian sure will ne'er consent
But I must sharpen all my wit,
Content at last he will relent
And we, oh, joy! be wedded yet!"

This is followed by a solo, "With mild and docile air," in which Rosina, while representing herself as a dove for meekness, has still a mind of her own when crossed, and her brain is a hive of subtle tricks which are loosed like bees to accomplish her ends, and which sting with a fierceness that leaves no doubt as to the source of the pain.

While Rosina is bewailing her fate and threatening to end suspense, Figaro enters, whom she welcomes cordially. She confesses that she is dying of ennui, for her chamber is so closely guarded that it is become a very sepulchre. Figaro draws her aside to speak of his mission, which she is all eagerness to hear and no less desirous to ask him about Count Lindor, but their interview is broken up by voices which Rosina recognizes are those of her guardian and Don Basilio. To avoid detection, Rosina and Figaro hastily run out of the room, promising to resume their conversation on a more opportune occasion.

Doctor Bartolo now enters, with Don Basilio, explaining his design to wed Rosina on the morrow, with or against her wishes, for as her guardian he claims the right to select her husband. Basilio is in agreement with this conclusion, and tells the Doctor that he has come to advise with him on this same matter. The conference partakes of supreme confidence, therefore Don Basilio reveals that Count Almaviva, who is the unknown lover of Rosina, has arrived, and that something must be done

"We must deftly begin by inventing some story
That may disgrace him in the eyes of the public."

forthwith to break the attachment. Concerning means how this may be done, Basilio suggests that some plausible story be invented that will disgrace the Count in the eyes of the public. Bartolo thinks well of the proposal, but professing ignorance of the word calumny, fearing legal consequences, he asks a definition.

This request gives Basilio opportunity to make his explanation in a wonderful basso aria, which is one of the lyric features of the opera, in which he likens calumny in its beginning to a zephyr, which gains force with every added breath until it develops into a storm of scandal and sweeps the victim into certain ruin.

> "Thus calumny, a simple breath,
> Engenders ruin, wreck and death;
> And sinks the wretched one forlorn,
> A victim of the public scorn."

When Bartolo and Basilio retire to draw up the marriage agreement, Figaro ventures forth cautiously, followed by Rosina. He has overheard all that has taken place between the conspirators, and quickly conceives his plans. Rosina is innocent of the designs of her guardian to make her a wife, and Figaro now acquaints her fully with Bartolo's resolution, and when she expresses doubts, he declares that the Doctor and the music-master are at this moment closeted to prepare the marriage contract. Rosina tosses her pretty head defiantly of her guardian's designs, and asks Figaro to tell of the gentleman with whom he was speaking an hour ago below her window? He answers indirectly, that her curiosity may thereby be increased, but presently tells her he is a cousin, a likely young man come to Seville to finish his studies, and with fair prospects, save that he has one very great fault, which lies in his heart, for he is dying of love. Figaro does not misjudge the effect of his circumlocution, for Rosina becomes all eagerness to know particulars about the love-lorn swain, and the lady of whom he is enamored, where she lives, and if she be beautiful? To these eager inquiries of the love-excited girl Figaro mischievously replies with assurance that the one upon whom the Count has centered his affections lives not more than two paces distant from where they are standing; that she is of extremely graceful figure, possesses a handsome face, has rosy cheeks, a roguish eye, most winsome manners, and the name of this fascinating maiden can be no other than—Rosina! This information fills the very romantic girl's heart with a joy she is no longer able to suppress, and the two thereupon express their feelings in a florid duet.

> "What am I, or dost thou mock me?
> Am I, then, the happy being?"

Very much concerned with this young man, whose name she learns is Lindor, Rosina exhorts Figaro to tell her how she may contrive to speak with him, and betrays the utmost anxiety to have Lindor come quickly and declare his passion. Figaro counsels patience, by which all things may be accomplished, and suggests that she give some sign of her affection and assent to her lover's wishes, by sending a note. She affects too much modesty to write the first letter, and Figaro, realizing the need of haste, rushes to a desk and offers to indite an invitation himself. Rosina calls him back, however, and drawing a letter from her bosom, quietly informs him the note which he suggests has already been written. Figaro is amazed by her action, and confesses that with finer wit than he possesses she is master where he would be teacher. Figaro takes the letter and passes out, as Doctor Bartolo pompously enters, and demands to know what prompted this visit of Figaro? Having no good excuse to give on the instant, Rosina stammers and contradicts herself, until Bartolo, growing more suspicious, bluntly asks if he did not come with an answer to her note of this morning? Assuming blank amazement she querulously questions, "What note?" "Come, come, now," he replies, "that air from the drama, 'Useless Precaution,' which you dropped from the balcony! You blush—I have guessed it! How came your finger to be so marked with ink?" She tremblingly answers that she cut her finger and used the ink as a cure; when she is pressed to explain that one sheet of paper is missing from the five that lay on her table this morning, she declares it was used to wrap up some candy sent to Figaro's little daughter, and that the new pen was cut to trace the design of a flower on her tambour. These excuses, so lamely made, only increase the Doctor's belief that the "Useless Precaution" was really a note dropped to her waiting lover, and therefore, commanding her to be silent, he vows his determination to have her closely watched night and day, and her room carefully guarded, until she is firmly made his wife by the law. The interview concludes with a bass air rendered by Bartolo, which, however, is often omitted from the performance.

When Bartolo and Rosina quit the room, Bertha, a maid-servant, enters, pitying the poor girl who she fears will be driven to some rash act if she is longer kept confined in this sepulchral place. In a moment a knocking on the door is heard, and a voice demanding immediate admission. Bertha promptly admits Count Almaviva, who reels into the room disguised as a soldier, and loudly calls for the master of the house. Bertha runs out in alarm and Doctor Bartolo rushes in, surprised to find a bewhiskered drunken fellow in possession, and demands to know his business? The Count staggers up to the Doctor, saluting him affectionately by many such names as Balordo, Bertholdo, Barbaro, advances which Bartolo indignantly repels. The persevering lover embraces him nevertheless by force, declaring that he is surgeon of the regiment and hence they are comrades. The two scuffle about until the noise attracts Rosina, and when she comes in the Count manages to whisper his name, and tries, but in vain, to pass her a note. Opportunity must yet be sought, so the Count tells Bartolo he has a mind to take permanent lodgings in his house, a privilege which is allowed an officer. Bartolo, greatly vexed, denies him such permission, and produces a parchment duly stamped, which exempts his house from use or search by the military. The Count treats the paper with contempt by knocking it out of Bartolo's hand, and repeats his intention to remain. Several times the Count tries to convey his note to Rosina, but is as often frustrated, until in despair he offers to fight the Doctor. During the scuffle the Count drops his note and simultaneously Rosina's handkerchief falls upon it, by which ruse she gains possession of the letter, but Bartolo has noticed the paper, and when Almaviva, with a bow to Rosina, picks up and hands her the handkerchief and the note, Bartolo insists upon seeing the latter. Rosina deftly changes the paper, and to her guardian's request she passes to him the substitute, which is a harmless wash-list. Bartolo is now as much astonished as indignant, and is made more ridiculous in his own eyes by the compassion Count Almaviva expresses for the treatment which Rosina is compelled to so often undergo at the hands of a suspicious and brutal guardian.

[illegible]

The storm of invective and remonstrance is renewed, and Figaro comes in, with a basin under his arm, to interpose as a peace-maker. The Count assumes greater anger, and drawing his sword makes a pass at the terrified Bartolo, vowing to run him through, but Figaro interferes to prevent the threatened murder. The quarrel noisily continues, by the calling of names and threatening, until a tremendous knocking announces the arrival of an officer with guards. All parties speak at once, accusing and counter-accusing, but as Count Almaviva is the only armed disturber, he is placed under arrest, to the great delight of Bartolo and the consternation of Rosina. To protect himself from an indignity, the Count privately shows his decoration, as a Spanish grandee, to the officer and whispers his real name. All are astonished by this revelation of Almaviva's identity, and after one of those stirring and spirited choruses of concerted confusion and pre-arranged surprise, for which Rossini is famous, the curtain is let down upon the first act.

Act II.—The second act begins with a representation of a room in Bartolo's house, in which the Doctor is seated alone, ruminating upon the adventures of the evening and wondering who the drunken soldier can be, for diligent inquiry of the members of his regiment has failed to find one who knows him. Naturally, the Doctor is in a state of extreme discomfort, for certain rueful presentiments are hovering about him, pertinaciously forcing themselves into gloomy vistas that terminate in woeful tableaux, one representing the marriage of his ward to the unknown Count Almaviva, and the other displaying himself most reluctantly, producing unsatisfactory accounts of his guardianship. Unable to understand the soldier's actions by any theory, he suspects that it is a ruse adopted by an emissary of the Count to sound the affections of Rosina. While Bartolo is thus soliloquizing, the Count enters, disguised as a music-teacher, and effusively salutes the Doctor, "May Heaven send you peace and joy!" but as if this were not enough, still more generously patronizing he wishes Bartolo "joy and peace for thousands of years"—of course contemplating prayers for the repose of his soul—with such sincerity as might be expected from a rival. Bartolo receives his visitor civilly enough, but is somewhat disturbed by the belief that he has somewhere seen that face before, which almost seems familiar, though he cannot bring his poor wits to recall the time or place.

[illegible]

The Count, not immediately knowing how best to act to make his plans more certain and keep his identity completely concealed, gains time by continuing his peace salutations until Bartolo's patience is quite exhausted by what he takes to be the greatest of simpletons. Despite these protests, the Count persists in going through a whole litany of supplications, until in self-defence against the most annoying of impositions, Bartolo threatens him with chastisement if he do not leave his wishing and come at once to the point. Thus adjured, the unknown visitor represents himself as one Don Alonzo, a professor of music, and a pupil of Basilio, who, having been taken suddenly ill, regrets extremely that he cannot appear to give Rosina her accustomed music lesson. Good and true man as Basilio is, so thoughtful of his promising pupil, he sends his respects. Bartolo proposes to go instantly to see Basilio, accompanied by his informant, but this does not accord with the Count's wishes, as we may well believe, and so, taking Bartolo aside, the Count whispers inaudibly in his ear. Unable to understand his words, Bartolo begs him to speak out loud, which order the Count very literally obeys, crying out, "Then you shall know who Don Alonzo is. I come from the Count Almaviva," and brusquely turns upon his heels to depart. Bartolo at once becomes interested to know more, and so restraining the Count begs him to tell what is on his mind. The opportunity is now at hand, which the Count improves fully by relating to the credulous old dunce that, "this morning, by chance, Almaviva came to the same inn, and by accident I took up this note, which I found directed to him by your ward!" Basilio eagerly snatches the note and a glance shows him it is indeed addressed in Rosina's handwriting. The disguised Count continuing, reminds Bartolo that Basilio being now engaged with the lawyer, knows nothing of this letter, and that he, the Count, having been substituted for Basilio to give Rosina a music lesson, may make a merit of the letter if he be permitted to see the young lady and convince her that Count Almaviva has betrayed her confidence. The contrivance succeeds admirably, for Doctor Bartolo is so pleased with the proposal that he puts the letter in his pocket and goes at once for his ward, leaving the Count to congratulate himself on his stratagem. Bartolo quickly returns with Rosina, whose sharp eyes and keen anticipations penetrate the Count's disguise, and in her ecstatic astonishment she exclaims "Ah!" but excuses herself by ascribing her utterance to a sudden cramp in the foot. The Count requests her to take a seat beside him at the spinnet, where in the place of Don Basilio, who is quite ill, he proposes to give her a lesson. This she is much pleased to receive, and when asked to sing she cheerfully acquiesces, and receives praise from the Count for her charming voice. The flattery of the disguised teacher touches Bartolo, who jealously declares the song just sung by Rosina to be far inferior to the airs heard in his day, and thereupon, to illustrate the degeneracy of music, he proceeds to give a ludicrous example:

"With that bewitching mien, ah!
Oh, come to me, Rosina!
And on my arm, oh, lean, ah!
There let me chant my lay.
Or, if you more incline, ah!
To dancing, so divine, ah!
Then thus in grace we'll twine, ah!
In the minuet's sway."

When Bartolo concludes his very bad song, Figaro enters in time to hear the last bars, which he mimics, but immediately excuses himself and announces that he is come to shave the Doctor. But Bartolo is in no humor to be shaved to-day, and bids the barber come on the morrow. Figaro, however, desirous of diverting attention from the young couple, insists that the Doctor shall be shaved this day and at once, on pain of losing his services hereafter. Under duress the Doctor yields himself to the petulance of his servant and orders him to go into the room and bring the cloth and shaving materials. On second thought Bartolo resolves to go himself, but fearing to lose sight of his ward for even an instant, he finally trusts the keys to his closet to Figaro. The sly barber discovers that in the bunch is the key to the lattice-window leading from Rosina's room to the balcony, and he manages to extract it from the lot. While Figaro is gone for the soap and towels, and gaining possession of the particular key desired, Bartolo observes to the disguised Count that this barber is a very rogue, adept in intrigue, who was in fact the same rascal who brought the Count's letter to Rosina, but promises that rogue, rascal and intriguer though he be, he cannot trick an old doctor schooled in the ways of dissemblers. His self-praise is interrupted by a great noise of breaking crockery, for Figaro has had the misfortune, in searching for the soap, to overturn the china-closet. Bartolo, in a rage, runs out to see the damage, which gives the Count and Rosina a chance to better devise their plans. Figaro returns quickly and shows the Count that he has possessed himself of the key, and is followed in a moment by Bartolo, in an outrageous passion at the havoc which the blundering awkwardness of Figaro has wrought, but is at length induced to be seated in a chair, with his back to the lovers, and Figaro begins to lather and shave him.

Affairs appear to be proceeding in a manner particularly happy to the Count and Rosina, who are plotting an elopement, when to their consternation the supposed sick music-teacher, Basilio, enters; the audacity of Figaro, however, supports the imposture, for as the Count slips a purse into Basilio's hand the intriguing barber loudly upbraids him for venturing out in his feverish condition and implores him to go home quickly. Basilio tries to deny that he is ill, but the Count, Rosina and Figaro urge him to bed in such a clamorous manner that even Doctor Bartolo adds his own entreaty, being convinced, by the assumed sincerity of the others, that the poor teacher is really very ill. Thus persuaded by prayer and gold, Basilio allows himself to be driven out of the room, his departure being hastened by a duet, "Fare you well, then, good signore."

The excitement caused by Basilio's untimely visit having subsided, Bartolo seats himself again and bids Figaro proceed, while the Count and Rosina resume their plotting under the guise of a music-lesson. The scene now becomes richly comic by reason of the many devices of Figaro to prevent Bartolo from discovering the endearing attentions of the Count towards Rosina. The old Doctor becomes very suspicious, despite all explanations, thinking that a music-lesson should be marked by more music and less talk, and presently overhears enough to put him into a paroxysm of rage.

The Count has not had time to fully explain the use he made of her letter, or to direct her explicitly as to the elopement, but he has arranged a midnight assignation with Rosina before being turned out of the room. When all have gone out Bertha comes in, declaring that this house knows no peace, nor is it likely to be other than one distinguished for quarrels as long as the Doctor insists on marrying his ward. The song sung by Bertha is called by Italians the "Aria de Sorbetto," as the audiences usually managed to sit it out by eating ices, for the music and words are alike long and dreary.

In the succeeding scene Doctor Bartolo and Basilio appear, the latter to explain some very unpleasant things that seriously compromise the Count, Figaro, and, no less, Rosina. He assures Bartolo that he is not sick, and that he did not send the strange music-master, who was, in fact, no other than Count Almaviva himself, practicing a bold ruse in order to have an interview with Rosina. Bartolo needs no more, for his resolution is immediately taken to free himself from all further fears by marrying Rosina this very evening. He therefore dispatches Basilio with an order to bring the notary, before whom the marriage contract must be signed. Basilio makes some objection, that it is raining; and besides, this evening the notary is to attend Figaro, who is to give his niece in marriage. "Niece! Niece!" Bartolo cries, "why, the rogue has no niece. It is a plot which this very night the scoundrels will play me." He thereupon gives the key to his door to Basilio and bids him make haste and bring the notary. As Basilio passes out, Bartolo vows, to himself, that either by force or love Rosina shall yield. On the instant, thinking of the note given him by the Count, he takes it from his pocket and conceives a purpose to use it to excite Rosina's jealousy. The plan seems an excellent one, and to put it into effect he forthwith calls Rosina, and when she comes in he sympathetically addresses her: "I have some news from your lover to give you. Poor, unhappy girl! In truth you have placed your affections on a noble object! Know that in the arms of another he makes a joke of your confidence. Behold the proof!" Rosina is profoundly amazed, and is easily made to believe what Bartolo tells her, that Don Alonzo and the barber have conspired to deceive and trick her into a marriage with Count Almaviva, for Rosina does not yet know that Lindor, her lover, and Almaviva are one and the same person. This information, that exposes to her what she believes to be the treachery of Lindor, makes her so indignant that, "to teach him a lesson," she reveals the Count's proposal of elopement, which she explains is arranged to take place at midnight. Bartolo proposes to at once bar the door, but Rosina declares it would be of no avail, because the rogues have the key to her balcony-door, by which they have planned to enter. Bartolo is afraid that the two may come armed, so, to avoid personal danger, he advises Rosina to lock herself in her room, while he goes for assistance, and if the two carry out their design and enter her room, he will have them arrested as thieves. Having thus instructed his ward, Bartolo goes to bring the peace officers. Scarcely is he out of sight, and while a storm is blowing viciously, the veranda lattice is seen to open and one after another, Figaro and the Count enter, wrapped closely in mantles. When they get into the room the Count congratulates Figaro on the promising issue of their adventure on a tempestuous night, and then lights a candle. In a moment the Count discovers Rosina and rushes forward to embrace her, but she repulses him as a vile wretch, and tells him she will repair the fault of her too foolish credulity by marrying her guardian. The Count is aghast at this declaration, and beseeches her to explain this sudden change, to which she makes indignant answer, "You have pretended love in order to sacrifice me to the wishes of the vile Count Almaviva." The Count quickly undeceives her by explaining the arts he has used to gain her presence, and that he assumed the name Lindor, as he did that of Don Alonzo, to the better hoodwink her too watchful guardian. He thereupon declares that this is the sweetest moment of his life, and throwing aside his mantle, kneels at her feet, which is followed by a florid terzetto, in which Figaro takes to himself great credit as an accomplished intriguer, and Rosina and the Count give expression to their felicity, vowing never to part. Figaro being less absorbed, is conscious of the danger that threatens delay and admonishes the couple to fly quickly, but their joy is so intense that the Count and Rosina have no mind for anything but love, and so linger, rapt in contemplation of each other. Presently Figaro runs to the balcony and gives the alarm that two persons, with a lantern, are at the door, and that the ladder by which ascent to the balcony was gained has been removed, thereby preventing escape. What is to be done? This very dramatic situation is rendered extremely comic by a tuneful and delightful terzetto: "Step as soft as zephyr dying, through the window gently hying," etc.

Rosina is dying of fright, but the Count bids her be courageous and retire for a moment to wait the issue of this unfortunate interruption. All three withdraw to a side room, and the next moment Basilio enters, with a lantern, followed closely by a notary with a paper in his hand. Figaro, from his place of concealment, acquaints the Count with the fact of having engaged the notary himself, and then issues from his retreat to greet that functionary warmly as a person he has been expecting, saying: "This evening you were to settle in my house the marriage contract between the Count Almaviva and my niece. Here are the papers, will you kindly endorse them?" The notary thereupon takes out a paper, but Basilio interposes to ask first for Don Bartolo! The Count has need now to play his trick promptly and consummately, which he does by calling Basilio aside and threatening him with a pistol if he does not keep silent and obey orders. He therefore orders Basilio to take a ring, which he hands him, and to subscribe as a witness the marriage contract, with Figaro. Thus in the absence of Bartolo the marriage agreement between Almaviva and Rosina is signed and attested, and in the presence of all Rosina is pronounced the Countess Almaviva.

While the Count is kissing the hand of Rosina, Doctor Bartolo enters with the alcalde and police, and seeing the two rogues he points them out as thieves and demands their immediate arrest. The alcalde approaches the Count and requests to know his name, to which Almaviva gives no better answer than assurance that he is a man of honor and husband of this lady! Bartolo is astounded by so much insolence and appeals to Rosina, but she only increases his amazement and anger by confirming the Count's declaration. Again Bartolo demands that the rogues be arrested, which order the officer is about to execute, when the Count imperiously waves him back, and then reveals himself as the Count Almaviva, at the same time showing his decoration as a grandee of Spain. This last act completes the series of astonishments that have met poor Doctor Bartolo in his short career as a lover of his ward. He is dumfounded to find that Figaro, who had so long served him as barber, is so willing to sell his master to a stranger, but amazement is greater to discover that Basilio has proven no less perfidious, and in the last moment of confidence has united with Figaro to betray him. Being accused of baseness Basilio excuses his deed, not by exposing that he had been under the duress of a pistol, but by blandly confessing that the Count carries certain persuasives in his pocket which cannot be resisted. Bartolo is not long in making the most of a bad situation. Being tricked out of a wife, he must save himself from a too strict accounting as guardian, which he thinks to do by blessing the union of the Count and Rosina. The opera concludes with a joyous quartet and chorus, "May love our hearts beguiling," etc.

L'Africaine

(AFTER THE ORIGINAL PAINTING BY WILLIAM DE LEFTWICH DODGE)

SELIKA (discovering Vasco, and his peril) — "*Hold!*"

VASCO (surprised to see her) — "*Selika!*"

ACT IV. — SCENE III

L'AFRICAINE.

(THE AFRICAN.)

MUSIC BY MEYERBEER.——WORDS BY SCRIBE.

L'AFRICAINE has the distinction of being Meyerbeer's most pretentious effort in music composition, which if it be not his greatest work, certainly occupied him very much longer than any other of his operas. The libretto was given to him in 1838, and the work of setting it to music was promptly begun, but after the score was completed, Meyerbeer demanded that so many alterations in the plot and words be made that Scribe, offended, withdrew the libretto. Finally, in 1852, the author was persuaded to make the requested revision, whereupon Meyerbeer introduced many changes in his original score, but did not complete the work until 1860, though he gave to it patient attention, with the hope of making it the greatest of his operatic creations. Indeed, so earnestly did he cherish this ambition that up to the day of his death he did not cease to correct and retouch the music with a view to more perfect expression.

When "L'Africaine" was completed and submitted for production, great difficulty was found in securing a satisfactory cast, because six of the characters require the ablest talent for effective interpretation, and Meyerbeer was so severely critical that few prima donnas, especially, cared to engage to sing the opera. A rehearsal was had in the fall of 1862, but the result was to throw the composer into a paroxysm of anger, and the attempt to produce the opera was abandoned for the time being. Meyerbeer died in the following April, and nothing further was done towards bringing it before the public until the opera was taken up by the Paris Académie, where it had its initial representation, April 28, 1865, but the greatest singer in the cast was Mme. Marie Saxe, whose name is already forgotten. The first success was hardly flattering, if success it may be called, but a year later it was performed in London, on which occasion the famous Mlle. Lucca appeared as Selika, and the opera was received with unbounded enthusiasm, such as would have gladdened the heart of the composer had he been spared to see it. The public will probably give the preference to "The Huguenots," of all of Meyerbeer's works, but "L'Africaine" must be credited with showing the most perfect consistency, while gems of melody are scattered so profusely through the opera that its brilliancy is often dazzling. Opinions of able critics are divided as to which is really the greater.

The action of "L'Africaine" takes place in Portugal, thence to the coast of India, and the time is near the close of the fifteenth century. The story, in brief, is substantially as follows: Vasco di Gama, a famous Portuguese navigator, was the first voyager to double Cape Good Hope and discover a sea route to India, which trip he accomplished in the early part of 1498, thereby opening up a lucrative trade for his country with the Zamorin, or ruler, of Calicut. As the story of the opera goes, Vasco was the betrothed lover of Inez, the daughter of Don Diego, a Portuguese grandee, at the time that he undertook his India voyage, upon which he was gone so long that his return is despaired of. In the meantime Don Pedro, president of the Council, falls in love with Inez, and presses his suit for her hand so earnestly that he secures the king's sanction to the marriage. Her father also desiring that she shall wed Don Pedro, persuades her to believe that Vasco has perished at sea, and her consent being thus obtained the wedding is about to take place, when Vasco returns, bringing with him two slaves, Selika, a beautiful, though swarthy princess, and Nelusko, her passionate adorer. Summoned before the Council, Vasco recounts the wonders of the country he has visited, and petitions the government to send an expedition to make further discoveries in the strange land. Don Pedro discredits the story, which so angers Vasco that he denounces the Council, for which offence he is thrown into prison with his two slaves. While the three are languishing in a dungeon, Selika conceives a great passion for Vasco, which Nelusko observing, his jealousy is so aroused that he determines to murder the navigator, but Selika prevents a consummation of this treacherous design.

Inez has secretly preserved her affection for Vasco even during the time that she was about to wed Don Pedro, and the return of the explorer served to intensify her love. She now resolves upon an expedient to secure his liberation, which she accomplishes by offering her hand to Don Pedro as the price of the liberty of Vasco and his two slaves.

The story related by Vasco has so impressed Don Pedro that, having obtained possession of the navigator's papers, he determines to go himself in quest of the India isles as they are supposed to be, with the view to winning great honors for himself. Accordingly, he sets out on the voyage, taking with him Inez, who is now his wife, and the two slaves that he has purchased of their master, and makes Nelusko pilot of the ship. Vasco hoping that some adventure may restore Inez to him, and also with the purpose to extend and confirm his previous discoveries, fits out a ship at his own expense, and proceeds upon the journey soon after Don Pedro's departure. The two expeditions meet somewhere near the coast of Arabia and Vasco goes on board of Don Pedro's vessel to warn him of the treachery of Nelusko, who is directing the ship towards a dangerous reef. Don Pedro, rankling with hate, not only resents this friendly counsel, but orders that Vasco be tied to the mast and shot. Before this sentence can be executed, however, the vessel strikes upon the rocks, and as it is going to pieces, savages from the African shore swarm on board and kill Don Pedro and most of his men.

It happens that Selika is princess of the land where the shipwreck takes place, and her influence with her people saves Vasco and Inez; hoping now to gain him for a husband, Selika prepares for her nuptials with Vasco, but when the rites are about to be performed, he hears the tender voice of Inez, which revives his old passion, and causes him to desert Selika for his first attachment. Harboring no jealousy, the love of the dusky princess is so devoted that she magnanimously permits Vasco and Inez to depart for Portugal in their ship; thus sacrificing her heart's aspiration for Vasco's happiness, she seeks death by inhaling the deadly odors of the manchineel tree, which Nelusko also breathes with like fatal results.

Act I.—The opening scene of "L'Africaine" represents a Council Chamber in the palace of the King of Portugal. Inez and her maid, Anna, enter, the former having been summoned hither by her father, who has a purpose to persuade her to abandon hope of Vasco's return and consent to become the bride of Don Pedro, her ardent suitor. Anna reminds Inez that her lover has been absent quite two years, and ventures to predict that some calamity scarcely short of death has befallen him, but to this Inez replies in a sweet ballad expressing her hope, devotion, and constancy through all vicissitudes of time:

"Vasco, true heart, will triumph yet,
My hopeful soul doth so declare;
'Tis years, alack, since last we met,
But love the test will patient bear," etc.

At the conclusion of the song, Don Diego comes in, and first greeting his daughter affectionately, informs her that she has been summoned to appear before the Council of Ministers touching the matter of her espousal to his grace, Don Pedro, the royal consent to such marriage having already been obtained. Creatly surprised, she protests that this cannot he, since her heart belongs to another. This rebellion against his wishes provokes Don Diego to anger, and he tells her that if she would escape his wrath, she will sacrifice her love for an ignoble youth, and celebrate her nuptials with one more suited to her station, the noble Don Pedro, who seeks her hand, and who better deserves the affection which she illy bestows. Inez, with some show of independence, makes bold to answer her father with a prediction that some day this despised youth will achieve greatness as a reward for his dauntless valor. At this moment Don Pedro enters, and to him Don Diego now turns to ask if the report be true, which is noised abroad, that Bernard Diaz has perished? Don Pedro assures him the news has been confirmed, and that particulars just obtained prove that he met [illegible] death at sea during a fearful storm. Inez, deeply agitated, anxiously appeals to know if the young officer, Vasco di Gama, who was known to be one of the ship company, also perished? Scornfully, Don Pedro examines a list of the casualties and thereon finds the name of Vasco, which he exhibits with much satisfaction to Inez. At sight of the document, the suffering girl's dread anticipations are confirmed, whereupon, uttering exclamations of intense grief, she leaves the room with Anna.

Don Pedro cannot understand why Inez betrays so much concern over the loss of the young officer, until Don Diego informs him that Vasco was her lover, but happily the rival is now no more. An usher now comes in to announce the arrival of the Council members, whose sitting is about to begin. Following quickly upon the announcement, the Grand Inquisitor, bishops, Don Alvar and other members file into the chamber, rendering in chorus a petition to God for wisdom to conduct their deliberations in justice, and for the benefit of the country. As the members take their seats, Don Pedro rises, and with dignity reminds the Council that ever since Columbus discovered a new world, their king, Emmanuel, has sought a means, through the enterprise of discovery, to signalize his reign, and so designing he has summoned the Council to obtain their opinion respecting the purpose he has in mind to send an expedition to ascertain the fate of Diaz, and to lend him succor if he be not dead. The Grand Inquisitor expresses his belief that the explorer has been dashed in pieces on the rock-bound coast of the Cape of Storms, but he calls upon Don Alvar to give his opinion. That gracious dignitary shares the general belief that all the members of the expedition perished, but begs to announce that a mariner stands without who craves the honor of addressing the Council. Permission being granted, a sailor enters and is immediately recognized by Don Diego and Don Pedro as Vasco di Gama, the bold navigator, who was believed to have been lost. Bowing respectfully to the august members, Vasco relates the story of his adventures in a newly discovered land, and asks assistance of the king to fit out an expedition that he may return and establish a commerce with the country of his discovery, and thereby extend the glory and empire of Portugal. Vasco speaks enthusiastically of what he has already done, and the greater things he hopes to accomplish for his king, but the Grand Inquisitor discourages his projects as those of a rash adventurer, and discredits the reports of a new country found. Don Alvar and the younger counselors are much impressed by Vasco's narrative, believing that such dauntless courage, joined with genius, may bring great honor to Portugal, and they recommend that the needful aid be extended; but the Grand Inquisitor cannot be made to believe the story told by Vasco until the heroic mariner brings forth his proofs in the form of two slaves, of a race till now unknown, which he informs the Council he purchased in a slave market on the coast of Africa, whither he had journeyed.

[illegible]

The Council betray the largest concern and interest when, at a sign from Don Pedro, an usher leads in Selika, a dusky princess, and Nelusko, a comely African. Urged to speak, in answer to many questions, Selika is finally induced to tell that she and her companion were overtaken one day by a fearful storm, while on the open sea, which drove them far from their native isle, and that their frail bark was seized by enemies in a larger boat who made them prisoners. Nelusko whispers a caution to Selika, begging that she will not forget her inviolable oath, and that though now wearing a tyrant's fetters, she is no less a queen, adored by her people, and the great Brahma himself. Don Pedro tries to compel her to speak of her country, whereupon Nelusko interposes to remind that masters who yoke the ox to their servile service, care only if it be strong for the work, indifferent where it was bred, then why should it be asked whence comes the man or woman who is made a beast of burden?

Vasco, observing how the pride of his slaves is being wounded, ventures to speak in their behalf, and to explain that manifestly, from their garb and hue, they are not Afric born, but are native of some clime where all of ship has never wailed and he promises if the needful help be given him, to discover that foreign land, however remote it may lie. The Grand Inquisitor and bishops again pray for wisdom to decide aright, but Don Pedro, after consulting aside with the Council, presents the verdict refusing Vasco's request, and takes occasion to add that the project for discovery is a senseless one. This insulting remark fires Vasco with such a rage that he gives expression to his indignation by telling the Counselors that the world has not forgotten how the great Columbus was spurned by such men as compose this junta. They command him to be silent, but he so far disregards their threats and orders as to persist in denouncing them as blind, partial judges, whose shame will one day be proclaimed. For his defiance, Don Diego, Don Pedro, the Inquisitor, and chorus declare that Vasco's life shall pay the forfeit, but Don Alvar espouses his cause, and in Vasco's name he appeals to posterity for an honest judgment of his designs, doubting not that the future will avenge him upon his inconsiderate critics. But this defence only serves to intensify the jealous hatred of the Grand Inquisitor, who launches an eternal malediction upon Vasco's head, and orders that he be carried hence, with his slaves, to prison, to await his orders, which scene ends the first act.

[illegible]

Act II.—The opening scene of Act II shows the prison of the Inquisition at Lisbon. A massive column rises from the centre, upon which a map is suspended, and at the back of the stage is a bench on which Vasco is seen asleep, with faithful Selika, who has learned to love him, keeping watch and singing a quaint but melodious slumber song:

"Child of the sun, from toil doth rest,
Peaceful visions now fill his breast.
Softly the night steals o'er the scene,
Leaving the world to sweetly dream.
Rest thee, warrior, safely sleep,
While my vigils I'll faithful keep."

She forgets her own sufferings, and even her native land, where loving subjects crowned her queen, in the greater joy she has found as companion of Vasco, who has become her heart's idol. Thus confessing her love, she is about to kiss the sleeper's forehead when suddenly she is startled by footsteps, and turning about is astonished to perceive Nelusko approaching from the right. Rising hastily, Selika quickly conceals herself behind the massive column to observe the actions of the slave, having a suspicion that his purpose can be no other than an evil one.

Advancing thoughtfully, Nelusko soliloquizes of his duty and honor to his sovereign queen, which justify his jealous hate of Vasco, whom he resolves to slay, and finding his purpose aided by sleep, he rushes with uplifted dagger upon his victim. The murderous design is arrested by Selika, who issues from her place of hiding, and begs him to spare the man who once saved them from a deadly peril, and who is now a prisoner like themselves. Nelusko, darkly scowling, reminds her that Vasco is of the despised Christian race, which it were a duty to slay, and that his great kindness, which she would so commend, was no more generous than buying them as slaves in the open mart, thus making merchandise of souls. Selika tearfully admits that this is true, but admonishes that their master's treatment has ever been most kind, and that at her entreaty Vasco sold his jewels and arms to buy her from her enemies, that she might not be separated from him whose fate is linked with her own. To her appeals Nelusko turns a deaf ear, and to her pressing to know if he has not other cause for hate than religious prejudice, if indeed there be not an ignoble feeling controlling his heart and inspiring to a deed that honor would shrink from in horror. To this accusing Nelusko responds in a vigorous aria:

"Daughter of kings, true homage I confess,
Nor slavery's chains can make my vows the less;
Thy woes I share, thy sufferings I endure,
Thy radiant queenship still to me is pure."

While acknowledging his obligations and declaring his loyalty as a devoted subject, Nelusko unveils the instigation of his hatred, and the raging passion that has taken possession of his soul, which proceeds from a fatal secret, discovery of which has given him to know that she has bestowed her heart upon this same Christian. His death, the slave declares, shall atone the sin of this misdirected affection, since jealousy can find no other cure. Selika's beseechings to spare the sleeper, more deeply aggravate the envious Nelusko, who again lifts his weapon to strike a fatal blow, but she arrests his arm, and wakes Vasco in time to avert the fatal thrust. Nelusko, abashed, conceals his dagger, and Selika, to prevent suspicion, informs Vasco that his slave has brought the morning meal! Nelusko thereupon retires, and Vasco falls to contemplating the map, and devising plans how he may consummate his ambition. While he is thus engaged, Selika approaches, and looking at the map, she points out the route by which he may sail to the land of Brahma, and indicates the spot where her frail bark was overtaken by a storm and driven upon a hostile shore. Passionately Vasco thanks and embraces her for informing him of the passage that leads to the fair land of the farther east, and assures her that his heart must ever grateful be for the helpful service she has rendered his ambitious project of discovery.

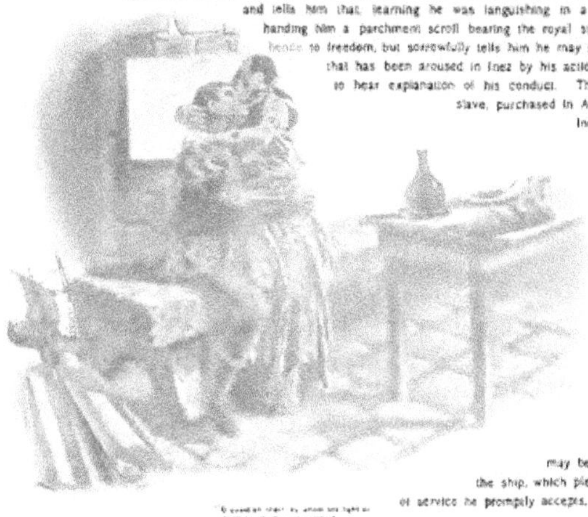

The affectionate demonstration of Vasco so cheers the soul of Selika that she reckons her fortune to be immeasurably great, believing that the loss of a kingdom is compensated by the finding of a true lover to whom her heart has been given. At this juncture, the prison doors are opened, and there enter Don Pedro and Inez, who are startled to behold Selika clasped in Vasco's arms. Don Pedro points to the two embracing as proof that Vasco has bestowed his affection upon a dusky slave, and of his unworthiness of the favors of his daughter, but Inez, though agitated by the sight that greets her eyes, still remains both loving and compassionate. She addresses Vasco tenderly, and tells him that, learning he was languishing in a dungeon, she has obtained his pardon, and handing him a parchment scroll bearing the royal signature, that grants him liberty, bids him go hence to freedom, but sorrowfully tells him he may see her no more. Vasco divines the jealousy that has been aroused in Inez by his action in embracing Selika, and begs her to stay to hear explanation of his conduct. Thereupon he informs Inez that Selika is his slave, purchased in Africa, and to prove his words he gives her to Inez. Selika at first shows indignation, though for the sake of Vasco, accepts the slavery imposed, but to mitigate her condition, Vasco permits Nelusko to follow her. Don Pedro is pleased with Vasco's sacrifice, and offers to buy both slaves, for he has need of their services, and explains that the king has entrusted to him command of an expedition to attempt the dread passage around the cape, for the quest of unknown lands of the far east. Vasco is profoundly astonished by this information, and reproaches Don Pedro for having gained, by artifice, possession of his charts to rob him of honors which were rightfully his. In an aside, Nelusko tells Don Pedro that the glory of discovery may be his if he will make him guide and pilot of the ship, which pleases the dignitary exceedingly, and the proffer of service he promptly accepts, for his purpose is to set sail at once. Having no mind to hold further converse with Vasco, Don Pedro asks Inez to give her hand, since they must depart immediately, and when Vasco demands to know by what right he thus commands her, Don Pedro replies that it is by the right that marriage gives him. Vasco, grieved and astonished, entreats Inez to acquaint him with the truth, or to explain her perfidy, whereupon she tells him how to save his life she has sacrificed her hand, for that marriage to Don Pedro is the price she paid for his pardon, and bids him now obey the voice of glory which calls him to pursue his projects of discovery. The act closes with a vigorous sextet, in which all express their respective emotions, and as Don Pedro and Inez pass out, Vasco, overcome by his grief, falls fainting on a seat. Selika rushes forward and attempts to succor him, but Nelusko interposes, and compels her to follow Don Pedro, which action furnishes the denouement of the second act.

"[illegible]"

ACT III.—The third act is played wholly on shipboard, which is incongruous, to say the least, from a dramatic point of view, but the music is of such powerful and melodramatic effects that one almost forgets the scenery in the intoxication of melodious charm produced. The opening scene shows the cabin of a large ship, with several naval officers, and Inez is reclining upon a couch attended by ladies. The action begins with a vigorous sailor chorus giving an impressive vocal greeting to sunrise, which is followed by a bell-stroke calling to morning prayer. The mariners pronounce an invocation to Saint Dominic, and Selika, Inez and attendants lift their voices in petition for heavenly guidance. The morning devotions ended, Nelusko appears on the main deck, and gives orders to man the yards quickly, and reef the sails, against a hurricane that is threatening, and cautions the helmsman particularly to keep well to the north. He then descends from the main deck as Don Pedro and Don Alvar enter the cabin, deeply concerned for the safety of the ship. Don Alvar expresses fear of treachery on the part of Nelusko, reckoning that he who has betrayed a former master may not hesitate to prove false to another, and reminds Don Pedro that already two of his ships have been lost through this same slave. Don Alvar at length ventures to question Nelusko whither he designs to steer the ship, and why he directs the prow northward? To this inquiry Nelusko returns no answer, but begins humming a gloomy air which he explains is the song of the dread Adamastor, whose mighty hand is even now suspended threateningly overhead. The sailors urge him to relate the legend of this monarch of the deep, whereupon he renders:

"Adamastor is monarch of the pathless deep,
Fierce are his actions when roused out of sleep.
Then his furious steeds he drives o'er the sea,
And the mad rushing waves are awful to see.
By the lightning's swift flash is revealed to the eye
How the storm-crested waters leap up to the sky.
All hope now abandon, prepare for your doom,
A grave in the ocean, 'neath the wave is your tomb!
Then beware, mariner! beware, mariner!"

Nelusko laughs with demoniacal glee as he pictures the raging storm, and predicts a speedy engulfment of the ship and all her human freight. A sailor on the poop-deck descries another vessel in the distance, and observes that she is sailing under Portuguese colors, announcement of which discovery disconcerts Nelusko, who conceives that it is a messenger sent upon his track to prevent the disaster which he has designed to bring about. In a few minutes a ship draws alongside of Don Pedro's vessel, and Vasco di Gama, after hailing, comes on board, where he is cordially received by Don Alvar, but Don Pedro regards him with suspicion, especially so when Vasco informs him that his ship had preceded, but seeing his danger returned to warn him against the treacherous promontory towards which Nelusko is steering, informing him also that savages ravage the coast, ever watchful for luckless vessels. Don Pedro, instead of showing gratitude, becomes enraged with jealousy, believing that Vasco has followed him with designs upon Selika, and therefore orders his sailors to seize the generous captain and bind him to the mast, there to dispatch him with their bullets. Selika and Inez utter cries of terror at this murderous command of the jealous Don Pedro, but Vasco betrays no sign of fear, and suffers himself to be bound without protest, as if wholly indifferent to his fate. As the mariners are drawn up in line to perform the execution, Inez and Selika fall upon their knees and plead in Mercy's name for Vasco's life, but Don Pedro remains obdurate, until as the storm increases, Selika, in desperation, angrily commands Don Pedro to set Vasco free at once, threatening, if he refuses, to kill Inez! By this bold defiance and warning, Don Pedro is for the moment terrified, and orders that the prisoner be carried to the hold of the vessel, there to remain until his punishment can be decided. Don Alvar reminds that Vasco's ship awaits him, but Don Pedro answers fiercely that he will not yield his prisoner, and that Vasco's ship may proceed without him; as to Selika, he promises to revenge himself upon her for rebellious conduct, in lifting a dagger above her mistress, and calls his sailors to bind and scourge her in the presence of the crew. Nelusko dares the anger of Don Pedro, and pledges his life to defend the princess against such a threatened outrage, but there is no need now for his interference, for at this moment the storm bursts over the ship with frightful violence, as she strikes the rocks, and at the same instant a swarm of savage Indians board the vessel, and, disregarding appeals for mercy, put nearly all the crew to death, and the curtain descends upon the third act.

Act IV.—The most beautiful music of the opera is heard in the fourth act, notably Vasco's solo, "O paradise on earth," the ensemble in the fourth scene, and the grand duet between Vasco and Selika, known as "The Espousal." The first scene of the act shows an Indian temple, on the right of which is a palace, and in the rear glimpses of magnificent buildings. Of all the ship's crews, there were spared by the Indian savages only Vasco, Selika, Nelusko and Inez, but the latter has been carried off by the piratical natives, and Vasco believes she perished with the rest, until a happy circumstance discovers her to him, as the sequel shows. In the first scene there appear Selika, Nelusko, a Brahma high priest, and Indians of various castes, who execute a march, and conclude the processional celebration with a ballet divertissement. Nelusko calls upon the people of all castes to swear by Brahma, Vishnu, Siva and all the gods of Hindustan, obedience to Selika, daughter of the ancient kings of India, and when the people pledge their loyal allegiance, Nelusko crowns her as queen, and commands her to take an oath, upon the golden book, to maintain the laws inviolate. Selika, with many misgivings, submits to this ceremony of crowning, but her mind is less occupied with the investiture of sovereignty than with Vasco, whom she has not seen since the tragedy of storm and piracy, and she wonders what dreadful fate has overtaken him. While her thoughts are thus distracted, the beating of a tom-tom is heard, followed by a piercing shriek, and the High Priest now advances to Selika to solemnly impress upon her the nature of the obligation she has taken, which, among other things, binds her to punish with death any stranger, whoever he may be, who by his presence defiles the sacred soil of Hindustan. Nelusko adds his reminder of how faithfully this law has been kept by all of India's kings, the sacred weapon having been used to destroy all strangers. A priest, in an aside, tells him that all perished save one, who was found chained in the hold of the vessel, and was rescued. Nelusko betrays great anger at this information, having no doubt that the one thus strangely preserved is Vasco, and he orders that he be dealt with speedily.

in obedience to which the priest goes out. Upon invitation of the High Priest, Selika enters the temple, followed by the worshipers and attendants. As the procession disappears inside the temple, a noise is heard, which a messenger explains proceeds from a stranger woman now being conducted to her death beneath the poison branches of the manchineel tree. A chorus of sacrificers sing in exultation of the rising sun whose flaming beams call for victims, and admonish that they shall forthwith prepare the steel and let the echo of shriek resound,—Death! Death!

In Scene II, of Act IV, Vasco appears, followed by soldiers, who attend him as he contemplates with evident admiration the scenery which surrounds him. Mindless of the dangers that threaten him, Vasco gives his mind to contemplation of the natural fascinations and marvels of this strange land warmed by the perfumed breath of perpetual summer. In an aria of exquisite melody, he expresses the rapture of gratified ambition:

"Oh, paradise of earth; oh, azure sky,
Oh, fragrant spices that enchant my heart,—
All these are mine by right of discovery,
The honor and glory shall be my part." etc.

Even while he is singing of the beauteous country, so little reckoning the perils that threat him, a chorus of Brahmins breaks upon his ears, and he hears the ominous song of the sacrificers. When the soldiers seize and prepare to execute him, he still remains immovably courageous, declaring that if die he must, it will be like a hero and a Christian. The soldiers raise their axes to dispatch him, but at this critical moment Selika appears upon the scene, and commands the soldiers to suspend the sacrifice. Nelusko, and the High Priest, who have followed her, protest against this mercy to a stranger whom by her oath as sovereign she is bound to destroy, but while the priest and soldiers cry lustily for his blood, Selika, determined to save him by a stratagem, takes Vasco's hand and declares that though he is foreign born, yet he is no stranger, but, by marvel strange, a—brother! To assuage their rising anger, she tells them that when a slave in far-off lands, her life was saved by this same stranger, whose deed so noble she rewarded with gift of her hand, and thus that ties indissoluble unite them. Nelusko is astounded, and would raise his voice in denial, but Selika anticipates his desire, and in an aside warns him if her claim be contradicted, that she will die with Vasco, and thereupon she asks him to confirm what she has told. Nelusko hesitates and looks appealingly to Selika, but his love for her is so great that, with weeping, he authenticates her story, and when pressed to do so, affirms it with an oath. The loyal subjects promptly accept Vasco as the husband of Selika and render him homage. In an aside, Nelusko threatens vengeance, and petitions heaven to aid him in bringing his rival to punishment; cursing his fate, he hurriedly goes out to concert his plans.

The High Priest gives loyal assent to his sovereign's conduct, but announces that it is an ancient law in Hindustan, which faithful Brahmins have never failed to obey, that marriages celebrated in foreign lands must again be solemnized at the sacred altar of the native faith when opportunity is granted, and he therefore requires Selika and Vasco to repeat their marital vows before the Hindoo Trinity, Brahma, Vishnu and Siva. At this request all withdraw except the principals.

In the succeeding scene Vasco appears as in a dream, forgetful of the peril he has just escaped, his soul steeped with ecstasy, his heart swelling with admiration for the incomparable natural beauties that surround him, and his mind dazzled by the glories he hopes to win as the discoverer of this fair country. Selika reproaches him for his cruelty in giving his thoughts to self-aggrandizement, rather than feelings of gratitude for her loving succor. Thus recalled to a sense of obligation, Vasco falls at her feet and praising her beauty and goodness, implores her pardon, while acknowledging his pledge as her husband to be. The interview develops into an exquisite duet, in which they make mutual vows of devotion, and manifest the joy of consummated love. Thereupon the priests and populace return, and the High Priest, with much solemnity, calls upon the gods to bless the fond pair, who by the sacred rites are now united as husband and wife. The ceremony is completed by a troop of India girls forming, by their veils, a circle of gauze around Selika, while others crown her with flowers. Vasco is gazing with ardent affection upon his bride, when he is suddenly startled by a mournful strain proceeding from a distance, and he catches the words "Farewell to the shores of Tagus," which sound so strangely familiar that his mind reverts to Inez, and he attempts to discover who is the singer. The group of maidens surround and coax him to follow Selika, who is moving towards the palace under an archway of gauze, formed by the veils of the bayaderes, creating a beautiful scene, heightened by choral accompaniment, which closes the fourth act.

Act V.—The final act of the opera opens with a charming view of the Queen's garden, in which tropical fruits, flowers, and trees are in rich abundance of gorgeous colors and inviting shade. On the left is Selika's palace, before the entrance of which she appears, with soldiers and Inez. The latter has escaped death through the interposition of the Queen, but since her freedom was obtained Inez has been sought and found by Vasco, which meeting has served to kindle afresh the fire of jealousy in Selika's breast, and she threatens her rival with a dreadful punishment. She demands to know by what base treachery, or subtle artifice, Vasco gained access to her in this same spot, to which Inez, trembling, answers that it was chance alone, and begs a pardon, which she urges the Queen may now well grant since Vasco has confessed his wedlock bonds, and pledged his loyalty. Selika expresses the fear that even though he is bound by marriage, Vasco still loves Inez, but the latter denies that it is so, for faithful he is to honor's law, and has forsaken for aye his old affection. Selika is not yet assured that she possesses the heart of Vasco, and continuing to express her indignation at the audacity that he has manifested in seeking a secret interview, Inez entreats the Queen to bear no anger against her husband, for if fault there lie, and love be a crime, such fault and crime may best be expiated by striking the guilty person, whom she confesses herself to be. This self-sacrificing spirit excites the compassion of Selika, who, pitying the woes of Inez, admits that impetuous love has led her to an act that is itself not free from fault, and which has brought a torment to her heart that no atonement can scarcely mitigate. Having lost Vasco, and become an outcast upon an alien shore, Inez implores Selika to end her woes by the dagger stroke she has threatened, and if her confidence be not yet restored, then remove all doubt by killing both. Selika shudders at the suggestion made to kill her husband, he for whom she would sacrifice all the sweetest ties of life, but the proof has entered deep into her heart that the attachment between Inez and Vasco has been renewed, and that henceforth she cannot hope to retain his undivided devotion. Her decision is therefore taken to magnanimously reunite them, and to sacrifice her own tortured heart to the happiness of her faithless spouse. Having thus resolved, as Nelusko enters, followed by soldiers, Selika orders him to remove Inez, and then to conduct Vasco far hence. Nelusko pauses to ask if the two shall be led away together, to which Selika, with a sigh, replies, "Yes, together let them be conveyed to yonder ship, which lies beyond the bar, and, mark me well, when Vasco is safe on board, deliver to him these tablets. When this duty you have performed and the ship is far at sea, return and join me on the promontory of the cape's farthest point." Nelusko, in terror, beseeches her not to venture to that dread

"Ye glittering [illegible]! Ye beauteous crimson flowers, [illegible] the temple of the new-made bride!"

spot, where death lurks most certainly in fatal odors of the manchineel tree—perfumes that intoxicate with fleeting ecstasy of celestial bliss, then plunge the mind in wild delirium until death ensues. Selika assures him that all this is common knowledge, yet however terrible the spot, she must seek it, since from this high vantage point she can best enjoy the spectacle of ocean's wide immensity.

In the next scene a lofty promontory is shown, towards which Selika slowly advances, silently contemplating the sea, until she comes beneath the shade of the poison tree, when she gathers some of the crimson flowers that have fallen from its branches, and lays them upon her breast, uttering:

"All envious feeling now forsake me,
And hate no longer racks my heart;
My pardon now, I freely waft thee,
Vasco, my love, forever we part!"

The symphonic prelude to this moving scene partakes of a funeral march, and the melody, of song and music, is universally regarded as being the finest of Meyerbeer's many exquisite orchestral numbers. The situation, too, from a dramatic point of view, is powerful for its intense pathos. The dying song, which begins with an apostrophe to the sea, and follows with a touching farewell to Vasco, a tribute to the fatal tree, and the celestial joy and visions inspired by the fatal odors, are examples of brilliant composition and orchestral accompaniment, which have few equals. As Selika, overcome by stupor, falls at the foot of the manchineel tree, the report of a cannon at sea arouses her, and she turns her failing eyes upon the disappearing ship, the sight of which brings her a fresh grief, and she utters a cry of distress. Nelusko has hurried back, and hearing her voice, he rushes in and clasps her in his arms, hoping to rescue her, but this hope is fleeting, for she makes no answer to his calling and her wandering senses and icy brow discover to him that death has already claimed her for bride. Overwhelmed by despair, he lifts his arms appealingly to heaven, and his heart breaking for his lost queen, he falls lifeless beside her, as the chorus render a finale:

"Released at last from earthly pain,
Love in heaven will endless reign."

Lee Woodward Zeigler

La Favorita

(AFTER THE ORIGINAL PAINTING BY L. W. ZEIGLER)

FERDINAND—"*And this sword, too, which, in battle,*
Lead for thee ne'er did lack,
At thy feet I fling.
Thus, broken, mighty king!"

ACT III SCENE XII

LA FAVORITA.

(THE FAVORITE.)

MUSIC BY DONIZETTI.——WORDS BY ROYER AND WAETZ

LA FAVORITA, the strongest of Donizetti's tragic works, had its first production at the Académie, Paris, December 2, 1840, and met with instant favor, and had a long run, but the opera was not sung in England until February 16, 1847, on which occasion the great Grisi appeared as Leonora and immediately captured the hearts of all London. The story of "La Favorita," adapted from a never popular French drama, "The Count of Commingues," has little to recommend it, and very much to condemn, for the sentiment, scarcely less than the plot, is perverted and repulsive, but Donizetti found in it the inspiration for his best work, in which his imagination had the most natural play, in marked contrast with the heavy affectations that distinguish his serious operas, though it must be admitted he is always a sweet singer.

The legend, tersely described, represents Ferdinand, a novice in the Monastery of St. James of Compostella, Spain, as being beguiled from his resolution to take monastic vows by a fair penitent, Leonora, who is mistress of Alfonso, King of Castile. His passion is so intense that he seeks release from his pious obligations, regardless of the admonitions of Balthazar, Superior of the monastery, and discarding his sombre habiliments he succeeds in gaining access to Leonora, who lives in splendor upon the island of St. Leon. He knows her only as a beauteous creature, for whom his infatuation is so great that the thought never occurs to him to inquire as to her past or present life. He pleads his suit with so much ardor and address that Leonora returns his love, but carefully guards the secret of her name and position, her desire being to live unblemished in his memory. It is necessary, for her own sake, that Ferdinand shall be persuaded, under some plea, to part from her, which she accomplishes by procuring for him a commission in the army. Believing that a way to glory is thus opened to him, and that he may prove himself worthy the hand of one whom he regards as a lady of rank, Ferdinand eagerly embraces the opportunity and takes his leave of Leonora, full of hope, to achieve his ambition in the war now being waged.

There is strong protest made by influential persons at the court against the King's amours, which presently develops an opposition by the Pope, who sends an order to Balthazar to pronounce an interdict on the King if he does not at once dismiss Leonora and restore his legitimate Queen to her wifely rights. In pursuance of this Papal commission, Balthazar appears before Alfonso, who at first resents the Pope's interference with his domestic affairs, but hesitates when he is threatened with anathema, and is given until the morrow to make his final decision. In the meantime, Ferdinand has distinguished himself in the war against Spain, fighting so valorously that he has saved the honor of the kingdom, and returns to claim reward for his services. Being asked to choose title or possession, Ferdinand claims the hand of Leonora, which Alfonso reluctantly grants, since, though he loves her dearly himself, he has observed that there is an attachment between the two, and that the wrath of the Pope forbids further continuance of his illicit relations. When Leonora learns the King's decision, she determines to no longer conceal from Ferdinand her guilty life, and dispatches a faithful servant, Inez, to inform her lover of her past history. Gaspar, the King's minister, glad that the Pope's anathema has been averted from his sovereign, has kept a close watch upon Leonora, and to prevent exposure of her past life, he intercepts Inez, and so arranges matters that Leonora is given in marriage to Ferdinand, she believing that the messenger has delivered her communication of confession. When Ferdinand returns to the court the nobles taunt him with having bound himself in marriage with a dishonorable woman, an accusation which Balthazar supports by refusing to receive him. Ferdinand is so exasperated and shamed by the truth thus first revealed to him that he concludes he has been made the victim of a base conspiracy by Alfonso and his mistress. In a rage he awaits their return from the Cathedral, and when they appear he publicly renounces all honors conferred upon him by the King, breaks his sword as a sign he will no longer serve so infamous a sovereign, and delivering a curse upon Leonora for her perfidy, he determines to at once seek refuge from the world's shams and disappointments in the cloisters.

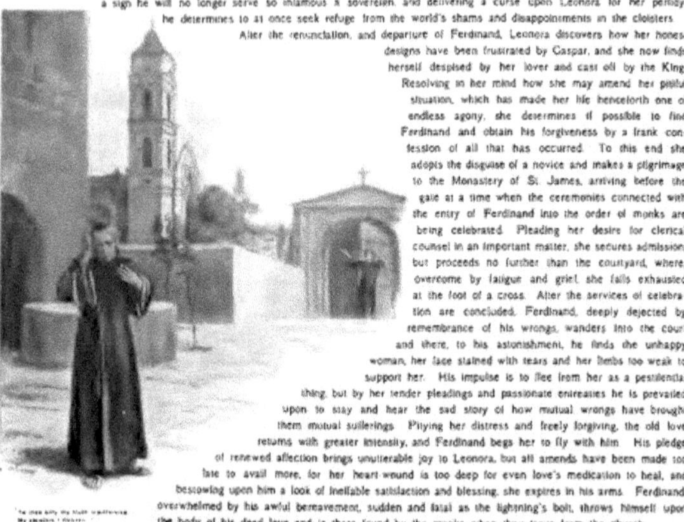

After the renunciation, and departure of Ferdinand, Leonora discovers how her honest designs have been frustrated by Gaspar, and she now finds herself despised by her lover and cast off by the King. Resolving in her mind how she may amend her pitiful situation, which has made her life henceforth one of endless agony, she determines if possible to find Ferdinand and obtain his forgiveness by a frank confession of all that has occurred. To this end she adopts the disguise of a novice and makes a pilgrimage to the Monastery of St. James, arriving before the gate at a time when the ceremonies connected with the entry of Ferdinand into the order of monks are being celebrated. Pleading her desire for clerical counsel in an important matter, she secures admission, but proceeds no further than the courtyard, where, overcome by fatigue and grief, she falls exhausted at the foot of a cross. After the services of celebration are concluded, Ferdinand, deeply dejected by remembrance of his wrongs, wanders into the court and there, to his astonishment, he finds the unhappy woman, her face stained with tears and her limbs too weak to support her. His impulse is to flee from her as a pestilential thing, but by her tender pleadings and passionate entreaties he is prevailed upon to stay and hear the sad story of how mutual wrongs have brought them mutual sufferings. Pitying her distress and freely forgiving, the old love returns with greater intensity, and Ferdinand begs her to fly with him. His pledge of renewed affection brings unutterable joy to Leonora, but all amends have been made too late to avail more, for her heart-wound is too deep for even love's medication to heal, and bestowing upon him a look of ineffable satisfaction and blessing, she expires in his arms. Ferdinand, overwhelmed by his awful bereavement, sudden and fatal as the lightning's bolt, throws himself upon the body of his dead love and is there found by the monks when they issue from the church.

Act I.—The opening scene shows the interior of a monastery, and the action begins with a chorus of monks, after which they retire into the Temple, leaving Ferdinand, who is about to take monastic vows, with Balthazar, the Father Superior. Noticing his troubled looks and hesitating manner, Balthazar asks Ferdinand why he does not join the rites, and lingers when the call to pious duty requires that he shall repair at once to the Temple to solemnize his vows? The novice confesses with shame that his thoughts are distracted, and that his holy resolves have been disturbed by dreams of earthly bliss, fond desires, mad affections. Balthazar is horrified by this admission, and exhorts him to make revelation of the cause of his sudden perfidious infatuation, to which Ferdinand makes confession in an exquisite aria.

"A vision! a spirit of beauty!
With a smile serene met my sight;
Forgetful, alas! of my duty
All trembling I thrill'd with delight," etc.

With a feeling of profound humiliation and penitence, he tells the Father that this morning, while passing through the crowded cloister, he saw among the pilgrims, lowly kneeling 'neath the dome, a beautiful creature whose hand he touched, when forthwith the ecstasy it evoked caused love to usurp his soul and broke his vows past all restoring. Balthazar, pitying his weakness, counsels him to put away such thoughts as wean him from holy purposes, but Ferdinand can make no other reply than "Ah Father! I love her." Persuasion, admonition being fruitless, Balthazar reminds him that this woman may be a lure of Satan, to induce him to forfeit his vow, and with hope of making him reflect he demands to know her rank, her name! To this Ferdinand admits he knows nothing except that he loves her, blindly, fatuously. Offended by this inapprehensible folly, Balthazar irritably bids him begone, nor longer profane these cloisters; but immediately compassionate, he charges him to beware, for his purblind infatuation cannot fail to lead him to destruction; as a drowning ship, broken by the storm, plunges to soundless depths, so will his soul, beaten by death's waves, sink to perdition. Ferdinand pleads for forgiveness, for support in his weakness, to which the Father replies with no more consolation than assurance that only mercy for his madness withholds a curse, and utters the prediction that if Heaven spares so vile a sinner it will be that he may bring back to the cloisters a broken heart as a punishment for his profane act. Nothing can persuade Ferdinand to forego the instincts of love, a power more potent than sense of religious obligation, and with a dear idol enshrined in his heart he painfully forsakes the monastery. After proceeding a little way, he turns and stretches out his hands imploringly towards Balthazar, who, however, averts his head as from a wretched sight, and the two exeunt from opposite sides of the stage, Balthazar returning in sorrowful mood to the cloisters, and Ferdinand, whipped of conscience, but irresistibly infatuated, goes to seek Leonora, the object of his mastering passion.

In the succeeding scene there is a beautiful representation of the Isle de Leon, upon which Inez and young girls are gathering flowers and singing a happy chorus, "Ye beams of gold, ye balmy zephyrs," etc. As the chorus subsides, Inez renders a pretty romanza, and then advancing to the riverside the maidens look out upon its placid bosom and sing an invitation to a lover who is coming soon in his bark, wafted by soft winds, redolent of the jasmine and orange. Presently a boat arrives at the shore bringing Ferdinand, who has a bandage over his eyes. The maidens courteously assist him to land, and then one of them removes the blindfold, a mysterious proceeding which he asks them to kindly explain, and begs them also to reveal the name of their mistress. Inez coquettishly tells him it is not for them to disclose their lady's secrets, but that she now approaches, and he may find an answer from her own lips. The girls now retire as Leonora comes forward and is hailed by Ferdinand as beauteous creature! form enchanting! for whom he has defied rebuke, and endured disgrace. Leonora receives him warmly, confessing she has discovered his ardent love and is not insensible to his advances, but curiously asks if he is quite sure that in seeking a bliss supreme he is not inviting destruction! The question surprises Ferdinand, and he entreats her to tell him of the threatening peril, though he promises to brave every danger for her sake. He asks her to reveal her name, and when she beseeches him not to urge this request, he implores that she will pledge to share with him her future life. Leonora is deeply moved by Ferdinand's ardor, and thoroughly reciprocates his affection, but realizing that she is bound to the King by illicit ties, and being eager to maintain herself unblemished in the eyes of the one whom she now devotedly loves, she freely confesses her feelings and offers him a means to achieve glory as an officer in the King's army. This recitative leads to a passionate duet, tender and tuneful, in which, first vowing his resolve never to part from her, Ferdinand is finally persuaded to leave her for a time, when, by valorous deeds, he hopes to make himself worthy to espouse so noble a lady. Leonora responds with a soulful farewell, begging him to remove her image from his heart, and with tearful sighs, that reflect remorse for her unhallowed relations to the King, she mournfully reminds:

"The rose, though fair to see,
If a canker it wears,
Can never restor'd be
By a shower of tears."

The painful parting is interrupted by the sudden entrance of Inez to announce that the King is coming. Ferdinand is surprised and wonders what can be the purpose of the King's visit, but Leonora gives no chance for inquiries, having much need for haste, and quickly handing his commission to Ferdinand, she bids him depart immediately. But he lingers confused in mind, and Leonora herself exits hastily. Left alone a moment with Inez, Ferdinand employs all his arts in a vain effort to induce her to expose the name and rank of the beautiful creature who has so completely won his heart; she makes no other response to his adjuration than a warning, by word and gesture, to be extremely cautious. When Inez goes out, Ferdinand marvels at his own audacity in aspiring to the hand of so lofty a person, one whom the King manifestly highly esteems for her gracious manner, no less than for her position. Thus soliloquizing for a moment, Ferdinand suddenly thinks of the paper which Leonora has given him, and examining it now for the first time, is joyously amazed to find that it is a commission conferring upon him a title of high honor, a captaincy, that transforms him from a sighing lover to a grim warrior, and in a very ecstasy over his great fortune, he renders a pleasing solo:

"Fame, thy voice inspiring, now my bosom firing,
This heart's best desiring: to seek with thee I'll rove.
War's trophies attaining, bright honors maintaining,
My soul true remaining to glory and to love!"

Fired by ambition, he speaks farewell for a time to the fair lady of his heart, and goes forth to win laurels—not for fame itself, but to lay at his dear one's feet, to prove his worthiness to possess her hand, this action concluding the first act.

Act II.—The second act is introduced by a view of the gardens of the Palace of Alcazar, which is overlooked by a gallery that is shown in the stage-setting. King Alfonso enters, with Don Gaspar, his prime minister, felicitating himself upon the glorious fortune that has given into his hands this delicious retreat, whose sylvan shades invite to dreams of love: gardens of loveliness where Moorish kings were wont to retire to bask in the voluptuous radiance of black-eyed graces, before Spanish chivalry laid low the proud crescent at Tarifa. Gaspar, with the obsequiousness of a servant, would give the glory of the conquest to Alfonso, but the magnanimous King disavows the honor, which he declares belongs alone to Ferdinand, who inspired to desperate valor the Spanish army and who won the battle that redeemed his country. For his gallant services the King declares he will reward Ferdinand with all the honor that it is in his power to bestow, to which end he waits the victor's coming to Seville, where the court has been ordered to assemble. An attendant now enters, whom Gaspar announces as a messenger from the monk Balthazar. Alfonso has poor grace for the father, whose mandates are often galling to the sovereign pride and license, and he makes a sign to Gaspar to retire. When the minister withdraws the King gives expression to his hatred of the sycophants who surround him, and who, jealous of his fortune, strive continually to separate him from Leonora, but he declares that their attempts, however strongly made, shall not divorce him from the real mistress of his heart.

"Leonora, from thee never
Could this fond heart, dearest, sever;
No! My throne, my home I'd fly forever,
For thee an exile I would be," etc.

As the song is concluded, Don Gaspar re-enters, and the King commands him to invite here at once all the court to a fête. The minister goes out, and immediately Leonora and Inez appear, speaking apart of the glories achieved by Ferdinand. The King makes a sign for Inez to retire and then addressing Leonora he asks why she appears with downcast eyes, as if despondent over some unhappy adventure? A very dramatic duet follows, in which Leonora reminds the King how she, a poor, simple maid, has been by him betrayed by promises to solemnize a vow that would redeem her honor, and make her wife instead of mistress. The King begs she will not be unmindful of his tender care to make her lot a pleasant one, by providing for her an abode where delicious peace reigns and all the sweets of nature abound. Leonora protests that neither jewels that glitter, nor flowers that beautify, nor music that charms the ear, can bring joy to a sorrowing heart, and refusing to explain the cause of her grief, she beseeches permission to leave the court, for though she may be beloved by the King, her lowly birth forbids that she should look so high, and in a rueful air she expresses the feelings that agitate her mind.

"Oh, love, alas! this bosom filling,
With secret woe each fibre thrilling
Consume unseen, mid deepest gloom,
As burns the death-lamp in a tomb!"

The King tries hard to disperse Leonora's melancholy by ardent declarations of his devotion, and begs her to enjoy the feasts, spread round her with a lavish hand for her diversion and happiness, but she has no heart to hear his encouragements.

The next scene introduces lords and ladies of the court, pages, guards, etc., assembled at the King's command to participate in the festivities of celebration. Alfonso takes Leonora by the hand and conducts her to a dais overlooking the fête, but at the moment the festival is about to begin Don Gaspar appears, and first asking permission to speak, with great agitation informs the King, in an undertone, that Leonora, whom he has loaded with gold and honor, has secretly betrayed him. Alfonso cannot believe this shocking report until a letter is handed to him, which has been intercepted by a slave and given to Inez. The King at once orders all his courtiers to retire, and then turning to Leonora demands to know who it is that dares to address her a message of love. Leonora recognizes the writing, and in a frenzy of terror, at the possible consequences, she cries, "Ah, spare me! I adore him!" This serves to intensify the King's jealous rage, and he orders her to reveal her lover's name, threatening her with the torture if she refuses. At this juncture Balthazar comes in, accompanied by a monk who carries a parchment with the Papal seal affixed. The King is astonished and angered by this intrusion, but Balthazar boldly represents the object of his visit to be to proclaim the wrath of Heaven, that the commands of God, through his Holiness the Pope, are pronounced against the King for his shame and disgrace in divorcing his lawful wife for an unhallowed union, which if longer continued will be punished by anathema of the holy church. The King hears these threatening words unmoved, and bids defiance to all the powers of Rome, reminding Balthazar that the royal diadem makes the King's will sacred, and that whoso dares the anger of a monarch will find a quick punishment. Emboldened by his rage at Papal interference, Alfonso declares he will wed this other lady (Leonora) despite the interdict of church and the protestations of noble hirelings of the clergy. Balthazar, more pacific, in a solemn aria warns the King not to invite the wrath of Heaven, which is now impending, and to make haste to obey the law ere a curse descends. Leonora trembles with fear at the threatened anathema, which will expose her to a sorry fate, and the King tries to console her with pictures of a bright destiny, but his heart wavers when Gaspar and chorus express their apprehension and despondency, which gives Balthazar the courage to utter a denunciation of Leonora and to warn the people to shun her as an adulteress, an outcast accursed of Heaven! The King asks by what right he threatens and speaks so mercilessly, to which Balthazar makes response, "In the name of the great High Priest, be malediction upon both of you, if by to-morrow's dawn you are not forever separated from her." The King exhibits in turn anger, remorse, and fear, while Leonora is overwhelmed by the awful curse that falls most heavily upon her own head, and she can think of no means of escaping her dreadful situation except to fly hence, with shame and grief raging, to some spot where she may die alone, where no human eye may look upon her miserable end. The chorus, frightened by the impending curse, propose that Leonora be driven out, to save them from the vengeance that Heaven will surely take upon her and upon all who give her shelter. Balthazar takes from the hand of the monk attendant the Papal decree of excommunication, which he solemnly unfolds before the King's eyes, marking the effect upon the trembling monarch. At sight of the awful instrument of anathema Leonora rushes from the stage in dismay, which action furnishes a climax for the second act.

Act III.—When the curtain rises it is upon a splendid saloon of the Alcazar Palace, to which Ferdinand has penetrated seeking Leonora. The fame that he has achieved he regards as a chaplet for the brow of the woman he loves upon whom he would bestow all earthly preferments and think not of glory for himself. King Alfonso enters pensively, followed by Don Gaspar, at sight of whom Ferdinand withdraws a pace. The King has debated in his mind the dread alternative imposed by Balthazar, and fearful of the judgment, he decides to yield obedience rather than brave anathema. He thereupon bids Gaspar to summon Leonora, but to conduct Inez, her accomplice, to prison. As Gaspar exits Alfonso discovers Ferdinand, whom he greets affectionately as the saviour of Spain, to whose services the King owes his crown, and so show his appreciation Alfonso asks him to request for recompense any honor or possession, and it shall be granted this hour. Happy at this promise from his King, whose favor has already been a rich reward, Ferdinand answers: "Though but a poor soldier, with my whole heart I love a noble lady; to her alone I owe my renown. Her hand is all I crave!" The King immediately grants the request, and asks her name. At this instant Leonora, pale, sorrowful, but beautiful in her grief, comes in, at sight of whom Ferdinand is enraptured, and he declares that in the presence of the King she blossoms the sweetest flower and shines more resplendent than any jewel of the palace.

The King is stupefied with amazement, and touched with jealousy by the discovery that Ferdinand is enamored of Leonora, and illy disguising his exasperation he coldly addresses Leonora: "Madam, thy lover, most adoring, through me his profession of devotion now conveys, and scarce a moment since demanded thy hand." Leonora, realizing her disgrace and fearing exposure, knows not how to demean herself in this trying situation, and can make no other response than a call for Heaven's assistance when she is apprised of Ferdinand's petition to claim her as wife. The King, feeling it hard to restrain his emotions, commands them to leave Spain to-morrow, and thus addresses Leonora, sadly reproving:

"Thou flower beloved, and in hope's garden cherished,
With sighs and tears refreshed, too, night and morn,
Fadest from my breast, since every beauty perished,
And in thy stead alone hath left a thorn."

Unable to comprehend this sudden tide of fortune sweeping back the sea of grief that broke so resistlessly upon her an hour ago, Leonora fears that it is some sweet delirium, a hopeless dream; but Ferdinand is enchanted by the prospect of gaining his heart's ambition, and when the King bids them prepare for the church rites that will bind them at once in wedlock, Ferdinand falls at the King's feet in eternal gratitude, a feeling that is shared by Leonora. The King counsels Leonora to be more faithful to her husband than she has been to him, and forgiving her deceit, he goes out with Ferdinand.

[illegible]

Leonora, left alone, throws herself upon a couch, and soliloquizes of the strange events of the past few moments. She cannot divest herself of the thought that her senses are deceiving her, that her marriage with Ferdinand is some dear delusion arising from her love, for it were more than strange that she should escape so quickly from the deeps of misery and gain a bliss her heart has sought in fondest moments. From these suspicions of the verity of her realized hopes, she suddenly turns to a contemplation of her sensual life, of which Ferdinand knows nothing. This thought plunges her at once into a new grief; her honor blighted through a King's deception, she resolves that Ferdinand shall not become her husband ignorant of her past relations, and determines to expose the whole truth, concealing no act or circumstance, that he may fully know her character and be the better able to test her devotion. Thereupon she describes her love and conflicting emotions in an aria, that is a favorite with all contraltos, and remarkable for its sweetness in melody and sentiment; moving to pity, the song expresses the alarm of a distracted heart while protesting its undying devotion:

"Dear Ferdinand, were mine this earth's whole treasure —
Mine, too, each star, and orb in heaven,
Each star a world, to purchase thee one pleasure,
All to thee by this fond hand were given!
All should be thine, save my poor name degraded;
And thine should be, too, my life's latest sigh!
But ere I give to thee a fame o'ershaded,
And thou deceive, I'll say farewell and crave to die."

Inez enters at the close of the song, and betraying great interest in the fortunes of her mistress, begs to know if Ferdinand has come to wed her? Sorrowfully Leonora answers that honor and love forbid such bonds, and with a heart breaking of grief she requests Inez to forthwith seek Ferdinand and say in frankness that poor Leonora, whom he loves, is not fit to be a bride, since all men call her Favorite of the King; but that he may know the truth, tell him that she was torn from her home when very young, and innocent as a nestling dove, and that it was her sad fate to be betrayed, unconscious, and kept in wrong against her will; that hearing this sad tale, if Ferdinand is still disposed to seek her hand, regardless of the stain upon her character, to tell him Leonora will be his slave, his everything that devoted wife can be. Thus charging Inez to expose her shame, Leonora implores her to return quickly with Ferdinand's answer, however dread it may be. Having thus instructed her maid, she passes out, and Inez is about to follow her when Don Gaspar, with guards, appears, and by the King's order, places Inez under arrest, by which she is prevented from conveying the message of her mistress to Ferdinand, for the soldiers rudely take her away immediately to prison despite her cries.

Don Gaspar and all the attending courtiers render a chorus felicitating Ferdinand, who is now about to receive a reward for his glorious services to the nation by bestowal upon him of the hand of a deserving woman, which he has elected to receive in preference to all other honors within the gift of the King. Ferdinand now enters, delighted with the prospects of his good fortune, and is followed by the King, who addresses him: "Thus to prove to the court how much thy deeds I honor, in conquering the Moorish foe, henceforth thou shalt be known by the proud titles 'Count of Zamora and Marquis of Montreal,'" at the same time investing him with proper decorations that excite great envy in the breasts of the nobles. Gaspar is especially jealous, and he being the only one who knows that Ferdinand has chosen Leonora to be his bride, discloses this purpose now to the other nobles and inveighs against the shameful act of the King in matching a dissolute woman raised to the rank of marchioness by a base decree, to a warrior who has served the state so gloriously. Leonora enters, dressed in nuptial robes, but looking extremely pale and dejected, and advances with fear and hesitation towards Ferdinand, who contemplates her with looks of tenderness. She feels no doubt that Inez has delivered to him the message that reveals her past relations to the King, and wonders what her lover's answer will be, but her anxieties are quickly allayed by Ferdinand, who takes her trembling hand, saying: "Blessed with a husband's love, every fear from thee will fly," and leads her joyfully from the room, the King retiring mournfully before them. When the principals have departed, Gaspar turns loose the phials of his venomous jealousy upon the mistress of the King, and the favored captain who has been created Prince of Alcantara and given treasures in great plenty for a lucky service. The nobles express similar sentiments at this sudden elevation to highest rank of a person of common blood, who is at best a gilded adventurer. While the nobles, with Gaspar, are conspiring how the honors may be nullified, lords enter and gravely announce that the nuptials between Ferdinand and Leonora have been solemnized, which the

nobles receive with indignation, exclaiming in chorus: "So, let us all pride of birth, rank, consulting," etc. Ferdinand comes in, filled with joy, paying compliments of every kind to the bride of his hand and heart and invites the noble lords to share with him his happiness in a festival celebration, but they hold him coldly, and when he offers his hand to Gaspar that envious minister scornfully refuses to take it, and spitefully declares that the title of marquis does not always entitle the one who bears it to the respect of an honorable man. Ferdinand resents the insult and threatens to make Gaspar pay dearly for his conduct, but the nobles are about to rush off without giving him any satisfaction by deed or explanation, and Ferdinand, in a great rage, is pressing them, when Balthazar enters and begs him to withhold his intemperate fury. Ferdinand embraces the holy man, his friend and counselor, when Gaspar tauntingly remarks: "Behold Leonora's bridegroom!" Balthazar astonished, repels Ferdinand, and shames him for linking his name with the King's favorite. Ferdinand is thunderstruck by this declaration, and, trembling with emotion, beseeches to know why so infamous a charge is made against the woman he loves and has just made his wife. Balthazar thereupon assures him that it is true, and wonders why a scandal so well known has been withheld from his knowledge. Ferdinand immediately concludes that he has been made the victim of a conspiracy, and vows that not even Heaven can thwart his purpose to take a bloody vengeance. At this juncture the King comes in, leading Leonora, and followed by ladies. Ferdinand advances, and repressing the fury that burns within him, addresses the King: "Your majesty, to you I owe my fortune, my life, the rank of a count; all this splendor, new to me, wealth, dignity, and the supreme gifts that man aspires to. But thou hast willed, oh, Heaven, that I should buy them at the heavy price of my honor!" The King not yet discovering the real cause of Ferdinand's anger, and believing that it is only his own infamy that prompts to this display of indignation, applauds the candor and noble soul of Ferdinand and confesses remorse for the wrong he has done an innocent woman. Leonora, unconscious of Ferdinand's wrathful feelings towards her, commends him for having made a sacrifice of his honor, and prays that she may prove herself worthy of so true a lover. But Balthazar knows the motive that urges Ferdinand to utter his protests, and he trembles for the result, while cursing the King for devising so great an outrage. Unable longer to control his rising passion, Ferdinand launches the thunderbolts of his rankling fury against the King, whose explanations and excuses he refuses to hear, since he has been made the dupe of the most cruel of conspiracies. Leonora becomes alarmed by this outburst, for the charge of conspiring causes her to fear that Inez has not acquainted Ferdinand with the facts of her disgrace. The King tries to stay his anger by calling him sharply, "Marquis!" to which Ferdinand replies in fiercest tones: "That name I scorn—resign, with every gift thou gavest, and will serve thy cause no more." He then turns to the nobles who insulted him and craves their pardon for his rashness, begging to be restored to their respect, for shame, dishonor, he had unwittingly incurred, and will now go hence forever. At these words Leonora frantically calls Inez, but being told that her maid is now a prisoner, the dreadful truth is revealed, and she is overwhelmed with grief. Ferdinand furiously tears off his decorations, and breaks his sword, exclaiming, "Oh, cruel sire, take this badge—of disgrace 'tis the trophy! I give it back; and this sword, too, which in battle zeal for thee ne'er did lack, at thy feet I fling, thus broken, mighty King. Tyrant! I disdain thine anger!" These words put the King into a terrible passion and he commands that Ferdinand be at once exiled, or for his daring insult be made to suffer a well-merited death. Leonora interposes to assuage Alfonso's wrath against her deceived husband, imploring that if vengeance be demanded it may fall upon her. Balthazar makes bold to charge that the wrong is all upon the King's head, a guilty, shameful sovereign, who had better be appealing for mercy than threatening

with direful punishment a loyal subject who is made the victim of basest treachery. This concerted finale, which is intensely dramatic, closes the third act, Ferdinand and Balthazar departing together while the chorus express sympathy for Leonora.

Act IV.—The concluding act is distinguished for its thrilling effects and beautiful music, probably the most melodious that Donizetti ever composed. When the curtain goes up there is shown an impressive scene in the cloisters of St. James, to which Ferdinand has retired in refuge from the world forever. On the right is a portico of the church, in front of which is a large cross set in a stone block. There are also tombs marked by smaller crosses of wood, and in the background several monks are observed digging their graves. The action begins with a solemn chorus participated in by Balthazar, pilgrims and monks, the latter prostrating themselves before the large cross, where Ferdinand is also bowing. The pilgrims and monks presently enter the chapel, and Balthazar admonishes Ferdinand that he has need to take only one more vow to divorce himself forever from the cares of this vain world. Ferdinand, fully penitent, admits the Father's prophecy has been verified, that he has returned in shame, to seek the peace that a quiet grave affords in this holy place. Balthazar tries to console him with assurances that by consecrating his thoughs to Heaven he may overcome his griefs. Then excusing himself to go and comfort a trembling novice, who has arrived this hour craving aid, Balthazar goes out. Left alone, a flood of bitter thoughts pour in upon Ferdinand, through all of which, however, there is still visible the sweet vision of Leonora, for whom his heart has not ceased to long, and he pours out his grief in song:

[illegible]

"Spirit of light, so fondly courted,
Once heavenly bright, but now departed,
All joy is fled thou didst awaken,
Love's hope is dead—I am forsaken."

Balthazar now returns, with several monks, and invites Ferdinand to repair to the sacred fane, where heaven will be revealed to him. Following his good monitor, Ferdinand passes into the church with the monks, whereupon Leonora appears, in the habit of a novice, and places herself in a position where she is able to scrutinize the faces of the monks as they pass, but the cowls upon their heads render recognition difficult, so she fails to perceive Ferdinand. Being alone, she discloses, in soliloquy, the object that has brought her to these cloisters—that it is to find Ferdinand and obtain his forgiveness before she dies. While she is anxiously searching for the husband lost at the very altar, a chorus of monks intone, from the chapel, pious vows addressed to Heaven over the acceptance of a soul that is given to God. Leonora wonders who is this candidate that renounces the earth, and as if in answer to her mental inquiry she hears Ferdinand's voice, "To Thy service I consecrate myself, O Lord! Come, shed Thy rays into my heart." Recognizing that voice, Leonora understands that grief for the disgrace that he feels in having wed her has driven Ferdinand to fly the world and take refuge in the cloisters. This realization of his sacrifice and of her own sins overwhelm her with sense of shame, sorrow, despair, and she falls senseless at the foot of the cross.

While Leonora is lying as one dead by the cross, Ferdinand issues from the chapel in great agitation of mind, saying, "My vows I have pronounced, yet in spite of these I feel such a secret terror in my heart that I have fled from the altar!" As he utters these words, Leonora revives a little and complains of the deadly chill that congeals her heart. Ferdinand overhears the complaint and hastens to render assistance to the suffering person. As he stoops above her, Leonora turns and implores forgiveness, but at sight of her face he recoils with horror, seeing in her the cause of his present miseries and a being so attainted as to profane the sanctuaries where only holiness may abide. He commands her to remove her fatal beauty from these cloisters, marveling what evil spirit could have brought her thither, and dismisses her:

"Hence to thy palace, he doth invite thee—
His gilded crown awaits thy brow;
Love like his can alone delight thee;
Go, tempter, ere I curse thee—go!"

To these repelling words Leonora replies with streaming eyes, declaring that with soul pierced with woe she has sought him here to give her pledge that she had never a thought to deceive him, and that she had sent Inez to reveal to him the truth of her past life and tell the story of her wrongs. On her knees she implores him to take pity and utter words of forgiveness before death shall claim her, urging her prayers for mercy in a pathetic aria:

"Dear Ferdinand, this heart is breaking!
To my sad fate compassion show,
And, ne'er the penitent forsaking,
Oh! let thy breast with mercy glow.
I ask but to my grave to carry
Thy sweet forgiveness of the past.
Nor care I then how soon they bury
One whose joy has throbbed its last!"

The plaintively passionate entreating of Leonora, who pleads in the name of the love he once bestowed, and with the death-damp already gathering upon her brow, causes Ferdinand's heart to melt at length with mercy, and pitying the woman, broken with despair, the old affection returns, and in an ecstasy of rejuvenated love, he exclaims: "Joy, joy once more fills my breast," and he begs her to fly with him at once to some other land, where their bliss may be renewed, beyond the reach of jealousies and the artful designs of base intriguers. Leonora is enraptured by Ferdinand's forgiveness and her restoration to his heart, but her strength is rapidly departing, and the death which she craved is too near at hand to allow her to obey his counsel. With failing voice she begs him to remember his vows, and when he declares that to possess her he would brave earth and heaven, she bestows upon him her blessing: "May the grace of God be ever with you! The Lord in mercy has granted me one more delight, and I complain not of my fate. Heaven, my Ferdinand, hath willed it so. I leave thee—free of shame—by my death. I die assured of thy forgiveness. Unstained I enter the tomb. We shall be united, Ferdinand. Farewell!" Her breath comes hurriedly a moment from this last great exertion, and then fails completely. A struggle, a gasp, and death claims her for bride. Ferdinand is horror-stricken, heart-broken by the tragedy and calls loudly for help, and implores the now dead Leonora to open her eyes and to speak one more word. Balthazar and monks run out of the chapel, to render aid, but perceiving at once that Leonora is no more, he tenderly draws the cowl over her head and sympathetically informs the distracted Ferdinand that the novice hath surrendered her soul and is now at peace where the world's sorrows cannot enter, and where all transgressions are forgiven. They all kneel in prayer beside the poor girl's body, and Ferdinand, feeling that his end is also at hand, admonishes: "By to-morrow my soul too will need your prayers!" which very affecting scene ends the opera.

La Sonnambula

(AFTER THE ORIGINAL PAINTING BY WILLIAM DE LEFTWICH DODGE)

CHORUS—"*Mark her!*"

ALL—"*Pow'r almighty, guide now her falt'ring steps!*

It trembles—it quivers—ah—"

ACT III.—SCENE II

LA SONNAMBULA.

(THE SOMNAMBULIST.)

MUSIC BY BELLINI ——WORDS BY ROMANI

A SONNAMBULA, an opera in three acts, is the most delightful of Bellini's lyric compositions, abounding as it does with such charming melodies that once heard they linger forever like tender memories. Bellini was not over-gifted with dramatic power, but his genius was specially pronounced in elegiac writing, as manifested in the luscious beauty of his airs, into which the greatest singers have infused much dramatic force. The story of "La Sonnambula" shows weakness, but it is of idyllic character, and served Bellini perfectly for the best expression of his style of musical pathos. The rare gems of the opera which have made it so famous are Amina's arias, "O love, for me thy power," "While this heart its joy revealing;" Rodolpho's beautiful air for baritone, "As I view these scenes so charming;" Lisa's cavatina, "Sounds so joyful, notes of gladness;" the playful duet between Amina and Elvino, "Foolish doublings and all fears are o'er;" the humorous chorus of villagers, "Be observant, 'tis his number;" the duet in the next scene, "Oh, misery, how am I guilty?" the tenor aria, "All is lost now;" and Amina's joyous, melodious outburst, "Do not mingle one human feeling." "La Sonnambula" had its initial production at Milan, March 6, 1831, where, with Pasta, Rubini, Mariano, and Toccani, great singers of the time, in the leading rôles, the opera achieved an immediate success. So great was its popularity that the opera was brought out the same year in both London and Paris, and two years later it was given in English with the famous Malibran as Amina. Thirty years afterwards Adelina Patti made her début in the same rôle at the Theatre Italian, Paris, and so thoroughly indentified herself with the part, that for a long while her name was chiefly associated in the public mind with that charming character she personated so well.

The subject of the story of "La Sonnambula" is taken from a vaudeville and ballet by Scribe, the scene being laid in Switzerland. Amina, an orphan, is brought up by an excellent woman, Teresa, who is a miller's wife. When the action of the opera begins Amina is about to be married to Elvino, a rich young man of the same village. Affairs would progress favorably but for the fact that Lisa, a young woman who keeps an inn near the mill, is ambitious to capture Elvino's heart, and exerts her wiles to this end. It happens also that the situation is further complicated by the attempt of Alessio, a peasant lad, to win the hand of Lisa. Notwithstanding the designs of Lisa, a marriage contract is executed between Amina and Elvino, to confirm which he places a nuptial ring upon her finger, and gives her also a bunch of pansies. The wedding ceremony is to be performed on the following day, but meantime Rodolpho, a young lord of the village, returns incognito, after a long absence, for the purpose of making an investigation respecting his estates, and takes lodgings at Lisa's inn. He is inclined to gaiety, paying compliments to all the girls, but attempts to show special attention to Amina, whose charms of person and manner really fascinate him, which arouses the intense jealousy of Elvino, who is inclined to bring the stranger to account for his actions, but is restrained by fear of scandal.

Amina is a confirmed somnambulist, and she being often seen in white robes, wandering through the village about midnight, the simple residents have come to believe that the place is haunted by a walking ghost. This legend is told to Rodolpho, but he dismisses it as an idle tale, and retires to his chamber, hoping for a rest that will refresh him for to-morrow's duties. Scarcely has he entered his room, when Lisa comes in to inquire if he is in need of anything, and a playful scene of flirtation takes place. While the two are thus indulging an interchange of coquetry, a noise at the window attracts their attention, and soon the form of a woman, clad in a night-dress, is seen entering. Lisa immediately perceives that it is Amina, and to escape an embarrassing situation Rodolpho hurriedly abandons the room, and Lisa takes refuge in a closet, but in her haste she unconsciously drops her handkerchief. Amina, in a profound sleep, kneels as at an altar, and murmurs Elvino's name, after which she walks to the bed and throws herself upon it, whereupon Lisa escapes from the closet, and with a purpose to compromise her rival, she loses no time in informing Elvino of Amina's presence in Rodolpho's room. She has not miscalculated the excitement such information will provoke. The village is quickly aroused, and a large crowd, headed by Elvino, proceed at once to the inn, where they find everything as Lisa has represented. Having no doubt of the faithlessness of Amina, his first jealous misgivings being seemingly confirmed, Elvino declares she is guilty, and denounces her. The noise of so many excited voices presently awakens the unfortunate girl, who, looking about her, and unable to comprehend her situation, seeks the protection of Teresa's arms. Gradually the horrible truth is revealed to her that she has been found in Rodolpho's room, to the great scandal of the whole village. She protests her innocence, and appeals to Elvino to withhold his censure, but so intense is his anger that he tears the nuptial ring from her finger, and turns his back upon her. The neighbors show pity for Amina's situation, half inclined to believe her innocent, and to their persuasions Rodolpho adds his own, declaring upon his honor, that the poor girl is blameless; but Elvino is not to be disabused, and to better satisfy his jealousy, he straightway offers his hand to Lisa. Rodolpho has a great desire to explore the mystery, and the villagers are no less anxious, for the finding of Lisa's handkerchief in Rodolpho's room has raised a doubt of her innocence, and created a belief that some vile plot has been perpetrated. This wonder is soon to be explained, for on the following night Amina is again seen walking in her sleep, and the neighbors are promptly aroused. She is watched by the amazed people as she steps from the window of the mill and crosses upon a rotten plank, directly above the great water-wheel, from the window to the embankment. She carries a lighted lamp in her hand, and when midway the bridge a splinter breaks from it, and the lamp falls from her hand, which cause the people to fear she will be precipitated upon the wheel, but she finally descends in safety to the ground, where her lover, now convinced of her innocence, receives her in his arms. The handkerchief serves as a proof of Lisa's infamous design to ruin the girl, and Amina and Elvino are married amid the blessings and rejoicing of the whole village.

Act I.—The opening scene represents a village-green, on one side an inn, and a water-mill showing in the background. In the distance lofty mountains are to be seen, for the action of the opera is laid in the Bernese-Oberland region of Switzerland. As the curtain rises, a body of peasants are heard singing a joyful chorus, celebrating the fortune of Amina, whose nuptials with Elvino are to be performed on the morrow. Merry voices draw gradually nearer until the peasants come upon the stage in groups. At the same time, Lisa, the inn-keeper, enters, and seeing the people giving their congratulations to Amina, her spitefully jealous feelings are aroused, to which she gives expression in the air:

"Sounds so joyful, notes of gladness,
Fill my heart with bitter sadness;
Ev'ry tribute they are bringing,
As an adder through me stinging,
I nurse in silence deep despair," etc.

Alessio enters as Lisa concludes her song, and accosts her tenderly, but she turns from him petulantly and frankly pronounces him a horrid bore. Although his passion for her is great, Alessio resents the sneers and contumely of Lisa, and thinking of no better answer to make to her scorn, he tells her that one day she may wish to be a bride, then the bridegroom will most probably be lacking. Again sounds of choral festivity proceed from behind the scenes, and quickly a company of villagers of both sexes, clad in white, descend from the hill with baskets and wreaths of flowers, hailing Amina the while. Lisa is fairly consumed with envy for her successful rival, and her temper is not improved by Alessio's side remarks, and his participation in the greetings extended to Amina. Her rancorous spirit is intensified by the villagers, who, after praising Amina as the fairest of her sex, congratulate her upon securing for husband one who is both wealthy and devoted, the greatest catch in all the country round. Distracted by this reception and laudation of the girl whom in her jealousy she despises, Lisa shuts her ears against hearing more, and retires apart to nurse her rage.

When Amina enters, with Teresa, she hails the female peasants as dearest companions of her earliest friendships, and blesses them for their affectionate bounties in gifts of flowers, offerings for her nuptials, and tributes of regard. Then turning to Teresa, Amina pours out her gratitude for such a zealous guardian who has trained her orphan childhood in steps of virtue, which appreciation for these blessings prompts Amina to express her grateful sentiments in a pretty air:

"O love, for me thy power
Bright bids the day to shine," etc.

Amina lovingly embraces Teresa, and taking her hand places it on her heart to prove that it beats with loyalty for guardian and lover. At this the villagers break forth in another jubilant chorus, which is followed by Amina's cavatina:

"While this heart its joy revealing,
Faithful beats with grateful feeling,
Still my lips, in vain appealing,
Cannot speak my soul's delight."

Alessio draws near to Amina and making a profound obeisance, gives her a special greeting, and informs her that he has prepared the festival, composed the songs of welcome and imported from a neighboring village musicians who will esteem it an honor to perform before so worthy and charming a lady. Amina returns her thanks for this kindness, and expresses the hope that Alessio may very soon find reward in celebration of his wedding with Lisa. Alessio appeals to Lisa if this pleasing prediction may not be verified, to which she disdainfully replies that she is no slave to Cupid, and prefers a life of freedom. At this moment the notary arrives, but as Elvino does not accompany him, Amina's solicitude is excited; her anxieties, however, are quickly relieved by the appearance of Elvino, who comes in hot haste, and first greeting Amina fondly, he begs her pardon for the delay, and excuses his lateness by telling that he had tarried long before her mother's grave-stone, praying that the angel spirit would bless their union. This Amina considers to be a bright omen of future happiness, which belief the villagers share. The notary now prepares to attest the nuptial contract, by handing the paper and a pen to Elvino. He reads the contract aloud: "With all my fortune, with my cottage, with my fair name, with the wealth my broad acres lawfully measured, I thee endow." He signs without hesitation, and then passes the paper to Amina for her signature. Elvino's mother and other witnesses also attest the contract, after which he takes a ring from his finger and places it upon Amina's as a solemn pledge of engagement, which is followed by an exquisite duet between the two:

"Take now this ring, as a pledge; 'tis thine, love;
'Twill make thee before the altar mine, love," etc.

The sentiment, expression, and melody of this duet is distinctly the pronounced gem of the opera. To-morrow, it is declared, the nuptials shall be perfected by holy ritual, a pronouncement that deeply distresses Lisa, who realizes that only some desperate chance can prevent a consummation which will doom her to despair of winning Elvino for husband. She thereupon conceives a design to disparage the reputation of Amina, by assuming satisfaction at the prospective wedding, a purpose which is soon aided by an unlooked-for circumstance.

A cracking of whips and tramping of horses' feet are heard outside, which attract attention of the villagers, followed at once by the entrance of Rudolpho, a stranger, who complains of being exhausted by his long journey, and asks how far is yet the way to the castle? Lisa volunteers the information that it is quite three miles distant, and tells him the route is so rough and tortuous, and that the night is so dark, he had better tarry at the inn until

"With all my fortune, with my cottage, with my fair name, and broad acres lawfully measured, I thee endow."

to-morrow. Rodolpho accepts the suggestion, and embraces Lisa's invitation to take lodging at her hostelry. As he looks about, he discovers familiar sights: the old mill, the ancient fountain, the sturdy oak, beneath the shade of which he often played in childhood; and under the spell which these dear sights evoke, enraptured by remembrances of other days, he gives expression to his feelings in a picturesque romanza:

"As I view these scenes so charming,
All my pulses and heart are warming,
With remembrance of days long vanish'd," etc.

Rodolpho notices that some festival is in progress, and suspecting it is a marriage celebration points to Lisa and asks if she is not the fair bride? The villagers, with one voice, pronounce the name of Amina, and inform him that she is the one who to-morrow will be led to the altar by the best and wealthiest of the village beaux. Rodolpho is immediately attracted by the fresh, sweet face of Amina, and is so charmed by her pretty smile that he makes confession of his admiration, comparing her graces to those of one he had fondly loved, but of whom he was robbed by death.

"Maid, those bright eyes my heart impressing,
Fill my breast with thoughts entrancing,
By recalling an earthly blessing
Long since dead and pass'd away," etc.

"[illegible]"

Lisa's hate flares up afresh at seeing the stranger bestowing attention upon her rival, and Elvino's jealousy is aroused by observing that Amina appears highly complimented by the admiration of the new arrival, for all the villagers applaud him as a gallant possessed of a most seducing way. Elvino at length makes bold to address Rodolpho and to ask if he has not some knowledge of the country through previous visits,—having a mind to discover the object of his present coming. Rodolpho satisfies this curiosity by informing that in his childhood he lived with the lord in the castle near by, who was in fact to him a father. Teresa calls to mind that the lord of the castle had a son, who long ago disappeared without cause, since which time no tidings of him has reached the afflicted parent. Rodolpho tells the villagers that the long-lost son still survives, and promises that very soon he will be restored, and that all shall see and meet him.

The sound of a shepherd's pipe is heard on the hills calling the herds to their folds, and Teresa admonishes the peasants that it is time to repair to their several homes, for the hour is fast approaching when the dread phantom, so often seen wandering about the village, in ghostly apparel, may be expected to appear. This reference to a superstitious fear felt in common by all the villagers, greatly interests Rodolpho, though he affects to disregard it, and tries to impress upon the people that such belief is a folly born of ignorance. The peasants declare that the phantom is a verity, and insist on telling him the strange story, which they thus narrate in chorus:

"When dusky nightfall doth shroud the sunbeam
And half repulses the timid moonbeam;
When thunder boometh, where distance loometh,
Floating on a mist a shade appears,
In filmy mantle of pallid whiteness,
The eye once gentle, now glaring brightness,
Like cloud o'er heaven by tempest driven
Plainly confess the phantom wears."

Rodolpho dismisses the story as a creation of village gossips, to frighten youths, but the peasants stoutly maintain its truth, and declare that they all have frequently seen the ghostly visitant, the appearance of which is always attended by a strange stillness,—that the leaves cease to stir, the watch-dog cowers in his kennel, the brook stops its flow, the screech-owl hurries to her nest, and a pall of deepest dread falls over all, and whoso is rash enough to brave the apparition must suffer a woe more awful than tongue can describe. These terrible predictions give Rodolpho no alarm, and he assures the affrighted people that ere he departs he will relieve the village of this dreaded ghost, and make plain the mystery. Having made his promise, Rodolpho requests Lisa to show him the room he is to occupy, but before going he turns yearningly to Amina and bids her good night, expressing the hope that her lover is as devoted as he himself could be. Elvino resents this endearing address as bold presumption, and with show of irritation declares, boastfully, that no man can give Amina love and protection equal to such as he feels and will extend. Rodolpho perceives how he has stirred Elvino to jealousy, and turning away he enters the inn, followed by Lisa. All quit the scene except Elvino and Amina, she pausing to secretly say good-night to her lover, and he staying to accuse her of flirting with a stranger. He speaks to her coldly, asking why she made her adieu so tender to the stranger, to which, little suspecting his jealousy, she replies, "There shone in his farewell a grace that did bespeak him noble in all his nature." Elvino sneeringly retorts, "A noble lover! You're skillful in feigning. Did he not press thy hand; did he not caress thee? Such actions gave you some pleasure; when his smooth tongue addressed you, did not those furtive glances echo his passion?" Amina is stunned by these suspicions. Her first thought is that he is teasing, to test her fidelity, but later understanding that he is sincerely accusing her, she reproaches him for thus wounding her heart with cruel doubts, and pleadingly she asks, "Oh, have I thought, or eyesight, except for thee? Is not our one faith plighted? And thy ring on this finger? My affection, is it not all thine own? What more then, dost still continue jealous?" Thus uttering the grief that torments her heart, she gives way to tears, which moves Elvino to such compassion and shame that he falls at her feet and passionately pleads for forgiveness, declaring so fervid is his love that he is jealous of even the zephyrs that toy with her tresses, of the sun that kisses her cheeks, but he promises to banish such fancies from his mind forever, and to be suspicious no more, trustful now of her love. The scene concludes with a delightful duet of reassuring, "Foolish doubtings and fond fears o'er."

"Ah, mine angel!
E'er constant to thee, in this bosom
Be the fealty which love hath created.
And more pure than the spring rose's blossom
Shall the morn of our happy life be."

The two part after affectionately embracing, and speaking peaceful slumber and happy dreams, as the curtain descends on the first act.

Act II.—The beginning of Act II is with a scene showing a sleeping apartment in Lisa's inn, into which the moon is brightly streaming. Rodolpho enters, and after testing the bed, and examining the furniture of the room, expresses satisfaction with the comforts it provides, esteeming himself quite lucky in finding a place so pretty. The village, too, pleases him, for he has found the men courteous, the women lovely, and the bride he has just met fascinating enough to justify a stay of more than one day. And the hostess, though she is somewhat backward, he thinks quite agreeable, and not without charms. While he is soliloquizing about his situation, Lisa comes in. He immediately addresses her with a traveler's familiarity, calls her a blooming, blushing maiden, and invites her to draw nearer. Timidly, she ventures to tell that her object in entering is to inquire if the apartment suits his lordship. Rodolpho is surprised to be thus addressed, having a wish to conceal his identity, and desires to know why she thinks him to be a lord. To this inquiry Lisa answers boldly: "Why, the crier hath so discovered, that you are lord of the castle, and for your welcome the village officers have been convened. I am grateful to fortune, in that she, over the others, haply concedes to me the grace to offer my first tribute." Rodolpho wishes to repay her tribute with a kiss, and proffers such sweet speech of admiration that her vanity is profoundly excited, but she acts with so much coyness that, to gain her confidence, he asks if she has never had a lover? Lisa protests that her bosom is a stranger to the passion, though her heart is sincere which cannot be said of all women. Rodolpho gradually insinuates himself in her favor, and praising her beauty, he presently puts his arm round her waist, and asserts that he knows some one who holds a place in her affections, and begs that she will accept him as the substitute, for the moment, of that preferred lover. At this point of the ardent interview a noise is heard outside the window, which greatly disturbs the two, and Lisa especially, who fears she may be discovered in her guest's room, to the great scandal of the village. To escape a dilemma, she quickly secretes herself in an inner apartment, retreating with such precipitation that her silk neckerchief blows off. Rodolpho picks it up, and carelessly throws it across the top of the bedpost, then going to the window he is astounded by the sight of a female figure (Amina), upon the roof, making her way towards his room. He is slightly alarmed at first, thinking it must be a ghost indeed, but as the figure draws closer, he perceives it is the beautiful village damsel who an hour before smiled on him sweetly, in conscious innocence and joy at her approaching marriage. Amina, walking in her sleep, opens the window and steps inside, then moves, rigid and erect, to the centre of the room, where she pauses and utters the words, "Elvino! Elvino!" of whom she is evidently dreaming. Rodolpho, receiving no answer to his address, understands that the girl is a somnambulist, and prudently watches, without disturbing her. The girl, speaking in her sleep, betrays her thoughts, for she tearfully pleads that Elvino will not be jealous of the stranger, and begs her lover to reaffirm his confidence, solemnly protesting that she has no love for any other than he to whom her hand has been sacredly pledged.

Lisa has secretly observed the movements of Amina, and she conceives a heartless design to compromise the girl, thinking that by so doing she may prejudice Elvino and herself gain him for husband. With this end in view she escapes by another door without being observed by Rodolpho, and goes out to spread report among the neighbors that Amina is in the stranger's room! Rodolpho is undecided what to do, and while he is contemplating her, the sleeping girl, still dreaming, goes through the marriage ceremony, believing she is being escorted to the church by a joyful populace, where she receives her affianced with feelings of ecstasy, and then kneels before the altar to make her nuptial vow, after which she promises eternal love and truth, and requests Elvino to embrace her. Rodolpho watches her meantime, greatly impressed by the loyal devotion which she manifests, the dream motives clearly portraying the thoughts that engage her wakeful moments. Fearful that Amina may arouse and find herself in a compromising situation should he remain, Rodolpho commends her spotless youth to Heaven's guardianship, and then, extinguishing the candles, he quietly leaves by the window, noiselessly closing it after him.

Very soon after Rodolpho has quitted the room, Amina falls upon the bed in an attitude of peaceful slumber, and immediately steps are heard on the stairs, and a smothered hum of voices from the outside indicate that the villagers are approaching. These at once appear, headed by Alessio, exclaiming in chorus, with quizzical interest and comical concern, "Be observant; 'tis his number; due advantage let us take," etc. The peasants, who have been apprised by Lisa of Amina's invasion of Rudolpho's room, cautiously enter the apartment, and to their great astonishment they find the girl asleep on Rodolpho's bed. Lisa exultantly points to Amina in confirmation of her statement, saying, "See the proof; I ne'er dissemble!" Teresa, though deeply mortified by the discovery, stoutly declares her ward's innocence, and pitifully looks to her neighbors for some friendly sympathy. The confusion awakens Amina, who, opening her eyes, sees with consternation a crowd of people before her, and innocently beseeches to know the cause of this intrusion into her room. She shows bewilderment, but presently perceiving Elvino standing alone she rushes towards him and endeavors to throw her arms about his neck, but he repulses her harshly as the falsest of traitors. Unable to understand his conduct, she entreats him earnestly to inform her what guilty act she has committed? The peasants join Elvino in imprecating her as a base and treacherous woman, and expel her as a lost one henceforth unworthy the recognition of honest people. Overwhelmed by the fierce condemnation of Elvino, and her expulsion by her neighbors, yet knowing the innocence of her own heart, Amina is no longer able to support her misery, and sinks to the floor, piteously wailing, "How am I guilty? Oh, bitterest woe!" Thereupon follows a touching duet, between Amina and Elvino, in which she tearfully asserts her faithfulness, and he implores Heaven to forgive her guiltiness.

Though the circumstances indicate Amina's baseness, Teresa refuses to abandon confidence in the purity of the girl she has raised in honor, and beseeches her neighbors to suspend judgment for a while. Glancing about, she discovers Lisa's neckerchief on the bedpost, and thinking it may serve as evidence hereafter, she places it around Amina's neck. Again Amina seeks sympathetic recognition from Elvino, but he repudiates her, and before all the villagers renounces the nuptial vow he made, saying, "Shame and misery now are thine. Take from me thy hateful presence!" In vain are all her protestations and entreaties. Elvino turns his back upon her, and to make her humiliation the more abject, the impertinent and designing Lisa thus condemns and execrates the suffering girl:

"No more marriage; all disdain thee,
Infamous the world proclaims thee,
Loathings, scorn and hate eternal
Make thy life on earth infernal."

Teresa, hoping yet to vindicate Amina from the aspersions that are heaped upon her, asserts sublime faith in the innocence of the girl, and with maternal confidence and devotion promises that all the world's abuse and the poison tongue of calumny cannot avail to destroy the trust and love which she feels. This outburst of compassion and unalterable affection upon the part of her foster-mother, deeply moves Amina, who still entreating, by passionate appeals to her lover, gives expression to her agony of mind in a touching air, "Where the life that knows no sorrow," etc. Conflicting emotions arise in Elvino's heart, and unable longer to view the anguish of Amina, he rushes from the room. The others, however, stand and continue to regard her with looks of execration, by which reproaches she is overcome, and falls into Teresa's sheltering arms as the curtain is rung down on the second act.

Act III.—The opening scene of the last act represents a shaded valley, that lies between the village and the castle. A party of peasants enter, singing in chorus of their purpose to repair to the castle, where Count Rodolpho is sojourning, to ask him by what circumstance Amina came to visit his room. They vouch for her goodness and beauty, and express the hope that Rodolpho will give them some explanation relieving Amina from the stigma that now attaches to her. When the group of villagers exeunt, Amina enters, supported by Teresa, who is now her only friend. Teresa tries to comfort her suffering ward with assurance that his lordship, Rodolpho, will yield to the pleadings of those sent to see him, and will give a truthful statement absolving her from all taint of suspicion, but Amina's dejection is so great that the most encouraging promises of the faithfulest friend cannot assuage her sorrow. She is compelled to endure the double grief that comes from scandal and the loss of a lover for whom her heart still possesses profoundest attachment. She feels faint, with sorrow and fatigue, and as she is near Elvino's farmstead, there is a rush of sweet memories, of dear days when she sat with Elvino under a spreading beech tree near by, and while the murmuring stream sang quietly of joy, she listened to his vows of constancy, and believed that happiness would bless their united lives; but alas, with sighs, she is brought to fear that all her dear hopes are now lost forever, that she has wakened from a dream of bliss to realize the deceptions that sometimes appear, like beautiful mirages, to dazzle with hope, and then dissolve in disappointment.

Teresa exerts her efforts to cheer the melancholy girl, and has no doubt that Elvino suffers an affliction no less deep, for that grief is plainly written upon his face since disavowal of his nuptial pledge. While Teresa is thus consoling her wretched ward, Elvino is seen approaching in the distance, and Amina is quick to note his deep dejection, which immediately creates fresh hopes that he still loves her. Teresa retires a little way as Elvino moves forward bewailing his ill-fortune, and expressing the affliction that has robbed his mind of peace, and made his heart a desolation. Amina waits anxiously until he draws near, when she addresses him timidly, and asks to be heard, but he at once assumes an irreconcilable attitude, and though she swears she is innocent, he positively dismisses her as an ungrateful and wretched deceiver, who has made his life miserable for all time. At this juncture a group of villagers, who have just returned from a visit to Rodolpho, come upon the stage shouting, "Vive his lordship!" Elvino turns away angrily at mention of the man to whom he believes all his sorrows are due, but the villagers and Amina beseech him to remain and patiently hear what the count has to say, for Rodolpho himself is coming to testify to the purity of the girl who is falsely maligned. This appeal serves no other purpose than to intensify the mad jealousy of Elvino, and in a rage he snatches the engagement ring from Amina's finger, at which rude act the villagers cry, "Unkind! shame!" Remorse also seizes Elvino when he sees the suffering girl fainting in the arms of Teresa, and his feelings he discloses in a tender air:

> "Still so gently o'er me stealing,
> Mem'ry will bring back the feeling,
> Spite of all my grief revealing
> That I dearly love thee still," etc.

[illegible]

But though remorseful, Elvino is too deeply jealous to meet Rodolpho, and leaves the place. Teresa draws Amina away, and in the succeeding scene a part of the village is shown, with Teresa's mill in the foreground, operated by a large water-wheel, which is revolving rapidly. A slight plank-bridge spans the space between the top floor of the mill and an embankment, with stone steps leading down to the stage. Lisa and Alessio come upon the scene, engaged in a dispute that furnishes a comic element as a relief to the pathetic conditions preceding. Alessio tries to persuade Lisa to reciprocate his passion, but having an ambition to form a better alliance, with Elvino, she repulses Alessio's pleadings, and frankly tells him if he had half the wit that nature intended, he would plainly see his attentions are annoying. He entertains the suspicion that Lisa has a preference for Elvino, and warns her that it is idle to centre her affections upon one whose heart is already pledged, but she gives him poor satisfaction by declaring that he will be ten thousand times more odious to her sight if her plans to marry Elvino miscarry. Alessio becomes in turn indignant at her insulting language, and assuming a cavalier attitude, he boastfully asserts: "You shall never wed him. I'll turn the village house-out-of-window; I'll submit to his lordship my cruel case, then shall my dainty madam have me her only bridegroom, please or displease her!" Their interview is interrupted by voices of villagers outside, who announce that "Lisa has been chosen!" When they enter, a gleeful chorus is rendered, giving a joyous welcome to Lisa, whose hand is now claimed by Elvino, his fortune and favor having been transferred from Amina, and in approbation they join in celebrating the approaching marriage. Elvino comes in while the peasants are rejoicing, and Lisa greets him with an extended hand which he lightly kisses, and to her question if she is esteemed worthy of his affection, he answers impassively by expressing regret that he has so long neglected her, and asks forgiveness. This she promptly grants and hopes the past will be forgotten, and that the flower of their former love may blossom in perfection. Elvino gives her a pledge of his devotion, saying, "Come then. Thou, O beloved, be my faithful companion; solemnest rite they prepare in yon temple. Be not thou tardy." Thus addressing her, Elvino leads Lisa towards the church, but he is stopped on the way by Rodolpho, who being told that the two are about to meet at the nuptial altar, he begs Elvino to pause and hear him. This Elvino has no mind to do, but Rodolpho persists, in the name of justice, of honor, in his purpose of declaring Amina's purity, a woman unknown by blemish, and pledges his word and reputation upon it. Elvino disdainfully replies: "Count Rodolpho, did not we all see the proof of guilt upon her, in your chamber fast asleep did we not find her?" Rodolpho thereupon explains that some there are who have a habit of walking in their sleep, and while in deepest slumber they are able to answer questions intelligently, of which after waking they have no remembrance,—such are called somnambulists, and Amina has this habit. The people are half convinced that Rodolpho speaks truly, but Elvino rejects the statement as a story invented by a lover to protect his mistress from shame and scandal. Rodolpho adjures him not to reject a worthy and innocent girl, but Elvino disregards the count and leads Lisa away towards the church as the villagers, with sudden change of sentiment, jocularly sing of a story that is as difficult to swallow as a nauseating pill.

As the villagers are passing out, Teresa enters, and pointing to the mill, she tells them that Amina is there sleeping, having need for quiet since grief has so exhausted her, and she begs that they will suppress their noisy voices. They tell her that the tumult is celebration of Lisa's marriage, but they have no wish to disturb the shameful sleeper, however little deserving she may be of their regard. Teresa is astonished, and asks Lisa if it is really true she is to be married, which inquiry Elvino himself answers with a modest "aye," whereupon, to show her elation, Lisa complacently remarks: "Yes, I deserve it; was I ever discovered all alone, too, after dark in a night-gown. Did any one ever find me sleeping in the chamber of a lord?" This language so incenses Teresa that she determines to declare her conviction, therefore taking Lisa's neckerchief from her bosom she holds it up saying, "This was found hanging upon the bed of Lord Rodolpho's chamber!" and pointing to Lisa, she calls attention to the crimson flush of shame that mantles her cheek, and remarks that the count would contradict the charge of suspicion if it were untrue. All the villagers regard Lisa with amazement, and Elvino, concluding that every lass has been the prey of Rodolpho, drops her hand abruptly, despairingly observing, "Banished from the world is affection, all faith and love are dead." A charmingly tuneful quartet between Teresa, Lisa, Elvino and Rodolpho ensues, in which each one gives expression to their respective feelings. Rodolpho stoutly declares that Amina is pure, whatever may be the grounds of suspicion, hearing which Elvino, in an agonizing tone, entreats to know who can prove it? At this moment Amina, in a night-dress, and with lamp in hand, emerges from a window of the mill, and passes over the plank-bridge that conducts, above the rapidly-revolving water-wheel, to the embankment. Rodolpho is first to catch sight of her, and exclaims: "See there! She herself will prove the falseness of your cruel suspicions!" Perceiving that she is walking in her sleep, he cautions the people against making the slightest noise, for to wake her suddenly may cause her death. The astonished villagers watch Amina as she sets foot upon the treacherous bridge, and fearing for her safety they fall upon their knees and offer up a prayer, "Power Almighty, guide now her faltering step!" The frail plank trembles perceptibly with her weight, and when she reaches the centre it bends almost to the point of breaking, and sways so much that the lamp falls from her hand into the raging torrent below. But she makes the crossing in safety, amid breathless suspense of the horrified spectators, and descends to the stage. Still sleeping, she advances to the midst of the villagers, and dreaming of Elvino, she softly murmurs, "Oh, were I but permitted only once more to see him, ere that another he doth lead to the altar!" Rodolpho and Teresa remind Elvino that all her thoughts are of him and of his cruel actions. Amina continues in her dream, and pictures the bridal procession that leads with solemn music to the church; then calling heaven to attest her purity, she offers up a prayer, "Great power of love and mercy, pass this cup from my lips. I do forgive him. Though joy forsake this bosom, may he be happy. Grant to a heart that dieth its last poor supplication." She rises, and examining her hand for Elvino's ring, recalls how he wrested it from her, but finds some solace in the knowledge that he cannot deprive her of his image fixed forever in her heart. Clasping her hands on her bosom, she takes therefrom a little bunch of violets which Elvino gave her the day before, and which she has since sacredly treasured, and marking how they are faded, kisses them as emblems of affection, and a pledge of passion, which though profaned by violated vows, she promises to keep them as long as her life endures. Weeping over the now drooping and scentless flowers, she plaintively sings:

"Scarce could I believe the power,
To wither so shortly a blossom;
Thus love is born within the bosom,
And dies unwept the self same hour."

Elvino can no longer resist the prompting of his revived passion, anxious alike to make amends for his disproved suspicions, and to reclaim the girl for whom his heart is starving. He therefore breaks from the count's restraint, and would embrace Amina, but pauses when she speaks again, anxious to hear her loving words. Tenderly she beseeches Elvino to look upon her, and if her prayers avail to prove her innocence, she entreats that he will restore the ring. Rodolpho counsels Elvino to obey this timely request, which he at once fulfills by placing the ring on Amina's finger, whereupon her dreams anticipate the reality, and in an ecstasy she utters, "I am thine, thine again, love; now at last I am happy," falling back into Teresa's embrace as Elvino drops upon his knees before her. At this the chorus set up a shout "Vive Amina," which wakens the somnambulist, and she startles to find herself in the midst of the villagers. She is immediately plunged into the deepest grief, believing the sweet dreams that revived her hopes are the contrary reflections of her despair, and covering her face with her hands, she implores the people, in good mercy, not to wake her, for in sleep alone can she find surcease from misery. Elvino, still kneeling, warmly assures her that her dream of joy is verified by a lover's appeal for pardon, who prays that her visions of bliss may be quickly completed by celebration of the interrupted marriage. Amina looks earnestly into his face, afraid to trust her senses, until gradually the happy realization comes to her that Elvino is indeed a suppliant for her hand, and in a transport of ecstasy, as they approach the altar she pours out her enraptured soul in song in exultation and praise-giving for the blessings of heaven:

"Do not mingle one human feeling
With the rapture o'er each sense stealing;
See these tributes to me revealing—
My Elvino is true to his love.
Ah, embrace me, and thus forgiving,
Each a pardon is now receiving;
On this bright earth while we are living,
Let us form here a heav'n of love."

Graves

Rigoletto

(AFTER THE ORIGINAL PAINTING BY C. D. GRAVES)

COUNT MONTERONE—"*On both of you be my malediction!*
Vile is he who hounds the dying lion,
But viler thou, O Duke, and the serpent there,
Who the anguish of a parent can deride!
A parent's curse be on you both!"

ACT I. SCENE I.

RIGOLETTO.

MUSIC BY VERDI.——WORDS BY PIAVE.

RIGOLETTO is one of Verdi's greatest compositions, holding rank probably next to Aida, though in point of popularity "Il Trovatore" undoubtedly has precedence. The opera, which Verdi himself regards as his best work, is an adaptation from Victor Hugo's tragedy "Le Roi, s'Amuse," and had its premier production at Venice, March 11, 1851. Those who have heard the delicious music of this charming creation of the great master will not be surprised to learn that the opera created a sensation when it was first given. So great was the admiration of the singers for the many exquisite airs which distinguish it, that despite all injunctions laid at the rehearsals, to refrain from repeating the music where the public might hear it in advance of the performance, the airs escaped, as it were, onto the streets and were at once seized by Venetians and were soon in everybody's mouth, to the chagrin of the famous composer. The initial night was little less than an ovation for Verdi, and a mighty acclamation of the opera by one of the most enthusiastic audiences that ever assembled. The history of the opera has an interest apart from its splendid reception, as there were trials to endure and political prejudices to surmount that almost disheartened both librettist and composer. Verdi himself suggested the use of Hugo's tragedy, which he thought admirable for lyric treatment, but to disguise the origin of the plot a new title was adopted, "The Maledicton," and upon these suggestions the original libretto was prepared. When the opera was completed and announced for representation, the civil authorities promptly interdicted it as being opposed to public policy to permit the characterization of a king on the stage in the situations which Francis I was made to assume in the original tragedy. This objection Verdi tried in vain to have removed, and the opera would probably never have been given in Italy but for the timely recommendation of the Minister of Police, who advised a change in the libretto, whereby the King should be replaced by a Duke of Mantua, and the title "Rigoletto" be adopted, which latter is represented as a buffoon in the tragedy. These alterations were accepted by Verdi, though the changes required considerable rewriting, of both the score and words.

The story of "Rigoletto" is little short of revolting, nor is it to be defended upon the ground of probability, for it would be difficult to conceive a more inconsistent, even unreasonable, happening in any state of society; but we must not deny to the dramatist the license that the poet exacts as a right, else romance would be reduced to a level with ordinary events. As he is represented in the opera, Rigoletto is a hunchback jester to the licentious Duke of Mantua, and his character is as distorted as his body, for he is panderer to the libidinous vices of his master. Besides his many other crimes, he has assisted the Duke in seducing the wife of Count Ceprano and in deflowering the daughter of Count Monterone. It is not surprising, therefore, that by his villainous contrivances Rigoletto has made himself hated by the courtiers, who have a desire to avenge themselves upon him. Count Monterone, burning with hate and indignation at the disgrace put upon him, appears before the Duke to demand reparation for the dishonor, but instead of obtaining satisfaction he is taunted insolently by the jester, and to complete the Count's humiliation, the infamous Duke orders his arrest.

It happens that Rigoletto has a beautiful daughter, Gilda, for whom his love is so great that he has concealed her from public observation in order the better to preserve her innocence from the corrupting influences of the court. Rigoletto is not known to be a father, and as he has been discovered making clandestine visits to Gilda, the courtiers conclude that she is his mistress, and as a punishment for his crimes they conclude to assist Count Monterone in his desire for vengeance by stealing her away. Notwithstanding Gilda has been kept closely confined, the Duke by chance observes her; stricken by her great beauty, he adopts the disguise of a student and contriving to enter her dwelling place he wins her affections, by which act the Duke is made an interested party to the tragic events that are soon to follow.

The courtiers conceiving their purpose, appear before Rigoletto, masked, and persuade him to believe that they desire to abduct the wife of Count Ceprano for the Duke's benefit, a design which the vile intriguer promptly agrees to further. By this means Rigoletto is made to assist unconsciously in the carrying away of his own daughter, for masked and bandaged he is induced to follow them, and to hold the ladder by which two of the courtiers mount to Gilda's room, where, covering her mouth to prevent an outcry, they seize and convey her to the ducal palace. When the abduction is accomplished the courtiers desert Rigoletto, who, upon removing his mask, discovers to his great consternation, by a scarf dropped in the flight that he has been robbed of his beloved daughter, and his anguish is intense. The Duke joyfully receives Gilda, believing her to be the mistress of his jester, and the unfortunate girl soon falls a prey to his infamous passions.

Rigoletto, distracted by overmastering grief, hurries to the palace and demands his daughter, but the courtiers resist his attempt to gain access to the Duke, and exhibit towards him the greatest disdain. While her father is clamoring for admission at the Duke's door, Gilda makes her appearance, and being restored to her father she departs with him, he cursing the authors of his sorrow. Not satisfied, however, by recovering his daughter, who has been disgraced, Rigoletto determines to obtain revenge, a purpose which he means to accomplish by hiring an assassin, Sparafucile, to kill the Duke. In furtherance of this murderous design, the Duke is enticed by Maddelene, sister of Sparafucile, to a lonely inn. Gilda, though betrayed by the Duke, still entertains a deep affection for him, but to extinguish this feeling for her seducer, she is brought to the inn, where, by looking through cracks in the wall, she witnesses his inconstancy. It happens also that Gilda overhears Maddelene earnestly imploring Sparafucile to spare the life of her handsome guest, but the assassin cannot be persuaded from fulfilling the terms of the contract unless, as he tells her, some person shall chance to come to the inn before midnight, whom he may kill instead and deliver the body in a sack to Rigoletto as that of the murdered Duke. Gilda is exhorted by her father to disguise herself in male attire and flee to Verona, where she may be safe from the Duke. Pretending to obey his will, she resolves instead to save the life of the unworthy Duke by sacrificing her own. She accordingly repairs again to the inn and knocking on the door, near the midnight hour, she is stabbed to death on the threshold by Sparafucile. Believing that the murdered person is a man, the assassin quickly places the body in a sack, and when Rigoletto calls to pay the reward, he is given the sack supposed to contain the Duke's body. He is about to throw it into the river that flows by the inn, when he hears the Duke's voice at a distance. Suspecting a trick, Rigoletto tears open the sack, when to his great horror he discovers that it contains the dying form of his own child, who revives to tell him how much she loved the Duke and to beg a father's blessing, and then expires. Rigoletto's anguish is so intense that he sinks down overwhelmed upon the body of Gilda, realizing the fulfillment of Monterone's curse.

Act I.—The introductory scene represents a splendid ballroom in the ducal palace, brilliantly lighted for a fête, which is in progress, attended by nobles and ladies in gorgeous costumes. The Duke enters with Borsa, an attendant, to whom he speaks of a beautiful young lady seen at church every Sunday for three months, whom he desires very much to meet. Borsa asks if her place of residence is known, to which the Duke answers that he has learned no more than that she lives in a remote part of the city, where she is visited nightly by a mysterious man who may be kindred or lover, the gossips have not revealed. At this moment a group of ladies and gentlemen cross the stage, among whom the Duke recognizes Count Ceprano's wife, and remarks that she is handsomest of all. Borsa cautions him to speak more softly lest the Count may hear, but he is indifferent to the tongue of scandal, and vaunts his capriciousness in love affairs by a delicious aria that forms an exquisite musical prelude to the play: "Though a fair throng gathers around me, not one o'er my heart holds sway."

As the Duke concludes his song of fickleness, Count Ceprano comes in, jealously watching his wife in the distance promenading with a cavalier. As the Countess draws near, the Duke very gallantly addresses her in most endearing terms, asking if she is leaving so soon? She replies that it is the will of her husband; whereupon the Duke more warmly praises her beauty, that sheds greater lustre than the sun, and confessing himself her slave, he kisses her hand passionately, and then offering his arm leads her off. Count Ceprano is immediately thrown into a state of jealous rage and starts after the couple, nor stops to answer Rigoletto's inquiry as to the cause of his troubled thoughts. Borsa observes that the Duke is having his diversion. "Very true," responds Rigoletto, "and there is little new in it, for all the pleasures gaming, feasting, fighting, coquetting are alike to his thinking, and just now he is laying siege to the Countess." Rigoletto makes his exit, and there appears another courtier, Marullo, who eagerly reports that he has an interesting bit of news which is the more surprising because it concerns Rigoletto. The others are all anxiety to know what it can be, and ask if the buffoon has lost his hump? Marullo at length relieves their suspense by declaring that, hunchback and idiot though the jester manifestly is, nevertheless, for all that, he has, incredible to state, but true, an inamorata who lives hereabout.

The Duke returns to the room, Ceprano in the background, as if dogging his steps with a sullen determination to defend his honor. The Duke remarks to Rigoletto that Ceprano is a particularly troublesome fellow to have a wife that is little short of an angel, plainly indicating his desire for a means to supplant the husband. Rigoletto, base panderer that he is, suggests that it might not be a difficult thing to carry off the fair Countess this very night, but to make the matter easier the Count could be sent to prison, or his head cut off, which would answer a better purpose. These recommendations are made in a voice loud enough to be overheard by Ceprano, who furious with rage, draws his sword and would make an end of the black-hearted villain but for the interference of the Duke, who tries to make a laughing matter of the jester's proposals. Rigoletto shows no fear, being protégé of the Duke, and taunts the outraged Count. Other courtiers present, in an aside offer their help to Ceprano to obtain vengeance on the vile buffoon, which he gladly accepts, and arrangements are secretly made to carry out their designs on the following night. A group of dancers now enter singing a gleeful chorus, followed directly by Count Monterone, who seeks the Duke to bring him to account for debauching his daughter. When the Count scornfully raises his voice in rebuke, Rigoletto insolently mimics his action, and with mock gravity reminds him of the Duke's clemency in pardoning his conspiracy, declaring it were madness to come in all seasons wailing about the honor of his daughter. This taunting and making sport of his grief so inflames Monterone that he dismisses Rigoletto as a despicable buffoon, to whom a dire punishment will come in due season, and then turns the vial of his wrath upon the Duke, declaring his resolution to continue to disturb his infamous orgies and to follow him with weeping and accusation so long as the disgrace put upon his daughter remains unavenged. The Duke tries to intimidate him by threatening him with arrest for this disturbance, but Monterone defiantly challenges the Duke to do his worst, and warns that if he be consigned to death his spirit will return to reproach the defiler of his child, even until the wrath of God shall atone the crime.

> "On both of you be my malediction!
> Vile is he who hounds the dying lion,
> But viler thou, O Duke, and thy serpent there,
> Who the anguish of a parent can deride!
> A parent's curse be on you both!"

[illegible]

Rigoletto is deeply agitated by Monterone's execration, for he is somewhat superstitiously inclined, but he assumes an audacious attitude and bitterly upbraids him as a devil sent to interrupt the fête, and cautions him that having invoked the sovereign anger, a fatal punishment will soon be meted. Halberdiers appear at the Duke's order, who place Monterone under arrest and march him off to prison.

In the succeeding scene the end of a blind street is shown, on the left an isolated house in a lonesome courtyard, beyond which is distinguishable a small part of the palace of Count Ceprano. The time is night, and Rigoletto, enveloped in a great cloak, enters, followed by Sparafucile, who carries a sword under his coat. Moving to the front of the stage, Rigoletto informs his lowering companion of Monterone's curse, which rankles in him to the exclusion of all other thoughts. Sparafucile, who lives by assassination, tells him it is not a difficult thing to rid himself of a troublesome person if he is willing to pay a good man for the service. The suggestion gives Rigoletto much satisfaction, and he immediately becomes so interested as to inquire how the work is managed and what danger of exposure is to be considered. Sparafucile assures him that he is an expert at the trade of killing, and has things well arranged to make his success certain; that he often does the work by waylaying, at night, but it is less risky and more agreeable to do the deed in his own house, a lonely inn, whither his sister,

Maddelene, who is handsome, and dances in the street, may be counted on to lure the victim. Rigoletto has no mind to engage the villain at once, while his enemy is in prison, but takes Sparafucile's address against future needs, and then dismisses him. Left alone, Rigoletto soliloquizes ruefully and compares himself to the assassin, "How very like are we; my tongue is my weapon, while the sword serves him no more fatally, and both are scoundrels. My vocation is to make people laugh, his to make them weep, and yet there is much in common between us. I am the butt of an imperious master who commands me to amuse and makes sport of my deformity. How I hate this life of shams and crimes, and all the sycophants that fawn about the shrine of power; so too am I harassed by Monterone's curse, though I am sure it is a foolish fear, a folly born of an unsettled mind." Having delivered himself of these disquieting thoughts, Rigoletto opens a door and passes into the courtyard, where he is met by Gilda, his daughter, who receives him joyously. She is quick to note a sad expression on his face, and beseeches him to open his heart in confidence and tell her the cause of his sorrow. She has often wondered why she has been guarded so closely, and kept in ignorance of her condition, and seizes this occasion to ask him to reveal his true name, and to speak of his family, at least of her mother. He refuses to enlighten her, and interrupts her entreaties by asking if she ever goes out? To which Gilda replies that no visit she ever pays, nor walks alone save to her devotions every Sabbath. Being commended for performance of her pious duties, Gilda renews request for knowledge of her dead mother, to which Rigoletto replies in a sorrowful aria, "Speak not of one whose loss to thee," etc., and continuing his grieving he admits that country, family, or friends he has none, save it be that all to him he finds in her, who is his sole consolation, treasure, and hope, which he prays may never be taken from him or dishonored, the tender interview concluding with a duet, "Safely guard this tender blossom." Committing Gilda to the care of Giovanna, Rigoletto is about to enter the house when he hears the noise of some one in the street, which causes him to pass through the garden-gate to make an investigation. At the same moment the Duke, disguised as a student, glides in, and throwing a purse to Giovanna, he secretes himself behind a tree. Rigoletto now returns and again questions Gilda, if any one ever follows her to church, and receiving a satisfactory answer, he cautions her on no account to admit any one to the house, not even should her visitor be the Duke himself, who of all others should be kept out. Having thus instructed his daughter, Rigoletto affectionately embraces her and departs. The Duke has been a spectator of the scene, and recognizing Rigoletto, concludes that Gilda is his mistress. When the jester has taken his leave, Giovanna expresses regret at not having informed him of the youth who pays clandestine visits to his charge, a remorse that Gilda represses by declaring her deep infatuation for the student, for whom her heart longs continually. Hearing this confession of love the Duke suddenly comes forward, and motioning Giovanna to retire, he kneels at Gilda's feet and pours out his passion, promising to love her forever and to protect her against all the world. Coyly, she begs him to go away, but her words only intensify his infatuation, and feelingly he delights her ears with an ardent aria, "Love is the sun by which passion is lighted." She accepts with feelings of ecstasy his protestations of devotion, and believing his purposes honorable asks his name, which, after some hesitancy, he tells her is Walter Maldé, a poor student. At this juncture the voices of Ceprano and Borsa are heard in the street, and taking alarm lest it be Rigoletto returning, Gilda orders Giovanna to conduct the disguised Duke to the bastion, where he may be concealed. The two separate after pledging unchangeable devotion, and Gilda being now alone gives expression to the joy that animates her, in an exquisite love-song:

"Dear name I treasure in this breast,
Thy memory sweet to me remain,
My love for thee I've frank confessed,
No power that love can e'er restrain," etc.

When Gilda concludes her tender air, she ascends the terrace with a lantern in her hand, lighting the way, whereupon Marullo, Ceprano and Borsa, accompanied by other courtiers, all armed and masked, enter the courtyard, and seeing Gilda, they remark upon her beauty, and marvel why she should give herself as mistress to such a misshapen fellow as the vile jester. While they are laughing at the strange alliance of beauty and the beast, Rigoletto reappears muttering to himself, "How fiercely that old Count cursed me!" The courtiers, who have come here to steal away Gilda, believing her to be Rigoletto's mistress, conceive a sudden thought to make him an accessory to the act. Marullo accordingly explains to the buffoon that the object of their visit is to steal away Ceprano's wife for the Duke's pleasure, which statement at once disarms Rigoletto's fears, and when his aid is sought he cheerfully acquiesces and asks to be supplied with a mask. This Marullo promptly supplies, but first fastens a handkerchief over the jester's eyes, and then commands him to hold the ladder steady while the others use it to scale the terrace-wall. Rigoletto is now placed in a position where he unconsciously assists in the abduction of his own daughter, and thus consummates the vengeance planned by the courtiers against himself. The party quickly ascend to Gilda's room, where they seize and bear her away, despite her frantic cries for help, an act that Rigoletto thinks is a capital joke, until, finding himself alone, a few minutes after, he snatches the bandage from his eyes, and discovers, by a scarf dropped in the flight, to his intense consternation and pitiful despair, that it is not Ceprano's wife, but Gilda that has been abducted, and that she has been taken to the harem of the Duke, which exciting incident furnishes a very dramatic dénouement to the first act.

Act II.—When the action is renewed the audience is introduced to a view of a large saloon in the Duke's palace, which is sumptuously furnished as becomes a person of very high rank. The Duke enters, very much agitated, bewailing the loss of Gilda and marveling by what means she could be stolen away, but vengefully promising that the parties to this outrage shall be apprehended and dealt with as their crime deserves, for he has not yet discovered that her abduction has been accomplished to serve his own base uses. His grief mastering his rage, he laments the loss of Gilda:

"Sweet maid, each tear of thine that falls,
Every sigh thy bosom heaving,
A prisoner in some dreary walls,
Fills me with grief past all relieving," etc.

On the next instant the conspiring courtiers run in to gleefully announce that they have just carried off Rigoletto's mistress, who is now safe within the palace, and being asked to relate how the deed was done, the courtiers tell the particulars of the abduction in a fine chorus. The Duke hears their story with great interest, perceiving that it is of Gilda they speak, and with a hope of speedily regaining her he eagerly inquires where the lady may now be found. Assured that she is well taken care of, and that he will soon see her, the Duke renders a happy air:

"To her I love with rapture I must at once away,
The crime of her base capture I will forget this day;
From her my name and station I may not now conceal,
Yet free from observation I will my love reveal."

As the Duke exits hastily the courtiers wonder what new thought has seized him, but their marveling is soon interrupted by the entrance of Rigoletto, who looks about anxiously and speaking to himself, "Whither can they have carried her?" The courtiers accost him cordially, but he answers them sardonically, with no better grace than congratulations that they took no cold from their escapade of last night. Marullo affects surprise, vowing that he slept through the entire night. Rigoletto glances at him contemptuously, and then moves away, carefully scrutinizing everything in the room to discover some sign of his daughter. A page comes in to ask if the Duchess may not speak to the Duke, but he is told by Ceprano that the Duke has gone hunting or at least he is at this moment so deeply engaged that an interview may not be granted even to the Duchess. Rigoletto immediately concludes that this precious engagement is with his daughter, and he creates a scene by loudly declaring that she must be here, and he will have her back. In his madness he rushes towards the centre door, but the courtiers bar his advance, for which interference he curses them as minions, panderers, thieves, who have sold his daughter for a price, and fiercely demands that they forthwith open the door or feel a desperate father's vengeance. This is probably the most dramatic scene in the opera, in which the musical alternations run the whole gamut of human emotion, from the fury of despair to the exquisite tenderness of prayerful appeal, for his anger being unavailing, the frantic father, with a gush of tears, begs for pity, and implores in mercy's name to be informed where his daughter is hidden, she who to him is more than all the world beside.

[illegible]

While Rigoletto is expressing his frantic grief, and entreating the courtiers, Gilda comes through the doorway and rushes into his arms. His joy at seeing her again is so great that it almost robs him of reason, and hugging her with soulful ecstasy he bids the courtiers look upon his angel child, who is his whole family, for other relatives and friends has he none. He is so glad, that vengeance ceases to rankle, and he is even willing to believe the abduction a joke, until he discovers Gilda to be weeping, and inquiring the cause, learns from her lips that in shame she has been maltreated. Hate, vengeance, immediately rises in his breast, and imperatively ordering the courtiers to leave the room, he falls into a chair and bids his daughter tell him of her woes. When they are left alone, mortified by her conduct, the deceits and confidences that have brought her father to grief, and herself to shame, Gilda makes a complete confession of how the Duke, in the disguise of a poor student, watched her at church, and contriving to gain her presence, by protestations of love won her trusting heart; that when he left her, a body of fierce men invaded her chamber and by force, against her struggles and cries for help, tore her from home and brought her to the Duke's palace. Rigoletto will hear no more, for the rest is told in the suffering face, the welling tears, the broken spirit that speak the ruin that has been wrought. He realizes now that Monterone's curse is following his steps like a hellish wraith; the wrong, deep, deadly, cannot be righted, but he will make amends so far as human power and parental love can perform. Consoling his daughter, he advises that it were best to quit this fatal place forever, since a day has changed their destiny. At this instant a herald enters, announcing that a prisoner has been ordered to the prison of Castiglion; behind him appears Count Monterone, who is marched across the stage, between two guards, led to execution. As the Count passes, his eyes chance to discover the Duke's portrait on the wall, and for a moment he pauses before it to remark: "In vain has been my malediction for your crimes, and since neither heaven nor earth has punishment for your infamies, I must remain unavenged; so, happy will you live, O lecherous Duke, when I am gone!"

Rigoletto hears the despairing Count's words, and in a frenzy of exasperation, of wrath that burns with unquenchable violence, he cries after the retreating form of the miserable man, who, like himself, mourns the disgrace of a daughter defiled by the Duke: "Thou shalt yet be avenged; henceforth the hope of my soul is to hasten retribution, and the hour is near when, like lightning from heaven hurled, the fury of a desperate man, aye, of the despised buffoon, will fall upon the head of the lecherous hell-hound, even though he wears a Ducal crown." Gilda is affrighted by her father's ferocious aspect, and his terrible threatening, and trembles for the safety of the Duke for whom, all unworthy, she still cherishes intense affection. With tender beseechings she tries to dissipate Rigoletto's glowing anger, and implores that pardon be given as we would pray heaven to pardon our own offences, to be merciful to him who has himself failed to show pity, for to God alone is the right to repay. This very emotional scene concludes the second act.

Act III.—The last act opens with a scene that shows a desolate place on the banks of a small river. On the right is a dingy, repulsive and dilapidated two-story house used as a cheap inn. Some of the weather-boarding is broken off, leaving crevices through which a glimpse of the interior may be had. The city of Mantua is distinguishable in the distance by the lights, for it is night. Rigoletto and Gilda appear in an altercation, for she has confessed that her love for the Duke is not yet dead, and her father is trying by reasoning of her wrongs to destroy her infatuation. The girl, with a woman's devotion, refuses to believe that the Duke is the incontinent her father pictures him, and implores that a merciful judgment be given. Unable to dispel her delusive dream of love by other means, Rigoletto asks if proof of the Duke's perfidy be presented to her own eyes, will she then discard him from her heart, and when she promises to do so he leads her close to the old inn, and challenges her to keep her eye to one of the crevices a little while. In a moment the Duke, dressed as a private soldier, enters through a door on the left, and imperiously commands that a room be assigned him, and some wine be brought forthwith. Gilda trembles with surprise, and dark suspicion, for she fears and dreads the discovery that will verify her father's charges. Sparafucile goes off into an adjoining room for the wine, and during his absence the Duke cheers himself by rendering the famous air, "How fickle women are."

Sparafucile returns, with a bottle of wine and two glasses, which he places on a table, and then strikes the ceiling twice with his sword. The signal quickly brings Maddelene, a sweet girl, in gypsy costume, who descends to the first floor by means of a ladder. The Duke rushes forward to embrace her, but knowing the value of a woman's wiles, with assumed modesty that counts so much in winning an ardent man, she repulses him, notwithstanding the girl has lured the Duke to this lonely place for a murderous purpose. Sparafucile goes out into the road to inform Rigoletto that the man (he does not know it is the Duke) has arrived, and asks if, according to the agreement made, the fatal blow shall be struck at once. Rigoletto prefers that the deed be postponed a little while, until the Duke's infamy may be thoroughly exposed to his watching daughter. The revelation is not long delayed, for believing themselves to be unobserved, the Duke declares his passion for Maddelene with all the ardor of protestation that distinguished his avowals of love to Gilda, and swearing to be her slave he attempts to kiss her. Unwilling to be so quickly won by flattery, Maddelene repels him, and a scene ensues of blandishment and coquetry that is intensely amusing. All his cajoleries failing to win the girl, the Duke calls her loveliest of her sex, and gives his solemn pledge, upon the honor of a soldier, to marry her, and beseeches for one word from her beautiful lips to assuage his sufferings of heart. Maddelene, accustomed to lovers' sighs, laughingly receives his vows for no more than they are worth, counting them as stories of little cost, and no greater value than utterances of a cavalier who has told his tales of love to a hundred listening maidens. Gilda has been an unwilling witness to this scene of gallantry, by which she is made to know how basely her faith has been betrayed by a heartless deceiver, and in anguish she exclaims:

"Oh, what a weak credulity is mine,
To place my trust in such a libertine!"

"For shame, father! I have been undeceived!"

Rigoletto now compassionates his daughter's shame, but he begs her to no longer nourish a useless grief, and to place her dependence in him to terribly revenge her wrongs. Encouraging her to abide the day of retribution, so near at hand, he counsels Gilda to return to the house, and there obtaining the gold that she requires, provide a horse, and in the apparel of a youth flee to Verona, where he will meet her on the morrow. She entreats him to come at once, but he refuses to depart, whereupon Gilda goes out and Rigoletto seeks an audience with Sparafucile. The Duke and Maddelene continue their dalliances, while Rigoletto makes a bargain with the assassin, by which he agrees to advance ten crowns, and to pay as much more when the dead body of the Duke is delivered to him at midnight, that he may cast it into the river. The compact being completed, darkness suddenly increases, and mutterings of thunder are heard in the distance. Maddelene startles at sounds of the coming storm, and struggles to escape from the Duke. Sparafucile now enters and warns that the rain is coming, but infatuated by desire for a conquest that he has been unable to complete, the Duke defiantly declares that he cares not for the storm, for he will spend this night at the inn. Maddelene exhorts him to leave, but he obstinately refuses, which pleases Sparafucile, for it were easier to do the deed at home, and graciously he lights the Duke to his chamber, which has plenty of air, even if it lacks other comforts.

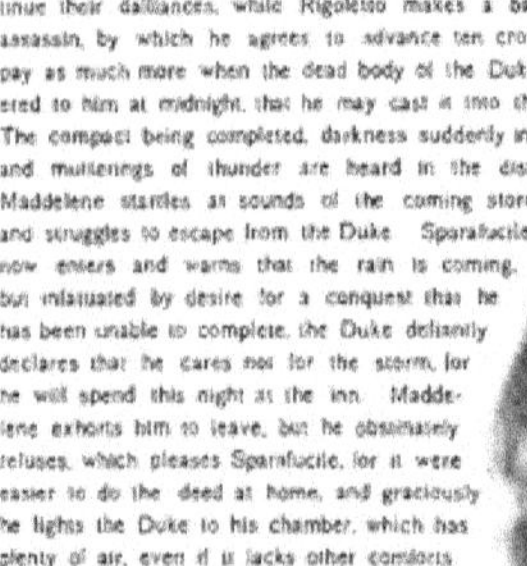

Having reached his room and dismissed Sparafucile, the Duke very deliberately removes his hat and sword, and then throwing himself upon the bed, soon falls asleep. The assassin returns to Maddelene, and with much satisfaction tells her of the agreement by which he is to receive twenty crowns, and bids her repair to the room and bring away her visitor's sword, that he may be defenceless, which order she reluctantly obeys, protesting that "it is a great sin to murder so fair a youth."

Gilda has followed her father's instructions, so far as to apparel herself in male clothing, but though deeply indignant at her lover's perfidious acts, her heart still inclines towards him, and jealousy brings her back to the inn to see the outcome of the Duke's wooing. She approaches slowly, and peeping through a crack in the wall, sees Sparafucile at a table drinking. The storm rises, and peals of thunder cause her to shiver with terror, but she appears chained to the spot, and watches Maddelene as she descends with the Duke's sword, and hears with unsuppressed horror the awful words of the girl, "This youth is handsome as Apollo. I love him as I never loved man before, and surely he loves me. I pray you, Sparafucile, do not kill him!" The assassin reproves her as a pigeon-hearted child, more fit to listen to tender tales than to perform deeds of vantage, and declaring he must slay this Apollo, and cast his body into the river, sternly orders her to mend the holes in the sack. Maddelene, still pleading for the life of the stranger, suggests to Sparafucile that he may win the reward and yet spare the youth, and with a woman's wit she explains: "Ten crowns have already been paid you by the hunchback; mark, now, how easy a thing to secure the rest. In a little while this cowardly fellow will return, when you may slay him and possess yourself of what he has." Sparafucile recoils at the suggestion, and soundly abuses his sister for aspersing him as a highwayman, reminding that he never betrays a client. Maddelene thereupon threatens to give a warning to the stranger, but he cautions her against an act that would lose them half the reward, which causes her to hesitate, for she sets money above conscience. Sparafucile, moved somewhat by his sister's entreaties, and taking pity on the handsome cavalier, at length agrees to accept another victim, provided a visitor shall appear before midnight, which is still half an hour distant. Maddelene realizes that no one is likely to come to so lonely a place, fit indeed for murderous deed, and the occasion doubly auspicious, for it is midnight's ghostly hour, and the angry elements are fiercely challenging the trembling earth with lightning, thunder, and blast of wind, as if all the fell demons of the air are holding carnival. So ominous appear the threatenings of heaven, so awful the crime meditated, that Maddelene is terrified beyond control, and unable to repress her horror and fears, she begins to weep.

Gilda has been an earnest and terrified listener to all this fearful conversation, and every moment her agony increases. When Maddelene begins to cry, Gilda is so deeply touched by this show of devotion that she no longer hesitates to make herself a sacrifice for the man who has shamefully betrayed her, but for whom pity has renewed her love. Having taken this resolution, she knocks on the door. The sound startles Maddelene, and she looks up in astonishment to ask, "Who knocks?" Sparafucile, giving no heed, tells her "it is the wind, or spirit of the storm,—no more." Again the knock is heard, so unmistakable that the assassin clutches his poignard and looks wildly, as if expecting that some fiend has come to claim toll of the criminal. Maddelene, more anxiously concerned for the life of her lover, calls, "Who's there?" to which a feeble voice, scarcely rising above the wind, begs pity on a stranger, and craves hospitality for the night against the beating, bitter storm. Sparafucile responds, "Wait a while!" and goes to the cupboard as if in search of something, during which brief interval Gilda gives expression to her anguish and passionately implores a pardon for the merciless assassin who will slay her for a price:

"So near am I to death, and yet so young!
Pardon, O God, the wretch to crime a slave;
Forgive, O father, thy poor hopeless child,
And happy live the Duke! die to save."

Maddelene begs Sparafucile to hasten and quickly do the deed, which, saving one life, will destroy another! He expresses indifference as to who may be the victim, so only that he receives the reward, and thereupon, to prepare himself for the fell purpose, he grasps his dagger and goes behind the doorway ready to strike. Maddelene, trembling with awful dread, throws open the door, and as Gilda enters, the assassin buries his weapon in her breast; the door is then closed again, and the two murderers make haste to crowd the body into a sack, as the storm sweeps more furiously, and the thunder peals as if heaven would avenge the terrible crime.

When the dreadful deed is committed, Rigoletto comes upon the scene enveloped in a cloak. First looking anxiously and fearfully about him, he timidly approaches the door of the inn and lightly knocks. Sparafucile answers the call by requesting him to remain without a moment, and the interval he improves by dragging the sack out of the house and depositing it at the feet of Rigoletto. The latter expresses satisfaction that the expiation has been done so cleverly, and requests that a light be brought, but Sparafucile demands that the ten crowns still due shall first be paid according to contract, after which he will cast the body into the river. Rigoletto hands the assassin a purse, but reserves the right himself to make disposition of the hateful remains, whereupon Sparafucile recommends that a better place to hide the body may be found higher up the stream, and then retires into the inn, no longer concerned for the man he has served.

Left alone with the corpse of what he believes to be that of the Duke, Rigoletto contemplates the sack for a moment, and gloats over the consummation of his dreadful revenge,—the buffoon's triumph over a lecherous master. Determined to subject the remains to the greatest indignity, he will treat them as he would those of a despised dog, and attempts to drag the sack towards the river. At this moment he hears the Duke singing in the distance, a sound that fills him with unutterable fear and foreboding, for he imagines that it is a demon of hell pursuing him with malediction. After dragging the sack a little way, he suddenly resolves to look upon the body, appalling though the sight may be, and hastily, but with great agitation, he tears open the bag, when a flash of lightning reveals to his terrified sight the face of his daughter! His distraction and anguish become at once uncontrollable, and in the torment of his awful agony he knocks violently upon the door of the inn, and calls for help, but the response comes from Gilda herself, who revives somewhat, though wounded mortally, and speaks in a feeble voice, telling him a dagger pierced her breast. To his request for explanation of this mystery, the dying girl answers feebly: "I have deceived you! I am guilty! Too much I loved him, and through my love I now die for him!" This revelation intensifies Rigoletto's despair, for the agonizing realization overwhelms him that she has fallen a victim to his own vengeful feelings, and that Monterone's malediction has been verified. With a breaking heart he beseeches her to speak further, but her strength is fast failing, and with the little that remains she begs her father to pardon the Duke, and to bestow his blessings upon a misguided but still loving child, whose latest breath is given to prayer that heaven may help him bear the sorrow for her acts and the grief for her death.

The scene concludes with a deeply touching duet, in which Gilda promises that when her soul shall gain the realm of heaven, there she will first seek out her sainted mother from the angel throng, and thus united they will join their prayers before the throne of God for His grace and mercy upon a father so strongly devoted to a hapless child. Rigoletto entreats her, his last and only treasure, not to leave him here alone, begging that she will stay and dispel the darkness that has gathered over his life. But his pleadings cannot heal the deadly wound, and Gilda expires with a half-finished prayer upon her lips. When at length he perceives that his daughter's spirit is fled, Rigoletto screams out, in a wail of despair, "His curse is on me!" and falls insensible upon the corpse of Gilda, which affecting scene concludes the opera.

GUIDE TO PRONUNCIATION OF OPERAS.

SYNOPTICAL TABLE OF OPERAS AND CHARACTERS.

[illegible]	[illegible]	[illegible]	[illegible]	[illegible]	[illegible]	[illegible]
Frederick	Buffo	MIGNON—Continued	Thomas	Carré and Barbier	35	Young cavalier infatuated with Filina, who uses him to her best advantage.
Antonio		do	do	do	35	Servant of a [illegible].
Giarno	Bass	do	do	do	35	See Lazarus.
Spirito	Mezzo soprano	do	do	do	35	See Mignon.
Wilhelm Meister	Tenor	do	do	do	35	See Coghlan.
Faust (Dr.)	Tenor	FAUST	Gounod	Barbier and Carré	47	[illegible]
Mephistopheles	Bass	do	do	do	47	[illegible]
Marguerite	Soprano	do	do	do	47	[illegible]
Valentine	Baritone	do	do	do	47	A soldier, brother of Marguerite. Is killed by Faust in a duel.
Siebel	Mezzo soprano	do	do	do	47	[illegible]
Wagner	Baritone	do	do	do	47	Soldier, friend of Valentine and Siebel.
Martha	Mezzo soprano	do	do	do	47	Friend and companion of Marguerite. [illegible]
Santuzza	Soprano	CAVALLERIA RUSTICANA (*Rustic Chivalry*)	Mascagni	Targioni-Tozzetti and Menasci	57	Sicilian girl, mistress of Turiddu. On his desertion informs Alfio of his [illegible] conduct with his unfaithful wife Lola, and falls fainting as [illegible] Turiddu has been killed by Alfio in a duel.
Lola	Mezzo soprano	do	do	do	57	Sicilian girl, promised wife of Turiddu. [illegible]
Turiddu	Tenor	do	do	do	57	Sicilian youth, son of Lucia, lover of Lola and Santuzza. [illegible] Turiddu in a duel.
Alfio	Baritone	do	do	do	57	Rich Sicilian carrier, marries Lola, and when he is informed of her unfaithfulness, fights a duel with Turiddu and kills him.
Lucia	Contralto	do	do	do	57	Sicilian woman, mother of Turiddu. [illegible]
Alberich	Baritone	THE RHINE GOLD	Wagner	Wagner	65	[illegible]
Wotan	Baritone	do	do	do	65	[illegible]
Fricka	Low Soprano	do	do	do	65	Wife of Wotan and sister of Freia.
Freia	High Soprano	do	do	do	65	[illegible]
Fasolt	Low Bass	do	do	do	65	[illegible]
Fafner	Baritone	do	do	do	65	[illegible]
Loge	Tenor	do	do	do	65	[illegible]
Thor	Baritone	do	do	do	65	Brother of Fricka and Freia.
Froh	Tenor	do	do	do	65	Brother of Fricka and Freia.
Mime	Tenor	do	do	do	65	[illegible]
Erda	Low Soprano	do	do	do	65	[illegible]
Wellgunde	High Soprano	do	do	do	65	Daughter of the Rhine Gold—Guarding the Rhine Gold.
Woglinde	High Soprano	do	do	do	65	Daughter of the Rhine Gold—Guarding the Rhine Gold.
Flosshilde	Low Soprano	do	do	do	65	Daughter of the Rhine Gold—Guarding the Rhine Gold.
Hunding	Bass	VALKYRIE	Wagner	Wagner	75	[illegible]
Siegmund	Tenor	do	do	do	75	[illegible]
Sieglinde	Soprano	do	do	do	75	[illegible]
Wotan (Wodan)	Baritone	do	do	do	75	[illegible]
Brunhilde	Soprano	do	do	do	75	[illegible]
Fricka	Mezzo-soprano	do	do	do	75	[illegible]

Rôle	Voice	Opera	Composer	Librettist	Page	Character
Loge	Tenor	VALKYRIE (Continued)	Wagner	Wagner	75	God of fire, vassal of Wotan—Spreads fire around Brunnhilde to protect her from none until a hero shall come to wake her
Fricka	Contralto	do	do	do	75	Goddess of wedlock—Wife of Wotan and mother of the Valkyries.
Wolfsung	Baritone	do	do	do	75	See Wotan.
Mime	Tenor	SIEGFRIED	Wagner	Wagner	85	Dwarf of the Nibelungs—Blacksmith with whom Siegfried is left in charge by Sieglinde when she is dying—Endeavors to obtain ring and helmet from Siegfried, who kills him.
Siegfried	Tenor	do	do	do	85	Son of Siegmund and Sieglinde—Reared by Mime—Forges magic sword "Needful," and slays the dragon, Fafner, who has possession of the ring and helmet—Kills Mime for trying to poison him, and searches for Brunnhilde—Is opposed by Wotan, but whose spear he breaks and overcomes all opposition—Finding Brunnhilde in her encircled bed of fire he falls in love with her.
Wotan	Bass	do	do	do	85	King of Walhalla—Endeavors to warn Fafner, in return for which he is to receive ring and helmet, but same is refused—Opposing Siegfried, his spear is broken, and he is made harmless.
Alberich	Bass	do	do	do	85	Former King of the Nibelungs, and possessor of magic ring and helmet; guardian of Fafner's cave—Endeavors to warn Siegfried but is hindered by him.
Fafner	Bass	do	do	do	85	Giant and dragon, possessor of ring and helmet; is killed by Siegfried, who thereby becomes master of both.
Erda	Contralto	do	do	do	85	Goddess of Wisdom—Mother of Valkyries, of whom Brunnhilde is one.
Brunnhilde	Soprano	do	do	do	85	Valkyrie—Daughter of Wotan—Condemned to slumber for disobedience, is wakened by Siegfried and falls in love with him.
Gunther	Baritone	GÖTTERDÄMMERUNG (Dusk of the Gods)	Wagner	Wagner	95	[illegible]
Hagen	Bass	do	do	do	95	[illegible]
Gutrune	Soprano	do	do	do	95	[illegible]
Brunnhilde	Soprano	do	do	do	95	[illegible]
Siegfried	Tenor	do	do	do	95	[illegible]
Woglinde	High Soprano	do	do	do	95	[illegible]
Wellgunde	High Soprano	do	do	do	95	[illegible]
Flosshilde	Contralto	do	do	do	95	[illegible]
Alberich	Bass	do	do	do	95	[illegible]
Stradella	Tenor	STRADELLA	Flotow	[illegible]	107	[illegible]
Leonora	Soprano	do	do	do	107	[illegible]
Bassi	Bass	do	do	do	107	[illegible]
Malvolio	Baritone	do	do	do	107	[illegible]
Barbarino	Tenor	do	do	do	107	[illegible]
Lady Harriet (Martha)	Soprano	MARTHA	Flotow	St. Georges	115	An attendant on the queen—Tired of the monotony of the court—Disguises herself and goes to Richmond Fair as a peasant—Is engaged by Lionel and runs away—Discovers that he is Count Derby and marries him.
Nancy (Julia)	Contralto	do	do	do	115	Maid of Lady Harriet—Goes with her to the fair disguised as a peasant, and is engaged by Plunkett—Runs away, but afterwards marries him.
Sir Tristan	Bass	do	do	do	115	An English noble—a Lover of Lady Harriet, but she dislikes him and finally deserts him entirely.
Lionel	Tenor	do	do	do	115	A young country farmer—Engages Lady Harriet at Richmond Fair as servant, and falls in love with her—She runs away, and he is arrested for following and insulting her, but discovering that he is Count Derby she repents and marries him.
Plunkett	Bass	do	do	do	115	Half brother of Lionel—Engages Nancy as servant—Falls in love with her—She runs away, but finally they are married.
Martha	Soprano	do	do	do	115	See Lady Harriet.
Julia	Contralto	do	do	do	115	See Nancy.

Role	Voice	Opera	Composer	Librettist	Page	Characteristics
Semiramide	Soprano	SEMIRAMIDE	Rossini	Rossi	125	[illegible]
Arsace (Ninias)	Contralto	do	do	do	125	[illegible]
Assur	Baritone	do	do	do	125	[illegible]
Azema	Soprano	do	do	do	125	[illegible]
Idreno		do	do	do	125	[illegible]
Nino	Contralto	do	do	do	125	[illegible]
Oroe	Bass	do	do	do	125	[illegible]
Mitranes		do	do	do	125	[illegible]
[illegible]		do	do	do	125	[illegible]
[illegible]	Contralto	do	do	do	125	[illegible]
Manon (Lescaut)	Soprano	MANON	Massenet	Meilhac and Gille	133	[illegible]
Chevalier des Grieux	Tenor	do	do	do	133	[illegible]
Lescaut	Baritone	do	do	do	135	[illegible]
De Brétigny	Tenor	do	do	do	135	[illegible]
Guillot (de Morfontaine)	Bass	do	do	do	135	[illegible]
Rosette	Soprano	do	do	do	135	Actress. Friend of Guillot.
Comte des Grieux	Bass	do	do	do	135	Father of Chevalier des Grieux.
Norma	Soprano	NORMA	Bellini	Romani	145	[illegible]
Pollio	Tenor	do	do	do	145	[illegible]
Adalgisa	Soprano	do	do	do	145	[illegible]
Oroveso	Bass	do	do	do	145	[illegible]
Flavius	Tenor	do	do	do	145	[illegible]
Clotilda	Soprano	do	do	do	145	[illegible]
Count Almaviva	Baritone	THE MARRIAGE OF FIGARO	Mozart	Da Ponte	155	[illegible]
Countess Almaviva	Soprano	do	do	do	155	[illegible]
Figaro	Bass	do	do	do	155	[illegible]
Susanna	Soprano	do	do	do	155	[illegible]
Cherubino	Soprano	do	do	do	155	[illegible]
Basilio	Tenor	do	do	do	155	[illegible]
Antonio	Bass	do	do	do	155	[illegible]
Marcellina	Soprano	do	do	do	155	[illegible]
Bartolo	Bass	do	do	do	155	[illegible]
Barbarina	Soprano	do	do	do	155	[illegible]
Don Curzio	Tenor	do	do	do	155	[illegible]
Aida	Soprano	AIDA	Verdi	Du Locle	165	[illegible]
Amonasro	Baritone	do	do	do	165	[illegible]
Radames	Tenor	do	do	do	165	[illegible]
Amneris	Contralto	do	do	do	165	[illegible]
Ramphis	Bass	do	do	do	165	[illegible]
King of Egypt	Baritone	do	do	do	165	[illegible]

Role	Voice	Opera	Composer	Librettist	Page	Character
Zamiel		DER FREISCHÜTZ (*The Sharpshooter*)	Weber	Kind	175	The Evil One—Master of Caspar—Causes his death by directing bullet fired by Max
Kuno	Bass	do	do	do	175	Master of the chase—Servant of Prince Ottokar and father of Agathe
Ottokar (Prince)	Tenor	do	do	do	175	Ruler of Bohemia—Patron of the shooting match
Agathe	Soprano	do	do	do	175	Daughter of Kuno—Sweetheart of Max—the prize for the winner of the match—Marries Max finally
Caspar	Bass	do	do	do	175	Huntsman gamekeeper—Enemy of Max—Minion of Zamiel—Leads Max into temptation and finally is accidentally shot by him
Kilian	Tenor	do	do	do	175	A peasant—Aspirant for the hand of Agathe and rival of Max
Max	Tenor	do	do	do	175	Champion marksman and huntsman—Aspires to be chief of chase and to marry Agathe, who is in love with him—Falls into Zamiel's power by Caspar through his love for Agathe and accidentally kills him—Finally breaks away from the evil influence and marries Agathe.
Annchen	Soprano	do	do	do	175	Relative and companion of Agathe
Hermit	Bass	do	do	do	175	Protector of Agathe and friend of Max against Zamiel
Dickson	Tenor	LA DAME BLANCHE (*The White Lady*)	Boieldieu	Scribe	185	A Scotch farmer—Friend of George Brown [illegible]
Jenny	Soprano	do	do	do	185	Wife of Dickson
Gabriel		do	do	do	185	[illegible]
MacIrton	Bass	do	do	do	185	[illegible]
Margaret	Soprano	do	do	do	185	[illegible]
Gaveston	Bass	do	do	do	185	[illegible]
Anna	Soprano	do	do	do	185	[illegible]
George Brown (Julien)	Tenor	do	do	do	185	[illegible]
Julien	Tenor	do	do	do	185	See George Brown
Sapho (Fanny Legrand)	Soprano	SAPHO	Massenet	Cain and Bernède	193	[illegible]
Jean (Gaussin)	Tenor	do	do	do	193	[illegible]
Césaire	Baritone	do	do	do	193	[illegible]
Divonne	Mezzo-soprano	do	do	do	193	[illegible]
Caoudal	Bass	do	do	do	193	[illegible] model of her and [illegible]
La Borderie	Baritone	do	do	do	193	[illegible]
Flamant	Tenor	do	do	do	193	[illegible]
Irene	Contralto	do	do	do	193	[illegible]
Fanny Le Grand	Soprano	do	do	do	193	[illegible]
La Gommeuse	Tenor	do	do	do	193	[illegible]
Sir Henry Ashton (Lord of Lammermoor)	Bass	LUCIA DI LAMMERMOOR (*Lucy of Lammermoor*)	Donizetti	Cammarano	205	Scotch lord—Brother of Lucy—To regain his lost wealth plans to have her marry Sir Arthur Bucklaw, which he forces her to do through perfidy—Challenges Sir Edgar, but fails to meet him
Lucy	Soprano	do	do	do	205	Sister of Sir Henry—In love with Sir Edgar—Believing him false, she marries Sir Arthur, but being convinced of Edgar's faithfulness, after her marriage she goes mad and kills her husband, and then dies herself
Sir Arthur Bucklaw	Tenor	do	do	do	205	A wealthy Scotch lord—In love with Lucy, and through her brother's intrigues marries her, but on their marriage night she goes mad and murders him.
Sir Edgar	Tenor	do	do	do	205	Scotch lord—Enemy of Sir Henry—In love with Lucy—Is sent to France on important mission, and returning finds Lucy married to Sir Arthur—Challenges Sir Henry, but does not meet him, for while waiting at the rendezvous he is informed of Lucy's death and stabs himself
Norman	Tenor	do	do	do	205	Steward of Sir Henry—[illegible] at the instigation of Sir Henry, [illegible] Sir Edgar's [illegible]
Raymond	Bass	do	do	do	205	Chaplain of Sir Henry—Friend of Sir Edgar
Alice	Soprano	do	do	do	205	Attendant and maid of Lucy
Orpheus	Contralto	ORPHEUS AND EURYDICE	Gluck	Calzabigi	215	A god, son of [illegible] and Calliope—Beautiful musician, mourns Eurydice, who dies. He decides to go to Hades after her, and Love gives him permission to obtain her, upon condition that he does not look at her until they are out of Hades. At her persuasion he disobeys this injunction, and thus loses her, but Love, in compassion, gives her back to him, and they are united again.
Eurydice	Soprano	do	do	do	215	Daughter of a Thracian shepherd—Is married to Orpheus and dies. He goes after her into Hades, but by her beseechings she induces him to look at her, and he loses her again, but she is restored to him by Love through compassion.
Love	Tenor	do	do	do	215	God of love, messenger of Jove—Leads Orpheus through Hades and returns Eurydice to him, after he has lost her through disobeying Jove's command.

Role	Voice	Opera	Composer	Librettist	Page	Character
Comte de Nevers	Baritone	LES HUGUENOTS (The Huguenots)	Meyerbeer	Scribe and Deschamps	225	A Catholic noble—Affianced to Valentine, but [illegible]
Tavannes	Tenor	do	do	do	225	Catholic noble, friend of De Nevers
De Cossé	Tenor	do	do	do	225	Catholic noble, friend of De Nevers
De Retz	Baritone	do	do	do	225	Catholic noble, friend of De Nevers
Méru	Baritone	do	do	do	225	Catholic noble, friend of De Nevers
Raoul de Nangis	Tenor	do	do	do	225	Huguenot noble—[illegible]
Marcel	Bass	do	do	do	225	Servant of Raoul—[illegible] to Valentine, but is killed by [illegible]
Marguerite de Valois	Soprano	do	do	do	225	Queen of France—[illegible] to Raoul, but [illegible]
Valentine de Saint Bris	Soprano	do	do	do	225	Daughter of Comte de Saint Bris—[illegible]
Comte de Saint Bris	Baritone	do	do	do	225	Catholic noble, father of Valentine, by whose order she is killed.
Urbain	Soprano	do	do	do	225	Page of Queen Marguerite
Maurevert		do	do	do	225	Catholic noble, friend of Comte de St. Bris
De [illegible]		do	do	do	225	Catholic noble, friend of Comte de St. Bris
Manrico (Trovatore)	Tenor	IL TROVATORE (The Troubadour)	Verdi	Cammarano	233	Son of old Count di Luna. Stolen by Azucena, a gypsy, who brings him up as her own child—Is loved by Leonora, lady attendant to the Queen—[illegible]
Leonora (Duchess)	Soprano	do	do	do	233	Lady attendant of Queen—In love with Manrico—Loved by di Luna—[illegible]
Di Luna (Count)	Baritone	do	do	do	233	Noble of Spain—[illegible]
Azucena	Alto	do	do	do	233	Gypsy mother, burned at stake by Count di Luna—[illegible]
Ferrando	Bass	do	do	do	233	Old servant of Count di Luna—[illegible]
Ruiz	Baritone	do	do	do	233	Gypsy companion of Manrico and lieutenant of his band
Inez	Mezzo-soprano	do	do	do	233	Maid of Leonora
Garcia		do	do	do	233	See Manrico
Frasquita	Soprano	CARMEN	Bizet	Halévy and Meilhac	245	Gypsy maiden, friend of Carmen
Mercédès	Soprano	do	do	do	245	Gypsy maiden, friend of Carmen
Dancaïro	Tenor	do	do	do	245	Gypsy chief
Il Remendado	Baritone	do	do	do	245	Gypsy chief
Michaela	Soprano	do	do	do	245	Spanish maiden—Affianced to Don José
Morales	Baritone	do	do	do	245	Spanish officer—In love with Carmen
Escamillo	Baritone	do	do	do	245	Spanish bullfighter—In love with Carmen and rival of Don José
Don José	Tenor	do	do	do	245	Spanish officer—Affianced to Michaela, leaves her for Carmen, whom he rescues when she is arrested, and falls in love with her; his love being unrequited, he stabs her
Carmen	Soprano	do	do	do	245	Spanish maiden [illegible]—Ensnares Don José and [illegible] and tries to leave Don José, but he follows and stabs her
Carmencita	Soprano	do	do	do	245	See Carmen
Albert	Bass	THE JEWESS	Halévy	Scribe	255	Officer of Imperial Guard, friend of Leopold
Ruggiero	Bass	do	do	do	255	[illegible]
Cardinal de Brogni	Bass	do	do	do	255	[illegible]
Leopold	Tenor	do	do	do	255	[illegible]
Eleazar	Tenor	do	do	do	255	A Jew—[illegible]
Eudoxia	Soprano	do	do	do	255	[illegible]
Rachel	Soprano	do	do	do	255	[illegible]
Samuel	Tenor	do	do	do	255	See Leopold
Mary	Alto	THE FLYING DUTCHMAN	Wagner	Wagner	265	[illegible]
Flying Dutchman	Baritone	do	do	do	265	[illegible]
Senta	Soprano	do	do	do	265	[illegible]

SYNOPTICAL TABLE

Rôle	Voice	Opera	Composer	Librettist	Page	Character
Tigellinus	Baritone	NERO—continued	Rubinstein	Barbier	315	Roman noble and friend of Nero
Balbillus	Bass	do	do	do	315	Roman noble, Augustan and astrologer
Poppaea	Soprano	do	do	do	315	Mistress of Nero [illegible]
[illegible]	Bass	do	do	do	315	Roman priest
[illegible]	Alto	do	do	do	315	[illegible] by Nero
Agrippina		do	do	do	315	Mother of Nero [illegible]
[illegible]		do	do	do	315	Roman noble and Augustan
Claudius		do	do	do	315	Former Emperor of Rome—Murdered by Nero
Britannicus		do	do	do	315	Murdered brother of Nero
Octavia		do	do	do	315	Murdered wife of Nero
Walton (Lord Walton)	Bass	I PURITANI (The Puritans)	Bellini	Count Pepoli	325	[illegible]
[illegible] (Sir Richard)	Bass	do	do	do	325	[illegible]
Sir George	Bass	do	do	do	325	[illegible]
Sir Arthur Talbot	Tenor	do	do	do	325	[illegible]
Henrietta [illegible]	Soprano	do	do	do	325	[illegible]
Elvira	Soprano	do	do	do	325	[illegible]
Bruno	Tenor	do	do	do	325	[illegible]
Walther	Tenor	THE MASTER SINGERS OF NUREMBERG	Wagner	Wagner	335	[illegible]
Eva	Soprano	do	do	do	335	[illegible]
Pogner	Bass	do	do	do	335	[illegible]
David	Tenor	do	do	do	335	[illegible]
Hans Sachs	Bass	do	do	do	335	[illegible]
Beckmesser	Bass	do	do	do	335	[illegible]
Magdalena	Soprano	do	do	do	335	[illegible]
Kothner	Bass	do	do	do	335	[illegible]
Nilakantha	Basso cantante	LAKMÉ	Delibes	Gondinet and Gille	345	[illegible]
Lakmé	Light Soprano	do	do	do	345	[illegible]
Mallika	Mezzo-soprano	do	do	do	345	[illegible]
Hadji	Second Tenor	do	do	do	345	[illegible]
Gerald	First Tenor	do	do	do	345	[illegible]
Frederick	Baritone	do	do	do	345	[illegible]
Ellen	High Soprano	do	do	do	345	[illegible]
Rose	Second Soprano	do	do	do	345	[illegible]
Mrs. Benson	Mezzo-soprano	do	do	do	345	[illegible]
Samson	[illegible]	SAMSON AND DELILAH	Saint-Saëns		355	[illegible]
Delilah	Soprano	do	do		355	[illegible]
Abimelech	Tenor	do	do		355	[illegible]
High Priest	Bass	do	do		355	[illegible]

Rôle	Voice	Opera	Composer	Librettist	Page	Comments
John (of Leyden)	Tenor	THE PROPHET	Meyerbeer	Scribe	[illegible]	[illegible]
Oberthal (Count)	Baritone	do	do	do	[illegible]	[illegible]
Bertha	Soprano	do	do	do	[illegible]	[illegible]
Fides	Mezzo-soprano	do	do	do	[illegible]	[illegible]
[illegible]	Bass	do	do	do	[illegible]	[illegible]
[illegible]	Bass	do	do	do	[illegible]	
[illegible]	Bass	do	do	do	[illegible]	
Robert	Tenor	ROBERT THE DEVIL	Meyerbeer	Scribe and Del a Vigne	445	[illegible]
Isabella	Soprano	do	do	do	445	[illegible]
Alberti	Bass	do	do	do	445	[illegible]
Alice	Mezzo-soprano	do	do	do	445	[illegible]
Raimbaut	Tenor	do	do	do	445	[illegible]
Bertram	Bass	do	do	do	445	[illegible]
Helena		do	do	do	445	[illegible]
Lucrezia Borgia	Soprano	LUCREZIA BORGIA	Donizetti	Romani	[illegible]	[illegible]
Duke Alfonso d'Este	Bass	do	do	do	[illegible]	[illegible]
Gennaro	Tenor	do	do	do	[illegible]	[illegible]
Orsini (Maffeo)	Alto	do	do	do	[illegible]	[illegible]
Gubetta	Bass	do	do	do	[illegible]	[illegible]
Liverotto	Tenor	do	do	do	[illegible]	[illegible]
Rustighello	Tenor	do	do	do	[illegible]	[illegible]
Astolfo	Tenor	do	do	do	[illegible]	[illegible]
William Tell	Bass	WILLIAM TELL	Rossini	Jouy and Bis	435	[illegible]
Gessler	Bass	do	do	do	435	[illegible]
Hedwige	Soprano	do	do	do	435	Wife of William Tell.
Jemmy	Soprano	do	do	do	435	Son of William Tell, from whose head he shoots the apple
Fisherman		do	do	do	435	Swiss peasant—Friend of William Tell.
Melchthal	Bass	do	do	do	435	Swiss patriarch—Father of Arnold—Instigator of rebellion
Arnold	Tenor	do	do	do	435	Son of Melchthal—In love with Mathilde, whom he finally marries
Mathilde	Soprano	do	do	do	435	Daughter of Gessler—In love with Arnold—[illegible] William Tell and finally marries Arnold.
Leuthold	Bass	do	do	do	435	Swiss peasant—Enemy of Gessler
Rudolph	Tenor	do	do	do	435	Captain of the guards.
Walter	Bass	do	do	do	435	Swiss peasant—Friend of William Tell.
Matteo	Bass	FRA DIAVOLO	Auber	Scribe	455	Innkeeper of Terracina, Italy—Father of Zerlina—Promises her in marriage to Francesco, a rich farmer
Zerlina	Soprano	do	do	do	455	[illegible]
Lorenzo	Tenor	do	do	do	455	[illegible]
Lord Allcash	Tenor	do	do	do	455	An English traveller—[illegible]

[illegible]	[illegible]	[illegible]	[illegible]	[illegible]	[illegible]	[illegible]
Pamela (Lady Allcash)	Soprano	FRA DIAVOLO [illegible]	Auber	[illegible]	[illegible]	[illegible]
Fra Diavolo (Lord San Marco)	Baritone	do	do	do	[illegible]	[illegible]
[illegible]		do	do	do	[illegible]	[illegible]
[illegible]	Tenor	do	do	do	[illegible]	[illegible]
[illegible]	Bass	do	do	do	[illegible]	[illegible]
[illegible]		do	do	do	[illegible]	[illegible]
Almaviva (Count)	Tenor	THE BARBER OF SEVILLE	Rossini	[illegible]	[illegible]	[illegible]
Rosina	Soprano	do	do	do	[illegible]	[illegible]
Dr. Bartolo	Bass	do	do	do	[illegible]	[illegible]
Figaro	Baritone	do	do	do	[illegible]	[illegible]
Don Basilio	Bass	do	do	do	[illegible]	[illegible]
[illegible]	Tenor	do	do	do	[illegible]	[illegible]
[illegible]		do	do	do	[illegible]	[illegible]
[illegible]	Soprano	do	do	do	[illegible]	[illegible]
[illegible]	Tenor	do	do	do	[illegible]	[illegible]
Inez	Soprano	L'AFRICAINE (The African)	Meyerbeer	[illegible]	[illegible]	[illegible]
Anna	Contralto	do	do	do	[illegible]	[illegible]
Don Pedro	Bass	do	do	do	[illegible]	[illegible]
Don Diego	Bass	do	do	do	[illegible]	[illegible]
Vasco di Gama	Tenor	do	do	do	[illegible]	[illegible]
Don Alvar	Tenor	do	do	do	[illegible]	[illegible]
Selika	Soprano	do	do	do	[illegible]	[illegible]
Nelusko	Bass	do	do	do	[illegible]	[illegible]
Ferdinand	Tenor	LA FAVORITA (The Favorite)	Donizetti	[illegible]	[illegible]	[illegible]
Leonora	Soprano	do	do	do	[illegible]	[illegible]
Alfonso	Baritone	do	do	do	[illegible]	[illegible]
Baldassare	Bass	do	do	do	[illegible]	[illegible]
Inez	Soprano	do	do	do	[illegible]	[illegible]
Don Gaspar	Tenor	do	do	do	[illegible]	[illegible]
Amina	Soprano	LA SONNAMBULA (The Somnambulist)	Bellini	[illegible]	[illegible]	[illegible]

SYNOPTICAL TABLE.

ALPHABETICAL LIST AND PRONUNCIATION OF CHARACTERS.

ALPHABETICAL LIST AND PRONUNCIATION OF CHARACTERS

ALPHABETICAL LIST AND PRONUNCIATION OF CHARACTERS

ALPHABETICAL LIST AND PRONUNCIATION OF CHARACTERS

www.ingramcontent.com/pod-product-compliance
Lightning Source LLC
Chambersburg PA
CBHW020555270326
41927CB00006B/844

* 9 7 8 3 7 4 4 7 9 3 0 6 3 *